TALL STORIES? READING LAW AND LITERATURE

Tall Stories? Reading Law and Literature

Edited by
JOHN MORISON

and

CHRISTINE BELL

Dartmouth

Aldershot • Brookfield USA • Singapore • Sydney

Published by
Dartmouth Publishing Company Limited
Gower House
Croft Road
Aldershot
Hants GU11 3HR
England

Dartmouth Publishing Company
Old Post Road
Brookfield
Vermont 05036
USA

British Library Cataloguing in Publication Data
Tall stores? : reading law and literature. - (Applied
    legal philosophy)
    1. Law in literature
    I. Morison, John, 1958- II. Bell, Christine
    809.9'3355

Library of Congress Cataloging-in-Publication Data
Tall stories? : reading law and literature / [edited by] John Morison
    and Christine Bell.
        p.   cm. – (Applied legal philosophy)
    Includes bibliographical references and index.
    ISBN 1-85521-741-4
    1. Law and literature. 2. Law in literature. 3. Literature-
    -History and criticism. I. Morison, John, 1958-   . II. Bell,
    Christine, 1967-   . III. Series.
    PN56.L33T35   1996
    809'.93355–dc20   96-1351
                                                                                CIP

ISBN 1 85521 741 4

Printed and bound in Great Britain by
Hartnolls Limited, Bodmin, Cornwall

Table of Contents

Series Preface

The objective of the Dartmouth Series in Applied Legal Philosophy is to publish work which adopts a theoretical approach to the study of particular areas or aspects of law or deals with general theories of law in a way which focusses on issues of practical moral and political concern in specific legal contexts.

In recent years there has been an encouraging tendency for legal philosophers to utilize detailed knowledge of the substance and practicalities of law and a noteworthy development in the theoretical sophistication of much legal research. The series seeks to encourage these trends and to make available studies in law which are both genuinely philosophical in approach and at the same time based on appropriate legal knowledge and directed towards issues in the criticism and reform of actual laws and legal systems.

The series will include studies of all the main areas of law, presented in a manner which relates to the concerns of specialist legal academics and practitioners. Each book makes an original contribution to an area of legal study while being comprehensible to those engaged in a wide variety of disciplines. Their legal content is principally Anglo-American, but a wide-ranging comparative approach is encouraged and authors are drawn from a variety of jurisdictions

TOM D. CAMPBELL
Series Editor
The Faculty of Law
The Australian National University

Introduction

The links between law and literature have a long history dating back as far as the metaphors and parables of Socrates on matters of justice, or the poet judges of the Irish Brehon law system. Over the past two decades the study of law and literature has re-emerged along with other interdisciplinary jurisprudence such as the Critical Legal Studies movement, Law and Economics and Feminism to challenge positivistic analytical studies of law. This renaissance has pushed law and literature on to the pages of law journals and the syllabi of law courses both in the United Kingdom and the United States, where it has gained popularity. This essay collection brings together a variety of perspectives on law and literature. These not only address the movement's claim for validity but seek to take forward the agenda of the Law and Literature approach by demonstrating, through the deployment of a variety of sustained examples, the value of looking at material outside the law library.

The essays here do not offer anything like a coherent manifesto for Law and Literature in a British or Irish context. Indeed we do not believe that there is one correct way to obtain or deploy the insights that literature may bring to our understanding of law. However all contributors are united by a belief that it is not just entertaining but necessary and useful to look beyond the materials which are the normal staple of lawyers in order to bring important insights to the essentially legal issues that we are concerned with. The literary critic Lincoln Faller maintains that

> [l]iterary texts are ... able to escape or smooth over strongly felt contradictions in belief or practice that other kinds of texts have difficulty dealing with. This can make them powerful instruments for 'solving' social and political problems ... or alternatively exposing the insufficiency in the face of such problems of other, supposedly more reality-oriented forms of discourse.[1]

We share the belief that key legal issues can be not only brought to life in literary texts but explored there in ways that orthodox legal materials can not rival. Notions of justice or injustice, the social creation and policing of concepts of difference and deviance or even standards of ethical lawyering are not ideas that can be fully explored by looking only at statutes, law reports, official crime figures or even Bar Council reports on standards. The proper mission of the Law and Literature movement is to read literature, not as ('wannabe') literary critics but as lawyers seeking to pursue the legal themes of power, authority, order, adjudication, penalty, justice and so on which occupy us all.

It seems to us that this eclectic approach to the materials considered relevant to the lawyer has clear dividends in teaching terms too. Especially at a time when legal education is more than usually uncertain and changing, it is important to offer an approach that promises to be lively and relevant. Many of the essays here owe their genesis to the experience of teaching not just specialist Law and Literature courses but more general, substantive subjects within the legal curriculum. In seeking to provide courses that provide a relevant understanding of the contemporary world of legal practice and beyond, and not least the sort of ethical context that the Lord Chancellor's Advisory Committee on Legal Education has recommended,[2] many of the contributors have found themselves moving beyond the standard fare of the law library. This is appropriate within the general direction of the Law and Literature movement which was inspired initially by dissatisfaction with legal education's preoccupation with technical professional requirements.[3] The turn to literature evidenced an attempt to supplement law studies with the wider humanistic concerns of the liberal arts degree. In its most general terms, it was hoped that the study of literature might create more rounded people and therefore more sensitive and thoughtful lawyers, leading in turn to the hope of justice and ethics in the operation of the legal system. Early work grappled with the validity of this project, questioning the Law and Literature movement's lack of a straightforward political project as with other legal theory movements, such as Law and Economics - the so-called 'no manifesto' debate[4]. The movement has emerged from this uncertainty largely through consensus as to the educational gains of studying literature and it is the movement's 'educative ambition' which continues to provide its justification as a legitimate field of study and research.[5] As Ward describes, rather than attempting to answer the question 'what is law', the recent focus of law and literature studies has 'simply attempted to reveal the possibilities presented by alternative approaches to the study and teaching of law'.[6]

Consideration of Law and Literature often begins by identifying two main strands of research: 'law *in* literature' and 'law *as* literature'. Law in literature is explicitly concerned with the depiction of legal issues in novels and plays. There are a variety of claims made for examining literature, but at its most basic, use of literature seeks to challenge the concept of law as finite and uncontroversial legal rules. The study of literature injects into legal studies questions about the nature of law and order, the complexity of issues such as justice, and the human context of law, all without using the formal vocabulary of traditional legal philosophy. Law *as* literature studies have focused on law as text, and the complex questions that this raises as to interpretation. They have been less concerned with literature itself and more concerned with the broader issues raised by literary interpretation and the lessons this has for legal interpretation.

This essay collection eschews a strictly categorised presentation. Instead we seek to expand the study of law and literature in several different directions. Firstly, we address the theoretical debate around the place of literature in legal education. Secondly, we extend the use of literature beyond the classical cannons of Kafka, Shakespeare and Dickens to less commonly considered authors such as Trollope, and to new genres such as crime fiction, romance novels, children's stories and newspaper accounts. Thirdly, we make several contributions to the 'no manifesto' debate and in particular make a bid for what we see as the logical next phase for Law and Literature, namely Law and Cultural Studies.

Educating Stories

Bonsignore has advocated starting every law class with a parable from Kafka.[7] He argues that not only is their content useful, but that they are 'cool, inviting and participatory' thereby contributing to a more active form of learning. Christine Bell provides an overview of the Law and Literature movement, using short stories from Kafka as illustration. She examines the claims for law *in* literature namely that it stimulates reflection on law, that it generates empathy with people, and that it provides a basis for critiquing the socio-political order. She also considers the contribution of the law *as* literature movement to legal education. In conclusion she examines the claim that we can learn legal skills from examining literature. It is argued that the unresolved debates within the movement rather than constituting a weakness, make law and literature a useful educational tool with the potential to harbour legal theory in the law degree.

Katherine O'Donovan's essay focuses in on the often asserted claim that use of literature in educating lawyers shapes the ethical sensibility of the aspiring lawyer. She interrogates the basis of the claim that literature can foster empathy with new and varied life experiences and situations. While ultimately concluding that there is some validity to this, she exposes the assumptions that ignore the choices and constraints shaping our identification with characters in literature, and which limit and therefore determine our empathy.

It has been argued that 'the liberal seizure of legal power ... conducted under the auspices of rationalism, and the 'myth of neutrality' suppressed more humanistic approaches to law in favour of more scientific approaches.[8] Thérèse Murphy takes the struggle between multi-disciplinary approaches and a more positivistic approach to law within the academy, as her starting point. She finds a parallel between too stark a division between law and 'not law' in legal education and binary pairs in other areas of legal theory, particularly Feminism. With regard to the latter she argues in addition that postmodern relativism has posed a problem which Feminism is failing to address. In an attempt to remedy this, she suggests a re-focusing on the female body. This is an approach which she envisages happening through legal education, and the multi-disciplinary courses of Law and Literature and Medical Law and Ethics. To date, she argues, these have been impoverished by their failure to seriously engage with women in a feminist way. She argues a new way forward for both, namely that Law and Medicine would find women beyond the present 'reproductive ghetto' and that Law and Literature embrace the arguably postmodern genre of 'Romance' fiction. Ultimately, she argues that this approach would collapse the binary pairs within both the academy's vision of law, and within feminism itself.

Criminal stories

The themes and ideas raised by these first three essays are explored indirectly through specific examples throughout the rest of the collection. The next four essays are concerned with the maintenance of order and the role of literature in illustrating how law marks out a society's limits, particularly with relation to crime.

Thanks to Glanville Williams,[9] *Dudley v. Stephens* is often part of the law student's early exposure to legal cases, dealing with whether necessity provides a defence to murder. Yet, its supposed interest lies not just in the legal ruling, but in the drama of its facts and the cannibalism of the sailors. While the role of the judge as decision-maker has been a central focus of legal theory, Ray Geary's examination of the case and related literature provides us with a picture of the judge as critic. He argues that Lord

Coleridge chose to ignore an extensive literature on cannibalism with implications for his judgment, suggesting that Coleridge's own moral framework necessitated this. Thus Geary illustrates O'Donovan's argument that identification is limited by who we are as people and our wider framework of views. Geary's account presents us with a working example of both tangible links between law and literature and also a study of cannibalism as a cultural construct and a mechanism for distinguishing between human and beast, hero and inadequate, Christian and pagan. He also demonstrates the part of law in underwriting these distinctions.

John Morison argues that children's literature exists as a cultural artefact bearing the mark of the wider society which produced it and in which it is consumed. Books for children are produced by adults and contain a distillation of how adults see the world, what adults want for children and how children themselves are constituted in that world. Morison maintains that that this genre of writing is thus uniquely placed to help us understand how our concepts of right and wrong, safety and dangerousness, consensus and otherness are created, transmitted and policed. His account looks at a variety of disciplines which have considered children's literature in order to see the sorts of ways that we might gain insights relating to how hierarchy and order is represented and communicated within this genre.

Murphy's plea that 'real women' are missing from law and literature is picked up by Marie Fox who uses literature to examine the case of women who kill those other than their abusive male partners. She argues that this is undertheorised in current debates leaving accounts of such women to fall into three possible pre-existing scripts, that the woman is more evil than men, that she is the dupe of men, or that she is mad. She traces these scripts from Victorian times to present 'True Crime' and newspaper accounts. Acknowledging the difficulties in re-envisaging female killers, and escaping these scripts, Fox argues that feminist fiction may offer a way forward focusing on Zhavis' *Dirty Weekend* (1992) and Dworkin's *Mercy* (1990). In these fictional accounts, more capable of experimentation than law reviews, we get pictures of female deviance and motivations that are often silenced in more traditional discourse. Fox concludes that it may currently be difficult to go beyond deconstructing present accounts of violent women, and therefore difficult to posit concrete solutions for legal reform. However, her essay initiates a process of breaking a taboo, and as such has implications for more researched areas such as battered women who kill, and indeed constructions of feminine identity in general.

Kieran McEvoy again bridges the gap between Law and Literature and Cultural Studies. His account examines the representation of crime in newspapers as constitutive of narrative thus telling stories about our culture and its need for order. He illustrates how the study of the representation of crime has expanded positivistic criminological studies and makes claims for inclusion in much the way that Law and Literature studies attack black letter law and legal analysis. He traces the study of representation of crime through straightforward quantification, to Marxist explanations of portrayal, and more complicated ethnographic discussions, and relativistic, postmodern postulating. McEvoy, while refusing to adopt a 'positively postmodern' position, underscores the interactive dynamic between newspapers and culture. He argues that within criminology the study of newspaper depictions of crime offer unique insight into society's identity.

Novel stories: from Grisham to Trollope

From innovation we return to a more classical analysis of law in literature. The essays from Peter Robson and Peter Ingram illustrate a view of law and lawyers that both raises questions as to tensions between law, lawyering, legal institutions and justice, and also provide a picture of how law is perceived. Robson focuses on the novels of John Grisham, and Ingram on the works of Trollope. Both authors are outside the traditional 'canon', and the contrast and context of each author is strikingly different. Robson deals with Grisham, one of the best sellers of the twentieth century with blockbuster Hollywood films of his books, a culture of excesses and fast talking lawyers. Trollope's novels are set in the contained conservative culture of nineteenth century middle England, and unlike those of some of his contemporaries they avoid the pressing social issues of the day. Yet, despite these differences, these two chapters provide in their conclusions indications of surprising similarities with respect to law. Within Grisham's world law is corrupt, and solutions are based not on justice but on the capacity of the client to pay. In the case of Trollope, law may be seen as a deeply flawed institution but yet the premium is on order rather than justice to the expense of reform.

Legal regulation: the law of literature

An important aspect of the law and literature debate has been examination of the 'law *of* literature', or the law that seeks to regulate literature whether through censorship, of obscenity, pornography or indeed defamation laws, or through the use of copyright. Norma Dawson examines some of the difficulties of copyright law by taking the case of folklore which provides specific problems to present rationales of copyright protection. Folklore has no one author, and comes from an oral rather than a written tradition. It thus defies the concepts of author ownership with written text for evidence on which existing law is predicated. With its contrasting communal basis, this discussion also has implications for notions of ownership and exploitation in developing and developed countries. Study of literature can give insight to the processes of creation that copyright seeks to protect as this study of the origin of folklore, and the ways in which it becomes changed, illustrates. However, the lawyer must also respond to this debate by offering pragmatic solutions as to how protection can be achieved, and whether it is desirable. This essay addresses these different aspects.

Law and art

The essay collection seeks to ground itself in the movement's claims to educational validity, both by exploring these claims and by providing new examples. However, in the last essay we return to the 'no manifesto' debate. In contrast to the other essays which do not proffer any particular way of reading or any specific theoretical end in view (and indeed actively argue against such an approach) Gary Bagnall seeks to provide the beginnings of a whole approach with its own theoretical agenda. He makes the point that Law and Literature approaches often reduce both law and literature not to art, but to *text*. He seeks to reject such anti-aestheticism and work out a reconstructed concept of art that can connect legal theory with a philosophy of art. Bagnall maintains that his argument for understanding law as an art form has the advantage over Law and Literature approaches of taking both law and art seriously. Both the Law and Literature movement and Bagnall's law as art thesis focus on language but, according to Bagnall, his avoids 'intellectualising excess' by concentrating not on the interpretative activity but on the experience of the art *work* that is the law. He is arguing for law to be regarded as art and for legal scholarship to be a multidisciplinary inquiry into complex, compound legal art works.

This is a wholly novel account and his argument is undertaken in sketch form in his essay here. Such ideas perhaps deserve or require to be afforded fuller treatment and such an account is in preparation. Bagnall maintains that a 'best explanation' must await such further exploration of these themes. He hopes that here he has achieved a 'plausible' account of his position. Let the reader judge if this is the case and if he has indeed offered a theory of law as art that can rival more conventional Law and Literature approaches.

The contributors

In pursuing this project, this work draws upon several of those who contributed to earlier essay collections which originated from the School of Law at Queen's University. Both *The Jurisprudence of Orthodoxy: Queen's University Essays on H.L.A. Hart*[10] and *Law, Society and Change*[11] are concerned generally to see law as much more than a set of abstract, impersonal norms which operate impervious to the social and political context which produces them. The complex and essentially social nature of law are themes which find their echo in all the essays in this volume too. This time, however, the authorship of the collection has been expanded to include a number of contributors who presently are not based at Queen's. However all have strong links with that institution. Most have taught there in the recent or not so recent past or, in the case of Peter Robson (and indeed Katherine O'Donovan - although she qualifies on both counts) have acted as an external examiner to aspects of the jurisprudence component of the law degree there.

The contributors are:

Gary Bagnall, Division of Jurisprudence, School of Law, The Queen's University of Belfast, BT7 1NN, Northern Ireland,

Christine Bell, Division of Jurisprudence, School of Law, The Queen's University of Belfast, BT7 1NN, Northern Ireland,

Norma Dawson, Division of Private Law, School of Law, The Queen's University of Belfast, BT7 1NN, Northern Ireland,

Marie Fox, Faculty of Law, The University, Oxford Road, Manchester, M13 9PL,

Ray Geary, Division of Jurisprudence, School of Law, The Queen's University of Belfast, BT7 1NN, Northern Ireland,

Peter Ingram, Division of Jurisprudence, School of Law, The Queen's University of Belfast, BT7 1NN, Northern Ireland,

Kieran McEvoy, Institute of Criminology and Criminal Justice, The Queen's University of Belfast, BT7 1NN, Northern Ireland,

John Morison, Division of Jurisprudence, School of Law, The Queen's University of Belfast, BT7 1NN, Northern Ireland,

Thérèse Murphy, Department of Law, The University, Nottingham, NG7 2RD,

Katherine O'Donovan, Faculty of Laws, Queen Mary and Westfield College, Mile End Road, London, E1 4NS,

Peter Robson, Law School, University of Strathclyde, Stenhouse Building, 173 Cathedral Street, Glasgow, G4 0RQ.

All of us, and particularly the editors, are most grateful to Grainne McKeever who provided patient and very efficient editorial assistance and to the School of Law at Queen's University which funded her endeavors.

Notes

1. Faller (1993), at p. xv.
2. Lord Chancellor's Committee (1994).
3. See further Ward (1993); Aristodemou (1993) and Posner (1988).
4. See further White (1988).
5. See Ward (1993) and (1995).
6. Ward (1993), p. 323.
7. Bonsignore (1988).
8. Ward (1993), p. 327.
9. Williams (1982), pp. 120-1.
10. Leith and Ingram (Eds.) (1988).
11. Livingstone and Morison (Eds.) (1990).

References

Aristodemou, M. (1993), 'Studies in Law and Literature: Directions and Concerns', *Anglo American Law Review*, Vol. 22, pp. 157-93.

Bonsignore, J. (1988), 'In Parables: Teaching Through Parables', *Legal Studies Forum*, Vol. 12(2), pp. 191-210.

Faller, L. (1993), *Crime and Defoe: A New Kind of Writing*, Cambridge University Press, Cambridge.

Leith, P. and Ingram, P. (Eds.) (1988), *The Jurisprudence of Orthodoxy: Queen's University Essays on H.L.A. Hart*, Routledge, London.

Livingstone S. and Morison J. (Eds.) (1990), *Law, Society and Change*, Dartmouth, Aldershot.

Lord Chancellor's Committee (1994), Lord Chancellor's Advisory Committee on Legal Education and Conduct, *Review of Legal Education: Consultation Paper*.

Posner, R. (1988), *Law and Literature: A Misunderstood Relation*, Harvard University Press, Cambridge.

Ward, I. (1993), 'The Educative Ambition of Law and Literature', *Legal Studies*, Vol. 13, pp. 323-31.

Ward, I. (1995), *Law and Literature: Possibilities and Perspectives*, Cambridge University Press, Cambridge.

Williams, G. (1982), *Learning the Law*, 11th Edition, Stevens, London.

1 Teaching Law as Kafkaesque

CHRISTINE BELL

Legal education, law and literature

The case for legal theory in the law degree 'remains unqualified'[1] and is roundly supported in documents such as the recent Lord Chancellor's Advisory Report.[2] However, given the tension between the law degree as a professional qualification, and the law degree as an academic pursuit, questions as to the aims of legal education persist.[3] Amidst the confusion, the pull of 'professional' aspirations coupled with current changes in legal education such as rising student numbers, modularisation and shorter courses,[4] mean that at best the exact location of legal theory, and at worst its place at all, is uncertain. A recent review indicating the demise of the compulsory jurisprudence course seems to bear this out.[5] In this essay I will examine the role of law and literature courses as a possible pragmatic response.

There are three broad connections between law and literature which might provide a rationale and mechanism for using literature in legal education. Firstly, many literary works are about law. Secondly, issues of interpretation are vital to the study and criticism of both law and literature. Thirdly, both lawyers and literary writers are self-conscious about their use of language and rhetoric.[6] Academic discussion often focuses on which connections support the study of literature for lawyers, and which do not.[7] This essay seeks to illustrate and interrogate this discussion using four of Kafka's short stories namely, *Before the Law*,[8] *The Judgment*,[9] *In the Penal Colony*,[10] and *A Fasting Artist*.[11] Through this I will address the contribution of law and literature to legal education and in conclusion suggest its potential to accommodate both academic and professional demands by carving out a dialectical common ground from which to teach.

I have chosen Kafka's writing as illustration for several reasons. Firstly, it seems to have entered what has emerged as the 'canon' of law and literature. This means that there is a fairly extensive legal writing both theorising how Kafka can be used by lawyers and directly using Kafka to illustrate legal points. Given that such a canon is under attack, as are the traditional canons of literature courses, Kafka forms a good example with

11

which to explore the uses and limitations of literature in law degrees. Secondly, Kafka's frequent and varied use of law in his writings means that in one writer we have a variety of examples to look at. Finally, on a more personal note, my choice of Kafka is based on my own relationship with his writing. It was particularly after experience of legal practice in a huge law firm when the term 'kafkaesque' sank home, and stories such as *The Trial* or *Before the Law* seemed less bizarre analogies than direct descriptions of the bizarreness of law at work. On returning to teach jurisprudence and trying to make a case for the relevance of jurisprudence to students whose expectations of entering practice tend them towards seeing core subjects as more important, Kafka's stories seem to explain better than I could what is at stake in the practice of law and its relationship to justice.

Literary works 'about law' ('law in literature')

One of the most obvious connections between literature and law, is the fact that many 'great works' of litcrature, are 'about law'. Legal use of literature turns naturally to these legal depictions. However, the use of literature has extended from that clearly 'about law', to that 'about legal institutions', and also into literature with no clear legal content at all, but about 'the alienation of the human condition'. This extension is linked to an extension in the claims made for literature's relevance to lawyers. At its most basic, this was a claim that the body of literature about law could stimulate fruitful reflections on law and legal concepts. This then became a claim that literature could generate empathy and understanding by exposing the lawyer to a wider life experience. And more ambitiously still, that literature could be used to critique the socio-political order. Often classified as 'law *in* literature' studies, the malleable, interpretive quality of Kafka's writing illustrates the impossibility of deciding whether there is law in the literature, thus implicating the ever expanding circles of possibility of literature for lawyers.

Stories 'about law'

Before the Law, a short parable in which a man seeks access to the law, arguably provides an example of a story 'about law'. A man presents himself at the door of the law but is refused entry by the doorkeeper who warns him that should he gain entry there are a series of barriers beyond which are increasingly impenetrable. The man waits by the door years and years, giving presents to the doorkeeper which are accepted 'only lest you should think you'd left some stone unturned'.[12] Years later, when nearing death, the man asks the doorkeeper, 'Everybody seeks the law, ... so how is it that in all these years no one but me has demanded admittance?' The doorkeeper, shouts at the now almost deaf, dying man, 'No one else could gain admittance here because this entrance was meant for you alone. Now I'm going to close it'.[13] On first appearance this story is directly 'about law'. As well as a short story it also makes a cameo appearance in the novel *The Trial*, where it forms a parable for, and perhaps a microcosm of, the process which protagonist of *The Trial*, Joseph, K. is undergoing. Like the man before the law, Joseph, K. is passive, his passivity colluding with the power of the law to destroy his life. Joseph, K. inevitably presents himself at the court, in effect processing his own case to the extent that we wonder would it continue at all without his active participation. Similarly the man before the law chooses to sit for an entire lifetime despite the continuing advice of the doorkeeper that his attempts are likely to be useless.

Before the Law, while clearly a parable, can used in the classroom to stimulate reflection as to whether it has any resonance in contemporary legal structures. At this level it may speak of the impenetrability of law for the lay person, and the obscurity of law's operation, with its legal fictions and technicalities that become sensible to the student, academic, or practitioner but remain a nonsense to the uninitiated. It may be used to initiate discussion about the practical obstacles to obtaining access to law, such as provision of legal aid, or the exclusionary nature of some legal doctrines. Although appearing as an extreme caricature, using the story to consider perceptions of law in practice may be used to de-centre complacency with the law and even remind the student of pre-law experiences of the impenetrability of the legal world which they have been striving to enter.

Stories 'about legal themes or institututions'

In the Penal Colony, provides an example of a story not directly 'about' law but ostensibly about a legal institution - that of punishment. In *In the Penal Colony* a traveller has been invited, apparently by the current commandant of the colony, to attend the execution of a soldier condemned for 'insubordination and insulting a superior'.[14] The officer in charge demonstrates the execution machine to the traveller. The device, designed by the colony's late commandant, works by inscribing the sentence, in this case 'Honour Your Superiors', onto the body of the accused prisoner with sharp needles which inscribe deeper and deeper until the prisoner dies. In his description to the traveller the officer revels in the intricacy of the machine's design, with its needles and sophisticated water and cotton wool system to ensure that it does not become clogged with blood and malfunction. He seeks to persuade the traveller of the merits of the machine, partly to enlist his support in advocating its use to the new and unsympathetic commandant, and partly because of a child-like wish that the traveller understand and cherish the machine as he does. The prisoner, whose insubordination was minor and lacking in intent, and who has apparently not had a fair trial with a chance for defence, is not to be told the sentence but rather is to experience it through its inscription on his body. After about six hours, just before the prisoner will die, the officer claims that enlightenment will dawn upon him, the judgment becoming complete on death. This inhumane and bizarre process is made further farcical by the low intelligence and primitive nature of the prisoner, who is portrayed as sub-human, and apparently beyond any form of enlightenment. Eventually the prisoner is strapped onto the machine, vomiting as a felt cloth, still soaked in the vomit of previous victims is placed in his mouth. Before the machine is switched on, the traveller who has been reluctant to intervene finally reacts to the officer's pressures to advocate the machine's use to the new commandant. He tells the officer that he does not support the machine's use. The officer realizing that he has failed to communicate the machine's merits and significance, in an existential crisis, releases the prisoner and climbs onto the machine himself, ready to have the inscription 'Be Just' engraved on his body. However, the machine now clogged with the prisoner's vomit, malfunctions and rather than scribing the sentence it disintegrates, stabbing the officer and finally killing him with an iron spike stuck in his forehead, depriving him of the sixth hour enlightenment which he seeks. The story ends with the traveller visiting the grave of the old commandant, and being chased from the colony.

Although seemingly a story about punishment, Posner has attacked attempts by lawyers to see this story as a commentary on due process and cruel and unusual punishment, claiming that the 'legal and political details in his fiction are metaphoric'.[15] Rather, the point of the story he claims 'seems to lie in the juxtaposition of the absurdity of the whole procedure with the utter seriousness with which the officer expounds its virtues'.[16] Does this mean that the student can, or more strongly, should, learn nothing about punishment from this story? While Posner's readings of the stories and their central emphasis is convincing, it begs the question of why law and legal institutions so often and so aptly provide a metaphor for the alienation of the human condition. One answer is that as a lawyer Kafka was merely writing about what he knew. But this does not suffice. The power of the stories is difficult to separate entirely from their use of law as metaphor.[17] The absurdness of the stories which for Posner seem to lift them from reality, and therefore out of the realm of legal discussion, also constitutes their compelling quality. Compelling because they resonate in some way with our own experiences. For example, while we abhor the officer's cruelty, we also comprehend his personal identification with the torture machine, and sympathize with his sense of isolation in failing to find someone who understands him. Yet, this disturbing identification with the torturer can be used to provoke introspection as to our reactions to punishment within our own society.[18] While it may not have been Kafka's main purpose his description of the punishment which is on initial examination shockingly extreme and nonsensical, on closer examination has connections with traditional and contemporary punishment debate. Punishment as deterrence is exposed as farcical given a prisoner who is perhaps innocent, and who has been told neither crime nor sentence. Punishment as retributive is similarly dismissed due to the sheer lack of proportion between it and the crime, and the failure of due process in regard to convicting the prisoner. Rather, the form of punishment is portrayed as a manifestation of particular constitutional set up or legal regime. The machine is intricately bound up with the old commandant's view of law, justice and social control. As the officer boasts:

> Have you heard of our late commandant? No? Well, I'm not exaggerating when I say that the entire set-up here is his work. We, his friends, knew when he died that the whole way the penal colony had been constituted was so complete, so self-contained, that his successor, no matter how many new projects he had in mind, would be able to alter nothing of the original concept for many years, at least. And we were right; the new commandant has had to admit as much.[19]

The new legal culture, is to be symbolised through punishment, much in the way that the old one was. The new commandant institutes a new form of punishment not just because of a respect for humane punishment but because it will consolidate his distinctive power. The story connects punishment with society, and legal control. Punishment is symbolic of governmental control and the imposition of law and order.

The absurdity of the inscription on the body of the sentence as the punishment, finds its echo no less absurdly perhaps, in Foucauldian ideas about punishment in the 'real' world. For example, Faller, drawing on the work of Foucault, contrasts punishment in England and France, noting that while in England the criminal biography was used to simultaneously eulogise and justifying their killing, in France the state 'inscribed its power on the bodies of criminals through torture, execution and the display of physical remains'.[20]   In contemporary society, elements of symbolic inscription remain. A startling example occurs in Northern Ireland where paramilitary groups shoot 'joy-riders' in the knees - immobilising those who have sought mobility, and often leaving a limp which can simultaneously stigmatise and heroise the young person. Frank Burton has described   another   'punishment',   taring   and   feathering,   as symbolic/dramatic, labelling it an 'expulsion ritual'.[21] Dismissal of such punishment as meaningless and brutal ignores the power dynamics at play between state and paramilitaries, and the connection between punishment and legality, as punishment is used symbolically to usurp legality, and place state legality in question.[22]   For students therefore, Kafka's *In the Penal Colony*, provides a way of examining punishment that may challenge their assumptions and 'knowledge' or denormalize phenomena that surround them. Through the very denial of its basis in reality, it disrupts traditional punishment discourse and brings its own insight, despite the fact that the primary intrigue and purpose of the story may not be its appeal to lawyers and these analogies, but the personalities involved.

Stories 'about the human condition'

While *In the Penal Colony* deals with a legal institution the next two stories are progressively less obviously connected to law; neither are 'about law' in any obvious sense. *The Judgement* contains nothing overtly legal apart from its title while *The Fasting Artist*, has no legal connection whatsoever. In *The Judgment*, Georg, a young businessman contemplates why he does not write to his friend who moved to Russia to gain his fortune. The young businessman has not known what to say to this friend, not wanting to be insensitive to his friend's comparative lack of business success. However, now Georg is getting married, and so he writes a letter informing the friend of his engagement. Georg then goes to talk to his own aging and ill father with whom he appears to have a distant and strained relationship. The father claims that while the son has been writing half truths to his friend, the father has been sending letters explaining the true situation all along. The father accuses his son of betraying and neglecting both him and the friend since he became involved with his fiancée. He claims the friend has not visited because he knows of the son's lies and duplicity. The father berates the son in an increasing tirade finally shouting, 'So now you know what else there was apart from yourself! You were an innocent child, to tell the truth - though to tell the whole truth you were the devil incarnate! Therefore know: I hereby sentence you to death by drowning'.[23] The son runs from the house and vaults over the nearest bridge into the water, saying softly, 'Dear parents, I did love you always'.[24] The story ends with the traffic streaming endlessly over the bridge.

The Fasting Artist concerns a man who makes his living by fasting in front of crowds of watchers. The manager of a fasting artist sets a limit of forty days on the fast, not because of any religious connection, but because after forty days, experience has shown that the crowd loses interest and profits drop. The fasting artist, like the officer in the penal colony, desperately seeks understanding and recognition of his strange art, the absence of which causes him to live his life in a state of gloom. While at one time the fasting artist drew crowds interest in fasting has now died out, and so the artist joins a circus where he sits in a cage to be seen by the visitors who stream past, mainly to see the animals in the cages alongside. Finally, the fasting artist tells the foreman of the circus that his fasting should not be admired because he has only fasted because he had never found any food he liked. With these words the fasting artist dies and his scant remains are removed by the keepers along with the straw in his cage. He is replaced by a young panther, whose vigourous pacing provides a stark contrast to the fasting artist's meagre, despairing existence and final hours.

If reading stories with some 'legal' content as about law in any meaningful sense has come under attack as illegitimate, what then is the legal end of reading stories with no legal content at all? One of the strongest defences of the use of literature in educating lawyers has been literature's humanistic value, that is, its value to supplement 'scientific' or 'technical' legal study. Thus literature not 'about law' can be used to inject a broader life experience than the lawyer can hope to achieve otherwise.

This largely rests on the premise that literature, and stories can be used to generate empathy.[25]   Part of the power of Kafka's stories is his ability to make us empathise with the most unlikely of characters and situations in a world that is simultaneously fantastic, real and surreal. While the central characters, for example, the officer from *In the Penal Colony*, the father and son in *The Judgement* and the fasting artist, are in one sense unreal and bizarre, they are also more 'real' and more 'normal' than the events and characters around them. As Nabokov writes, in many of the stories 'the absurd central character belongs to the absurd world around him, but pathetically and tragically, attempts to struggle out of it into the world of humans - and dies in despair'.[26]   Yet despite the absurd quality of the stories, they also resonate in the reality of our own fears and frustrations and the dream or nightmare quality life can take on, often when we are confronted with isolating events such as personal tragedy or circumstances beyond our control, or even in the surreal conversations and situations which surround us in the trivialities of life. Indeed it is this juxtaposition of the dream and reality and the humour, often grim, that accompanies it, that earns situations the label 'kafkaesque'.

The claim of 'empathy generation' more clearly opens the door to stories with little or no legal content. *The Judgment* and *The Fasting Artist* provide many possibilities for empathy both through their underlying themes of alienation and indeed with their specific situations and characters. Posner suggests that a son who acts on the father's judgment, and a hunger artist who deliberately starves have mental health problems, and cannot be assumed to 'make choices that will maximise [their] satisfactions'.[27]   However, law is full of passive, accepting characters, who participate in their own judgment for various reasons, not least of which is the power of the image of law. To take another literary example, Oscar Wilde took a libel suit, despite legal advice to the contrary, against the Marquis of Queensbery for calling him a 'somdomite' (*sic*).   Started voluntarily this process was eventually to take him to Reading Gaol and hard labour. Wilde's passivity in the face of self-interested pressures from the Marquis' son Bosie and his refusal to flee the country when prosecution became imminent, led to his eventual exile and death. Like Joseph, K., the man before the law, and the son in *The Judgment*, participation with legal processes combined with passivity as to the results of this participation contributed to his death. More recently, in the Irish case of *Attorney General v. X*[28] a 14 year old rape victim who had gone to England with her parents for an abortion returned to Ireland after the Irish Attorney General placed an injunction on her obtaining an abortion, despite its unenforceability outside of the jurisdication. Examples such as this reinforce that the power of law is more than just the threat of sanction, made stark by Kafka's stories.[29]

In *The Fasting Artist*, once again Kafka makes us empathise with the artist despite his 'irrationality'. This empathy with the artist occurs because we relate to the alienation his art form symbolizes, rather than because we relate to the wish to starve ourselves. However, it is not impossible that the story also forces us to reconsider our conceptions of rationality, even as confined to the specific act of starvation; would the story work if we were unable to identify at all with the need to fast? Ellman in a book entitled *The Hunger Artists* explores the political commonalities of self-starvation in contexts as varied as anorexia and hunger strikes.[30] Legal treatment of both these situations involves construction of rationality and irrationality which Kafka's story throws into question. In *In Re W*[31] a teenager's decision to refuse food was dismissed by the judge as irrational, warranting force feeding. Yet if, remembering identification with the fasting artist, we look again, the history of devastation in W's life makes one wonder if self-starvation was not a rational attempt to take back control in one of the few ways open with her. From such a standpoint, refusal to eat while physically self-destructive was perhaps mentally self-securing, and the judge's decision to force feed more controversial. Rather than a life-saving intervention, it appears as just one more instance of control being taken away, the very trigger for the fasting in the first place.[32] In the examples of the 1981 hunger strikes in Northern Ireland where ten men died, self-starvation was a response to conditions in prison, and an attempt to reform them by achieving political status.[33] Employed as a negotiation tactic with tremendously high stakes, the hunger strikes, while clearly emotive to the point of fascinating incomprehension, were simultaneously the epitome of rationality and calculated risk-taking that is the basis for the coldest law and economics reasoning. As in the case of the anorexic teenager, the act of fasting and questions around its rationality were intrinsically connected to questions about justice as hunger strikers and state vied for the moral high-ground.[34] Different conceptions of rationality conceive justice differently.

From using the stories to explore empathy with the characters, and the situations they find themselves in, it is possible to move to a critique of the socio-legal order which forms a part of their predicament. In *Before the Law*, it is possible to go beyond using the story as a platform for creating empathy with legal mystification, and problematise legal education itself which will normalise the operation of law and co-opt the student in its mysterious world.[35]   Indeed, a critique of legal education can be further extended, to a critique of liberalism itself, with its tensions between generality and individualism.[36] This critique also can flow from the story's absences. Specifics in the story are left out, what country is it, what sort of legal system is operating, is the state totalitarian or a dictatorship, or a democracy? These questions make accessible the theoretical debates about the nature of the rule of law. Both *The Trial* and *Before the Law*, present a picture of law's operation that is clearly at odds with even the narrowest requirements of the rule of law; requirements of openness, clarity, prospectiveness, and generality.[37]   This feature of Kafka's work has led some commentators to see it as prophetic of the Nazi era yet the discussion can be extended to critique liberal democracy itself. The essence of the rule of law's requirements lies in liberalism's demand that people should be able to exercise freedom of choice in their personal lives free from state interference. Critiques of the rule of law have argued that in practice the rule of law obscures and justifies injustice, and the subjective, fact-specific nature of decision-making that favours elites. The challenge to law's claim of general application of justice is presented in a direct and more accessible way by the doorkeeper's final explanation 'this entrance was meant for you alone. Now I'm going to close it'. With little theorising, it suggests that legal solutions often seem dependant on individual characteristics, such as race or gender, or other subjective factors, which are supposedly excluded from the decision-making process.

Such 'political' use of Kafka's work is contested. Posner has argued that it is a mistake to read *The Trial* as a book 'about law' in a literal sense arguing, one 'might as well read *Animal Farm* as a tract on farm management or Moby-Dick as an exposé of the whaling industry'.[38]   He finds its meaning to lie

> elsewhere, in K.'s futile efforts to find human meaning in a universe (symbolised by the court) that, not having been created to be accommodating or intelligible to man, is arbitrary, impersonal, cruel, deceiving, and elusive - like the doorkeeper in *Before the Law*, who not only thwarts the effort of the man from the country to reach the source of the 'radiance that streams inextinguishably from the door of the Law' but makes the man's effort ridiculous and pathetic.[39]

As such he finds efforts to link *The Trial* to critiques even of totalitarian justice, and lack of rule of law 'wide of the mark'.[40] He claims that it does not contain several necessary ingredients of totalitarian systems, namely, that it does not have the serious 'documentary' feel of works such as Arthur Koestler's *Darkness at Noon*, and that throughout *The Trial*, the oppression does not have any political agenda or point - Joseph K. is not a subversive. Posner therefore reflects a reading of these stories which would imply a critique of legal institutions.

Unsurprisingly, the legitimacy of using Kafka for such a political enterprise has been most explicitly and famously debated through use of the two stories least explicitly about law - *The Fasting Artist* and *The Judgement*. Here, West and Posner[41] have had a series of exchanges triggered by West's use of Kafka's writing to critique the assumptions of human behaviour and fulfilment which she argues underpin Posner's law and economics theory of law and society. She has argued that stories such as *The Judgment* and *The Fasting Artist*, describe the human alienation that flows from making decisions based on market forces and wealth-maximization and the impoverishment of life which this brings. Thus, 'Kafka's hunger artist is the ultimate Posnerian entrepreneur, and the artist's audience consists of Posnerian consumers',[42] and *The Judgment* with its young businessman, provides an indictment of capitalism. Posner in turn has attacked such use of Kafka's writing as misplaced. He defends the attack on law and economics by attacking West's interpretation:

> *A Hunger Artist* may also be about the world's indifference to Kafka's own artistic scruples. It may be about many things. But only superficially is it about hunger, poverty, the pitfalls of entrepreneurship, and the fickleness of consumers.[43]

For *The Judgment*, Posner rejoins,

> West conceives the story to be about capitalist alienation. How flat and dull her reading makes the story! If the story is not about the Oedipus complex, of Kafka's relationship with his own father, or why Kafka did not marry, then it is about the sense of guilt, about the disproportion between cause and effect, about the surreal, about life's unfairness, about how people tend to accept the valuation placed on them by other people, about the dislocated feeling of modern life to highly sensitive souls, about the indifference of others to our inner turmoil ... But ... in arguing that Georg kills himself because of guilt over 'his own self-imposed alienation from [his friend's] suffering', West has taken the father's side in the story, and this I find bizarre.[44]

It is not just Posner who is uncomfortable with the extension of literature as an empathy-generating tool to literature as a tool of political critique. Others who are less ambivalent about the use of literature by lawyers remain uneasy with literature's use for political ends. Weisberg, who like West has had a series of exchanges with Posner based on the 'anti-humanist' nature of the law and economics movement, seeks to limit the impact of literature on law to an ethical rather than a broader political ambition.[45] Dunlop and Ward, with specific reference to legal education feel that tying up literature with one specific political agenda is to defeat the broader educational purpose which launched the movement in the first place.[46]

In the classroom however, the discussion itself can be used as an active learning tool. Engagement with literature is not just more fun than engagment with law, it is different in type.[47] Parables such as Kafka's present moral choices without dictating what that choice should be, reversing teacher/student hierarchy by pressurising students to find their own source of wisdom. For example, it has been suggested that *Before the Law* was created deliberately by Kafka 'to defy any potential attempt to ascertain a certain interpretation of his treatment of legal issues in the [*The Trial*]'.[48] Reading Kafka's stories may ultimately fail to create feelings of empathy or convince us that the socio-political order is flawed, however, they may expand our understanding of the issues at stake in the choices we make around these arguments.[49] For example, the debate between Posner and West illustrates in a readable and entertaining fashion the competing underlying world visions which underpin both Posner's law and economics vision, and West's more critical legal, communitarian one. As Posner claims West could have grounded her attack on law and economics 'in the literature of the social sciences but ... instead she grounds it in Kafka's fiction'.[50] Posner in turn responds through use of the same fiction, and indeed it is through this defence that he claims to have been drawn into contributing to law and literature studies. Use of literature is therefore responsive to contemporary notions about what constitutes 'good' educational technique and participative learning, as much as to legal academic critique of legal education as obsessed with rules and 'right' answers.

The meaning of texts

So far, I have used Kafka's stories in a free-wheeling manner, with little reference to the vast body of literature which seeks to interpret his work. This literature interprets Kafka with relationship to his specific historical context, to his experience as a Jew in pre World War II eastern Europe, to Freudian analysis of his relationship with his father, to his relationships with women, to his experience as a lawyer, and to the city of Prague. However, the very existence of such a vast literature and such people as 'kafkaologists' raises the question of what we need to know to interpret works of literature, and whether there are correct and incorrect interpretation, or indeed better and worse ones. As the Posner/West debate indicates, differences of interpretation can be vital in deciding what is a legitimate use of the stories in the legal classroom. Literary critics have engaged with these questions over a long period of time, and the theories they have generated can very roughly be divided into three. Theories which focus around the author's intent and factors for discerning it as an interpretive source (Intentionalist); theories which focus on the text as the basis for interpretation, (New Criticism) and theories which focus on the text and the experiences and background of the reader herself as a source of interpretation (Deconstructionist).

These literary debates find their counterparts in legal interpretation debates, and it is this comparison that the law and literature movement has developed and is concerned with. Often described as studies in law *as* literature, rather than law *in* literature, the justification for borrowing from literary theory is provided by Dworkin who argues,

> critics themselves are thoroughly divided about what literary interpretation is, and the situation is hardly better in the other arts. But that is exactly why lawyers should study these debates. Not all of the battles within literary criticism are edifying or even comprehensible, but many more theories of interpretation have been defended in literature than in law.[51]

Posner, who unlike Dworkin denies that literary theories of interpretation can usefully help in legal interpretation, also continues to offer a minimalist justification for their place in legal education. He maintains that 'an understanding of the differences between legal and literary interpretation may improve our understanding of the former indirectly'.[52]

The focus of the debate as to legal interpretation has been North American in orientation, partly because of the questions posed by

Constitutional interpretation. It is here that originalist or framer's intent approaches to legal interpretation have been most explicit, and formed a parallel with 'author's intent' type literary interpretation. With the United States Constitution talk of author's intent raises questions such as who were the framers, how can we divine a single intent, and why should such an intent hundreds of years ago be relevant to reading the Constitution to-day?[53] Literary interpretation raises these same problems in a different and arguably more easily accessible way. For law students engaging with Kafka's stories perhaps for the first time, there are specific questions of interpretation which arise and which shake a simple author's intent mode of interpretation. The first is one of translation, cultural and lingual. Culturally, we might ask, why study Kafka with first year students in Britain or Ireland? They know nothing of his background, his personal life, his experience as a Jew in pre-war Europe, or his legal training. Does this not preclude them from informed comment? Furthermore, there is not just a problem of cultural translation, but of language translation. Kafka, though Czechoslovakian, wrote in German yet law students read the stories in English. Translation is itself a complex process of interpretation. The reader is therefore a step further removed from any possible author's intent and arguably must also grapple with the translator's concept of the author's intent, about which there may be little information. Do concepts such as a 'Fasting Artist', or 'Hunger Artist' even exist similarly in English as in German? Does the phrase, *The Penal Colony*, conjure up different ideas in the head of an English reader as that of *Der Strafkolonie* in the head of a German one? J.A. Underwood indicates in his preface some of the dilemmas he faced in translation, in particular the question of 'fidelity in translation' where he states '[a] translator's rule of thumb might be to seek to carry as much of the original across to the reader of the target language as is compatible with an equivalent level of readability ... One is continually trimming for a balance between content and equivalence, between the demands of fidelity and the requirements of readability'.[54] For example Underwood gives his translation of *ungeheures Ungeziefer* in *The Metamorphosis* as 'giant bug'. He acknowledges that the translation 'monstrous vermin' would better capture the 'cultural resonance of Kafka's [original] in terms of social and religious exclusion', but claims that 'the awkwardness of that noun in the singular might balk the reader in a way that is irrelevant to Kafka's purpose'.[55] As another example, Underwood makes 'no apology for anglicising the first names Georg, Gregor, Grete, Josef and Josefine (they are people, not foreigners)'.[56]

A second problem with author's intent is that before his death Kafka asked Max Brod, his friend and executor, to destroy almost all his writing. Brod did not comply. Should this request to Brod be taken as part of Kafka's intent and if so how? Borges' defence of Brod's refusal suggests that Kafka was 'surely relying on the devout disobedience of his friends', and that the request reflects the author's own personal and religious feeling of himself as an artist and a passing of existential responsibility more than a genuine desire to see the works destroyed, for 'a man who really wishes to see his work consigned to oblivion does not entrust the task to someone else'.[57] Therefore discerning the intent of the request itself, as well as how, if at all, that should affect the reading of Kafka's work is problematic. Kafka's work therefore seems to defy any simple application of an objective 'author's intent', thus undermining its force as a means of interpretation in other contexts.

A New Critic approach stands as an intermediate position between the objective stance of the author's intent school and the subjective reader-oriented stance of the deconstructionists. The New Critic takes the text itself as the primary tool of interpretation, and seeks to provide a 'coherent and satisfying meaning to the words'.[58] According to Posner,

[a] New Critic treats a work of literature as an artifact, coherent in itself and not to be understood better by immersion in the details of the author's biography or in the other circumstances of its composition (except that some slight knowledge of those circumstances may be necessary to understand particular references in the work).[59]

Certain writers, such as Dworkin, Fiss and to some extent Weisberg, have taken a view of legal interpretation that is akin to a 'New Critics' approach to literature. Dworkin, for example, argues that legal adjudication is an interpretative exercise and that judges should apply the interpretation that shows the rule in its 'best light' according to a principle of integrity. While interpretation is not therefore restricted to what framers intended neither is the judge's role an open-ended unconstrained one. Adjudication is constrained by the text itself, with some reference to community, and therefore is in some sense 'objective'. Fiss also rejects the 'textual determinism' of framer's intent type interpretation,[60] without reaching a conclusion that interpretation is subjective. He claims that rules governing interpretation, recognised as authoritative by judges 'transform ... the interpretative process from a subjective to an objective one, and they furnish the standards by which the correctness of the interpretation can be judged'.[61]

The Deconstructionist like the New Critic denies objectivity in interpretation, but takes it further to extreme scepticism, or what has been described as 'postmodern nihilism', whereby the text itself holds no objective meaning extrinsic to the meaning assigned to it by the reader.[62] Posner provides an illustration with reference to *In the Penal Colony*:

> The torture machine is a writing machine, and one way of stating the officer's problem of communication is that he puts too much faith in writing as a medium of communication, while an alternative interpretation is that, in good deconstructive fashion, it is the medium, not the communication that obsesses him. And those fearful arabesques that the machine traces out on the body of the condemned in order to protract the torture are a wonderful metaphor for overdetermination.[63]

The Deconstructionist approach to legal interpretation, like that of literary interpretation, challenges 'the assumption that interpretation should hinge on the preservation of an inherent meaning placed in the text by the author'.[64] This approach deconstructs the way in which judges and lawyers rely on framer or author intent arguments to legitimize particular interpretations. The Deconstructionist recognises that 'originally unintended meanings ... are assigned to the text by subsequent readers, and that such readings have as much validity as the author's intent'.[65] This approach is taken by writers such as Stanley Fish whose subjective approach to interpretation means that he rejects the search for finality and truth in interpretation. This is not to say that he believes that any interpretation is as good as any other, claiming to be able to defend his own views of interpretation of any text as right. As Levison writes:

> In this regard Fish seems similar to Ronald Dworkin, who views judging as including the phenomenological experience of feeling oneself to have achieved the uniquely correct solution even to a hard case. But Fish, more candid than Dworkin on this point, admits that his own conviction of rightness will provide no answer at all to anyone who happens to disagree with him, and that there is no way to resolve this dispute.[66]

While the Intentionalist and New Critical positions to legal interpretation seek to simultaneously describe and prescribe legal interpretation - they give the same answer to the questions how do judges decide cases and how should judges decide cases - the Deconstructionist approach is concerned with exposing the political biases of legal interpretation, rather than justifying interpretive processes.

All three prongs of the literary/legal interpretation comparison have been critiqued for failing to take sufficient account of the differences between law and literature.[67]   While literature exists to generate interpretation, and even to entertain, legal interpretation is usually linked to the making of a decision and the exercise of power. This can be illustrated through a comparison of literary and legal titles. In literature the title is involved in the interpretive process in a number of ways. It sets the framework for the reading of the story and indeed sets the reader's perceptions on certain tracks. As such it forms an integral part of the story. Umberto Eco has argued that the author's purpose in writing a novel is to generate multiple interpretations. He argues that the novelist should not therefore supply interpretations, but notes that 'one of the chief obstacles to his maintaining this virtuous principle is the fact that a novel must have a title',[68] which will itself suggest an interpretation, illustrating that his choice of *The Name of the Rose* 'rightly disoriented the reader, who was unable to choose just one interpretation'.[69] The titles in Kafka's stories are similarly ambiguous, although the issue of author's intent is complicated by the fact that Brod gave some of his works their title. *Before the Law* indicates the parable form of the story, and its analogy, while giving little else away. *In the Penal Colony*, suggests from the outset, a society that is different and 'other', it both smacks of the exotic, and sets the scene for the sinister and bizarre. It tells of a colony which is defined not by location or name, but by its system of punishment, and of a society with questions as to the legitimacy of its rulers. *The Judgment* as a title, forms an integral part of the story which gives it shape in focusing the reader by begging the question of what is 'the judgment' in question. Is it the father's judgment of the son, the son's continual judgment of his friend, the son's judgment of himself with reference to the judgments of others such as the friend or his father? Or is it a judgment on friendship and relationships themselves? Most obviously, a judgment appears in the last sentences with the father pronouncing death on his son, and while raising the above questions, the title prepares the reader for this twist in the tale, instantly redefining the characters as the judge and the judged, the unsympathetic son ultimately appearing as the victim. Similarly, in *A Fasting Artist*, the title as well as intriguing, opens the twist in the tail where the artist questions whether his has been an art form or something much more mundane - a dislike for the food on offer.

In legal interpretation cases and statutes have names and not titles. Far from existing to generate interpretations, these names are seen as all but irrelevant to the substance of the texts serving only as a descriptive label for accessing information. As such they are part of a process of exercising power rather than a process of creativeness. The name of the case tells us little about its content, although the parties involved tell us something about the form of the case, and whether it is for example, a criminal case, a family law case or a judicial review. This perhaps carries more significance than is often credited as the journey from the intricacies of the facts and events in a client's life to the pages of the law reports involves a series of decisions by the executive, the lawyers and the judges and the ultimate emergence of the problem as for example a civil or criminal or administrative matter determines the remedy affecting the exercise of power. Likewise statute names do not exist to generate interpretations but to inform the reader as to what the statute aims to deal with. Headnotes or abstracts may constitute a form of title for the case, but again these seek to delimit and summarise the decisions with reference to its effect in terms of an exercise of power.[70]

West has described the legal identification of adjudication as interpretation as a debate with two main strands, the crucial rift being 'over the nature of interpretation'.[71] She rejects both a subjectivist and an objectivist approach to interpretation as based on the same false assumption, namely that adjudication is an interpretive exercise. She claims that 'despite a superficial resemblance to literary interpretation, adjudication is not primarily an interpretive act of either a subjective or objective nature; adjudication, including constitutional adjudication, is an imperative act'. As such it involves an exercise of power in a way that literary interpretation does not. She claims that refusal to acknowledge and engage with this crucial difference, de-radicalises criticism of law, because it confuses interpretation of law with legal criticism itself, so to criticise is to interpret, and to interpret is to criticise. She argues that:

> The criticism of law, by contrast, should be grounded in a different text. It must rest on a claim regarding that which ought to be, not a claim regarding that which is, or how power has been used to date. It must be grounded in the text we didn't write - the text of our natural needs, our true potential, our utopian ideas.[72]

She suggests that the 'test of morality of power in public life as in private life may be neither compliance with community mores, as objectivists insist, nor political success, as subjectivists claim, but love. Imperativism, distinctively, frees the critic for this possibility.'[73]

Posner also claims that it is a mistake to closely connect the philosophy of literary criticism with the philosophy of legal criticism, because legal and literary texts have different *raison d'etres*. He contrasts an Intentionalist stance with a New Critics stance. The former limits interpretation with reference to the author's intent, the latter, allows for a more reader oriented interpretation, freeing up reading for the lay reader, rather than the historian or biographer, but not going as far as Deconstructionists who he feels have replaced obsession with the author with obsession with the reader. Thus he claims to be a New Critic when it comes to literature and an Intentionalist when it comes to law.[74] However, his purpose in making this distinction is quite different from West's. West is doing it to preserve radical criticism of interpretation and law, while Posner is doing it to preserve the idea of law as a science, where 'right' answers can be achieved, and humanitarian concerns about law are quite distinct and outside of the interpretive process.[75]

As Ward has pointed out, the law as literature debate contains the paradox that while it reasserts 'language as a living force', it also wants to 'intellectualise legal study' by introducing the various interpretive schools of thought.[76] Teaching through examples such as Kafka's short stories, provide an accessible way of raising the debate's basic precursers, if not their complexities, at an early stage in the curriculum thus problematising legal interpretation.

Language, rhetoric and persuasion

Ward also suggests that the above paradox is accommodated in the 'resurrection of rhetoric as a primary concern in law teaching'.[77] Posner states the case more broadly as one of literature teaching the lawyer about persuasion. The Law and Literature movement with its link to the humanities is often presented as the antithesis to the 'law as a profession' culture of technical science. In contrast, the growing emphasis on skills based training is often seen as a response to professional demands and therefore at odds with jurisprudence courses. However, the law as literature branch of the movement, raises the proposition of a more dialectical skills based training or legal skills as jurisprudential.

The link between law and literature and discussion of legal skills is to be found more explicitly in the extension of law and literature studies to 'narrative scholarship' as legal theory. As Farber and Sherry explain it:

> Once upon a time, the law and literature movement taught us that stories have much to say to lawyers, and Robert Cover taught us that law is itself a story. Instead of living happily ever after with that knowledge, some feminists and critical race theorists have taken the next logical step: telling stories, often about personal experiences, on the pages of law reviews.[78]

This approach focuses on law as telling stories and then deconstructs stories told by law, exposing their assumptions and consequences, and posits possible alternative stories as either a conceptual challenge or a possible reforming in-court challenge.[79] As a theoretical extension, this branch of scholarship has been challenged in ways similar to the challenges to the law in literature branch of the law and literature movement. Like those who ask whether literature can educate to empathy, critics of narrative scholarship question whether it has the capacity to impact on law makers, and why certain narratives should be prioritised over others. Yet, like law and literature studies, narrative scholarship retains its place as a part of legal theory through its ability to present new views on legal decision-making in a provoking and readable way.

Toddington has argued that skills training is presently based on a vacuum, where we cannot teach legal skills without knowing what law is, and therefore which skills are specifically legal.[80] He rejects a pragmatic answer to this question - law is what lawyers do - in favour of a philosophical position which would find some shared answer to the question 'what is law?' In fact, for teachers of jurisprudence, the job has often been to indicate the many different answers to the question of what is law and live with the unresolved dilemmas the contest poses for legal education. Also teachers play a part in constituting what law is by what they teach it to be. Why then not similarly teach different skills while problematising them as well much in the way that narrative scholarship explores? This approach would look at different theories of say, advocacy or negotiation, and show the consequences for lawyering, and therefore justice, underlying different ways of exercising these skills, much in the way that our previous examination of Kafka's stories has indicated the different consequences which flow from the various choices we can make as to interpretation. Particularly on the undergraduate degree, surely skills-based training can be presented in a contested way, just as specific courses such as tort law exist in uneasy harmony with the legal theory on the degree whether in the shape of the 'policy considerations' taught at the end of the tort lecture or the more abstract legal theory of the separate jurisprudence course. It is arguably not the teaching of skills themselves which poses a threat to the academic aspirations of the law degree, but competence rather than knowledge based assessment. Competence based assessment focuses uncontroversially on what lawyers do as the criteria of assessment, with no critique of whether the chosen performance is a useful standard, and therefore falls foul of Toddington's criticism.[81]   In providing a way of presenting both persuasive skills and their shortcomings and controversies, the law as literature debate contributes to current dilemmas in legal education. The price is coherence of goals - a more kafkaesque law world for the student.

Conclusions

Law and literature studies respond to the current legal education debate in several ways. Perhaps most cynically, the 'fun factor' makes them one of jurisprudence's best chances for competing in the modular world in which compulsory jurisprudence is no longer a reality. They provide a 'much needed focus' for students who 'find it difficult to engage in abstract reasoning when they are accustomed, from their other subjects, to problem and case-oriented discourse'.[82]   Law and Literature courses while presenting as a unit, also have an advantage over other single-issue jurisprudence courses such as Law and Economics. The 'no-manifesto' theoretical weakness is an educational strength in that Law and Literature can be used to provide a jurisprudential overview previously found in the compulsory jurisprudence course, thus avoiding the dangers inherent in presenting one specific theory.[83]

The quantity and diversity of literature 'about law', also arguably provides a mechanism for legal theory, or at least a 'call to context'[84] in more black-letter law courses. While there may not be time to address the underlying policies and politics in a 12 week land law course, a reference to *Bleak House* may well be manageable. Use of literature, especially when established in a course, has a way of filtering from pure law and literature courses into others, albeit in a short and perhaps simplistic fashion, with some of its power to disrupt the traditional discourse intact. This is responsive to discussion about whether jurisprudence should be in a self-contained course which can encompass a number of issues,[85] or injected into each course.[86]

Discussions about the relevance of literature to lawyers provide an interesting way to present current and traditional debates in legal theory, as both the law *in* literature and law *as* literature strands of the movement illustrate. The synthesis of these two strands in pursuit of persuasion arguably provides a way for skills education to extend beyond the narrowly vocational to the academic. This approach to skills teaching may seem hopelessly incoherent to those such as Toddington, in the absence of consensus as to what law is. However, the only alternative seems to assert some objective core no matter how contested. Such a project has not served to clarify goals in legal education generally, and therefore seems unlikely to be any more helpful in clarifying the goals of skills teaching. Ward writes, 'indeterminacy is not a monster that devours all possibility of a rational and fulfilled existence ... It is simply a fact of life which, when appreciated, can be used precisely to enhance our understanding of our own possibilities'.[87] Surely this holds true not just of law, but of educational goals themselves which are similarly dependant 'on the (moral) view we hold of the nature of society and the nature of man, and presuppose an ideal of a person to which education should lead or an ideal of a society for which education should prepare the individual member'.[88] In this sense teaching law as kafkaesque is kafkaesque in the fuller meaning of word which connotes humour, self-responsibility and context creation, as well as the oft-times futility and confusion more normally associated with the word.

Notes

1. Barnett (1995).
2. For example, the report suggests that law degrees 'provide a rigorous theoretical and analytical education to enable students to develop a constructive and critical approach to the processes of law'; and to 'enable students to see law within its social, economic, political, historical, ethical and cultural context'. (Lord Chancellor's Committee (1994) at p. 12.)
3. Aristodemou (1993) p. 190.
4. Toddington (1995) also documents the 'economic' problems of legal education which focus around legal practice.
5. Barnett (1995).

6.   A fourth connection is that law has been used in a variety of ways to regulate literature, for example obscenity laws and copyright laws, although I will not deal with this in this essay, the censorship of Kafka's work at different times for different reasons, provides some interesting examples.
7.   Posner (1988).
8.   Written in 1915.
9.   Written in 1912.
10.   Written in 1914.
11.   Written in period 1921-1924. These stories can all be found in *Franz Kafka Stories 1904-1924*, Trans J.A. Underwood, Foreword, Jorge Luis Borges 1988 at pages 194, 43, 147, and 242 respectively. In this edition *Before the Law* is given the title *At the Door of the Law*. All references to the stories will be cited to this edition.
12.   Underwood (1988), p. 194.
13.   Underwood (1988), p. 195.
14.   Underwood (1988), p. 149.
15.   Posner (1988), p. 117.
16.   Posner (1988), pp. 117-8.
17.   As Weisberg writes: 'Dickens, Twin, Kafka, Camus, and Faulkner (among many others) perceived that people felt so dominated by law, so mystified yet so involved, that the more legalistic they made the subject matter, the more compelling would be the work', (1992, p. xi).
18.   See for example, Sparks' analysis of the relationship between fictional crime stories in popular culture and punishment (1992, pp. 161-2).
19.   Underwood (1988), pp. 161-2.
20.   Faller (1987), p. xi; see also Foucault (1977), chp. 1.
21.   Burton (1978), pp. 108-9.
22.   Munck (1988).
23.   Underwood (1988), p. 56.
24.   Underwood (1988), p. 56.
25.   Ward (1993/i), p. 60.
26.   Nabokov (1980), pp. 254-5.
27.   Posner (1988), p. 188. However, he is prepared to have a working assumption that they are sane.
28.   [1992] I.R. 1.
29.   Although see Ward's analysis of stories such as *The Trial* or *Before the Law* as also about taking responsibility (1993/i).

30.   Ellman (1993).
31.   [1992] 3 W.L.R. 758
32.   Bridgeman (1993), p. 79.
33.   See Campbell, McKeown, O'Hagan (1994) for one of most recent accounts.
34.   Ellman (1993).
35.   Kennedy (1990).
36.   Unger (1975).
37.   Raz (1979).
38.   Posner (1988), p. 180.
39.   Posner (1988), p. 125.
40.   Posner (1988), p. 127.
41.   See West (1985), Posner (1986) and (1988) and West (1986). There is also an exchange between Weisberg and Posner, in which Weisberg looks at Kafka; Posner (1988), and Weisberg (1992).
42.   Posner (1988), p. 180.
43.   Posner (1988), pp. 180-1.
44.   Posner (1988), p. 184-5.
45.   Weisberg (1992). For a more detailed discussion of Weisberg's position and in particular, the difficulties inherent in deciding where the ethical stops and the political begins, see Ward (1994).
46.   Dunlop (1991), pp. 93-6; Ward (1994), pp. 399-400.
47.   Bonsignore 1988.
48.   Ward (1994), p. 398, n. 8.
49.   Even Posner would not quibble with this use. He acknowledges, 'If Kafka reminds Robin West of how much she dislikes capitalism, and thereby stimulates her to critical reflections about it, that is fine, too, but she is not entitled to wrap her criticisms in the mantle of Kafka's immense prestige', Posner (1988), p. 186.
50.   Posner (1988), p. 178.
51.   West (1987), p. 148
52.   Posner (1988), p. 355.
53.   Perhaps the specific history of the United States also provides an impetus for deconstructing these notions of intent as too much reliance on the framers' intent also potentially provides a moral crisis for the Constitution for 'an all-too-comprehensive Constitution might well be read to have protected slavery, and this fact alone would justify raising

the question as to why the Constitution is worthy of respect and obedience' (Levison (1982), p. 393).

54. Underwood (1988), p. 10.
55. Underwood (1988), p. 10.
56. Underwood (1988), p. 10.
57. Underwood (1988), p. 5.
58. Posner (1988), p. 219.
59. Posner (1988), p. 218.
60. Levinson (1982), p. 393.
61. Levinson (1982), p. 394.
62. Ward (1994), p. 391.
63. Posner (1988), pp. 214-5.
64. Camilleri (1990), p. 569.
65. Camilleri (1990), p. 569.
66. Levinson (1982), p. 384.
67. West (1987).
68. Eco (1994), p. 2.
69. Eco (1994), p. 3.
70. See Frug (1985), for discussion of structure of contract casebooks, and the patriarchy inherent in its structure.
71. West (1987), p. 206.
72. West (1987), p. 278.
73. West (1987), p. 278.
74. Posner (1988), pp. 209-68.
75. For a fuller explanation of conservatives approach to law and literature, see Thomas (1991).
76. Ward (1993/ii), p. 328.
77. Ward (1993/ii), p. 329.
78. Farber and Sherry (1980), p. 807.
79. The literature on 'narrative scholarship is too extensive to document here, but for the thrust of the debate see symposiums published in (1988) 66 *Texas Law Review*, pp. 577-645, and (1987) *Michigan Law Review*, Vol. 87, pp. 2073-2494.
80. Toddington (1995). He similarly argues that we cannot teach law in context without knowing what law is.
81. Jones (1994), pp. 19-20.
82. Aristodemou (1993), p. 191.
83. Barnett (1995), p. 126.

84. Massaro (1989), p. 2105.
85. See N. MacCormick (1985); MacCormick and Twining (1986) cited in Barnett (1995), p. 95, n. 57.
86. See Hunt (1986, 1988) cited in Barnett (1995), p. 95, n. 57.
87. Ward (1993/i), p. 60.
88. Aristodemou (1993), p. 190.

References

Aristodemou, M. (1993), 'Studies in Law and Literature: Directions and Concerns', *Anglo-American Law Review*, Vol. 22, pp. 157-93.

Barnett, H. (1995), 'The Province of Jurisprudence Determined - Again!', *Legal Studies*, Vol. 15, pp. 88-127.

Bonsignore, J. (1988), 'In Parables: Teaching Through Parables', *Legal Studies Forum*, Vol. 12(2), pp. 191-210.

Bridgeman, J. (1993), 'Old Enough to Know Best?', *Legal Studies*, pp. 69-80.

Burton, F. (1978), *The Politics of Legitimacy: Struggles in a Belfast Community*, Routledge, London.

Campbell, B., McKeown, L. and O'Hagan, F. (Eds.) (1994), *Nor Meekly Serve My Time: The H-Block Struggle 1976-1981*, Beyond the Pale, Belfast.

Camilleri, M. (1990), 'Lessons in Law from Literature: A Look at the Movement and a Peer at Her Jury', *Catholic University Law Review*, Vol. 39, pp. 557-94.

Dunlop, C.R.B. (1991), 'Literature Studies in Law Schools', *Cardozo Studies in Law and Literature*, Spring-Summer, pp. 63-110.

Dworkin, R. (1984), 'How Law is Like Literature', *A Matter of Principle*, pp. 146-66, Harvard University Press, Cambridge.

Eco, U. (1994), *Reflections on the Name of the Rose*, Minerva, London.

Ellman, M. (1993), *The Hunger Artists: Starving, Writing and Imprisonment*, Virago, London.

Faller, L.B. (1987), *Turned to Account*, Cambridge University Press, Cambridge.

Farber, D.A. and Sherry, S. (1993), 'Telling Stories out of School: An Essay on Legal Narratives', *Stanford Law Review*, Vol. 45, pp. 807-55.

Foucault, M. (1977), *Discipline and Punish*, Allen Lane, London.

Frug M. (1985), 'Feminist Analysis of a Casebook', in *The American University Law Review*, Vol. 34, p. 1065.

Hunt, A. (1986), 'Jurisprudence, Philosophy and Legal Eucation', *Legal Studies*, Vol. 6, pp. 292-302.

Hunt, A. (1989), 'The Role and Place of Theory in Legal Education', *Legal Studies*, Vol. 9, pp. 146-64.

Jones, P.A. (1994), 'Competences, Learning Outcomes and Legal Education', *Institute of Advanced Legal Studies (Univ. of London) Legal Skills Working Papers*.

Kennedy, D. (1990), 'Legal Education as Training for Hierarchy' in Kairys, D. (Ed.) *The Politics of Law*, pp. 38-58, Pantheon Books, New York.

Levinson, S. (1982), 'Law as Literature', *Texas Law Review*, Vol. 60, pp. 373-401.

Lord Chancellor's Committee (1994), Lord Chancellor's Advisory Committee on Legal Education and Conduct, *Devices of Legal Education: Consultation Paper*.

Massaro, T.M. (1988), 'Empathy, Legal Storytelling and the Rule of Law: New Words, Old Wounds?' in *Michigan Law Review*, Vol. 87, pp. 2099-2127.

MacCormick, N. (1985), 'The Democratic Intellect and the Law' *Legal Studies*, Vol. 5, p. 172.

MacCormick, N. and Twining W. 'Theory in the Law Curriculum in Twining, W. (Ed.) (1986), *Legal Theory and Common Law*, Blackwell, Oxford.

Munck, R. (1988), 'The Lads and the Hoods: Alternative Justice in an Irish Context' in Tomlinson, M., Varley, T. and McCullagh, C. (Eds.) *Whose Law and Order?*, pp. 41-53, Sociological Association of Ireland.

Nabokov, V. (1980), *Lectures on Literature*, pp. 251-84 Weidenfeld and Nicolson, London.

Posner, R. (1986), 'The Ethical Significance of Free Choice: A Reply to Professor West', *Harvard Law Review*, Vol. 99, pp. 1431-48.

Posner, R. (1988), *Law and Literature: A Misunderstood Relation*, Harvard University Press, Cambridge.

Raz J. (1979), *The Authority of Law: Essays on Law and Morality*, Clarendon, Oxford.

Richmond, M.L. (1989), 'In Defence of Poesie', *Fordham Law Review*, Vol. 57, pp. 901-29.

Shaw, A. (1994), 'Review of Legal Education', *The Lord Chancellor's Advisory Committee on Legal Education and Conduct*.

Thomas, B. (1991), 'Reflections on the Law and Literature Revival', *Critical Inquiry*, Spring, pp. 510-39.

Toddington, S. (1995), 'The Emperor's New Skills: The Academy, The Profession and the Idea of Legal Education', *The Hull University Law School Studies in Law Publications*.

Underwood, J.A. (1988), *Franz Kafka Stories 1904-1924*, Futura, London.

Unger, R. (1978), *Knowledge and Politics*, Collier Macmillan, London.

Ward, I. (1993), 'Responsibility in Critical Legal Theory: An Interdisciplinary Investigation', *Critical Legal Theory*, pp. 49-62.

Ward, I. (1993), 'The Educative Ambition of Law and Literature', *Legal Studies*, Vol. 13, pp. 323-31.

Ward, I. (1994), 'From Literature to Ethics: The Strategies and Ambitions of Law and Literature', *Oxford Journal of Legal Studies*, Vol. 14, pp. 389-400.

Weisberg, R. (1992), *Poethics: And Other Strategies of Law and Literature*, Columbia University Press, New York.

West, R.L. (1985), 'Authority, Autonomy, and Choice: The Role of Consent in the Moral and Political Visions of Franz Kafka and Richard Posner', *Harvard Law Review*, Vol. 99, pp. 384-428.

West R.L. (1986), 'Submission, Choice, and Ethics: A Rejoinder to Judge Posner', *Harvard Law Review*, Vol. 99, pp. 1449-56.

West, R.L. (1987), 'Adjudication is not Interpretation: Some Reservations about the Law-as-Literature Movement', *Tennessee Law Review*, Vol. 54, pp. 203-334.

White, J.B. (1988), 'Law and Literature: 'No Manifesto'', *Mercer Law Review*, Vol. 39, pp. 739-47.

2 Identification with Whom?

KATHERINE O'DONOVAN

In Colm Toibin's novel *The Heather Blazing*[1] the protagonist is an Irish High Court judge. Central to the fleshing out of this man's character by the author is a depiction of his exercise of the judicial function. The High Court case to be judged is straightforward: an application for a court order instructing a convent school to re-admit a sixteen-year-old after the delivery of her child as a single mother. Both the mother-to-be and her own mother give evidence of their belief that stigmatisation of unmarried parents is reserved for women, and that this youngster is the victim of injustice. The principal of the school argues that she has to protect the ethos of the school, despite its status as a state educational establishment. The judge is faced with a dilemma:

> in the end he was not the legal arbiter, because there were so few legal issues at stake. Most of the issues raised in the case were moral; the right of an ethos to prevail over the right of an individual. Basically, he was being asked to decide how life should be lived in a small town ...
>
> He went to the window again and stood there looking out. How hard it was to be sure! It was not simply the case, and the questions it raised about society and morality, it was the world in which these things happened which left him uneasy, a world in which opposite values lived so close to each other. Which could claim a right to be protected?[2]

The idea comes to him that the young woman and her child might be a family unit, entitled to protection under the Irish Constitution. The idea seems plausible, but would require a great deal of thought and research.[3] 'If he were another person he could write the judgment.' But he feels safer with the judgment he has written, in favour of the school which

> would be viewed as eminently sensible and well reasoned. But he was still unhappy about the case because he had been asked to interpret more than the law, and he was not equipped to be a moral arbiter. He was not certain about right and wrong, and he realised that this was something he would have to keep hidden from the court.[4]

In puzzling over his judgment the judge is uneasy because he feels he is being asked to depart from what he sees as the judicial function. This is a matter of personal definition of his role, but it is also a matter which continues to fascinate judges and academic commentators. It is not always possible to draw a line between judging law and judging morals.[5] It is with the role of adjudicator of law that the judge feels safe, with which he identifies. His view of his role is an internal view, yet he worries about the public reception of his decision. The author succeeds in presenting an external view of the man, with a suggestion that a more imaginative, or even empathetic, judge would have asked counsel to address him on the constitutional aspects of the case.

A particular twist to the story is given when, on leaving court the judge goes on holiday with his daughter, herself an unmarried mother. Throughout his cogitation about the case no reflections about his daughter's life enter his mind. He does not identify with her, or with his grandson, or so it seems to this reader. It is not intended, by this reading, to suggest that the judge *should* identify with unmarried mothers in particular, or in general. The literature on the role of the judge in a democracy constantly emphasises the need for objectivity. This chapter has as its object a discussion of the development of a capacity for empathy in legal education, and in the lawyering and adjudicative processes. To this end the place of literature in illuminating the study of law is examined.

The argument that literature can enable imaginative leaps and empathy, thus developing a sense of justice, has not been put forward in a sustained way by writers on law and literature. There have been such suggestions.[6] The case in favour posits that by allowing the reader to enter into the experiences of characters in drama or novel, in biography or autobiography, literature can broaden and deepen feelings of empathy. Arguments for the development of empathy in education are various. They include ethical arguments about deepening imaginative experience, sharing the feelings of others, understanding others, finding expression of one's own and others' experiences and emotions, foreshadowing and anticipating future experience of life.[7] There are also arguments about improving legal skills and the lawyering function.

The major argument is a moral argument. To understand the consequences of our actions on others, we need to understand the perspectives of those others. 'Do as you would be done by', is one version of a moral code. In Kantian terms this is expressed as follows: 'act only on that maxim through which you can at the same time will that it should become a universal law'.

Social and political aspects of what we think, who we are, our attitudes and values, may be opened up for exploration through the discussion of stories. Persons such as lawyers and politicians, who make decisions affecting others, may become better qualified to do so by such experience. As yet the importance of empathy, or at least sympathy, for a democratic society remains relatively unexplored. However it is often said that standing in the shoes of another, in one's imagination, facilitates social arrangements for sharing and for social justice. When theorists try to imagine a fair political or legal system their appeal may be on the level of 'imagine how it would feel';[8] or it may be 'how would you like it if you were poor/stigmatised/ill?'. The former appeal invites us to use our imagination in order to empathise with those less fortunate than ourselves; the latter appeal is closer to a Rawlsian strategy of risk aversion.

In discussing arguments about reading aiding the development of empathy I am conscious of objections. A critical assessment of such arguments is necessary. For example, entering into the experiences of another through imagination often involves identifying with the chosen subject. This suggests elements of choice for the reader. She may or may not identify with a particular character or *dramatis persona*. If citizenship of a society includes an obligation of abstraction - a stepping outside one's commitments and seeing one's point of view as one among many - then imagination is to be encouraged. But if we are limited persons, as indeed we are, we may lack the capacity to identify with those others who are radically different from us. Or we may, for personal reasons, identify with the oppressors rather than with the oppressed. There are, doubtless, a number of ways in which empathy can be developed, including creative use of case law. Arguments for law and literature studies as developing empathy are scrutinised particularly through advancing counter-arguments. If a core of conviction remains in favour, then a case will have been made out.

Empathy and experiences

'Legal decisions and lawmaking frequently have nothing to do with understanding human experiences, affect, suffering - how people *do* live.'[9] Legal discourse precludes affective argument in the view of Lynne Henderson. The ideology of legal education and legal argument excludes emotion and arguments based on personal experience.[10] In contrasting empathy and legality Henderson finds three phenomena captured by the language of empathy. She categorises 'feeling the emotion of another', and 'understanding the experience or situation of another, both affectively and cognitively' as ways of knowing; whilst the third form, 'action brought about by experiencing the distress of another' is presented as a catalyst.[11]

In urging reading as an aid to empathy it is sometimes suggested that the reader may thus enter into the experiences of another. But it is doubtful whether this can occur fully. It is more likely that we relate what we read or hear to our own experiences. This has been expressed as follows by John McGahern in *The Leavetaking*;

> 'It's like an American breakfast. Except the coffee is better in the States,' she said, and began to tell me her life. I finger her words like worn coins as I remember her voice in the little café. I try to animate them by turning them into my own life, I garland them with memory, embellish them with what I know, and remember in some dismay that we can only love what we know.
>
> A child is riding on a bus from her school in the Berkshires into New York. Her father is waiting for her at the terminal with tickets for a concert he has promised to take her to for her birthday. His eyes light on her gloveless hands as she gets off the bus and he is furious she is not wearing one of the pairs of white gloves he gave her for the birthday and he returns her to the school on the next bus back to the Berkshires. And that bus will be forever in my mind a green bus moving between the whitethorns of Ireland ... and the child riding back to the Berkshires is not my beloved when she was young but some sister on a day a waxen head of a doll had shattered. I watched my own words too pass behind the mask of the lovely face across the table; and if that sea-change happens to your coinage, my love, what may become of mine?[12]

From this passage what emerges is that, even as we try to imagine the lives of others, we return to our own experiences in so doing. The writer or the speaker does not control. Interpretation lies with the other, as does identification.

Identification

Sympathetic identification with others is a basis of ethical experience, but there is no law of reading which states that readers must identify with one character rather than another. So it is also in life. Peter Van Daan in his wartime attic hiding-place confides to Anne Frank his uneasiness in being a Jew and how he would have found it much easier if he had been a Christian, and if he could he would be one after the war. His hope for the future is to go to the Dutch East Indies and live on a plantation.[13] One interpretation of this desire for the future is that Peter hopes to find in colonial life an independence and power he cannot have as a Jew in Europe. This interpretation is not intended as a criticism of Peter. Given his miserable existence in hiding, and the threat to his life, it is hardly surprising that he dreams of another existence. Given the social stigmatization of his identity, it is not surprising that he seeks a different identity. But my interpretation is intended to illustrate the point that choice of identification is possible. Because of their stigmatization and victimization some identities are subordinate, or possibly dangerous. Such identities may not be identified with, even by those categorised by others as having such identities. So we may choose who we identify with and whether or not to identify with the victimized or the stigmatized. One of the more powerful arguments for reading imaginative literature is that it gives voices to those often not heard. It is in the pages of literature that we find the excluded.

It must also be acknowledged that the phenomenon of unreflective empathy exists, in which we identify with those persons or characters whom we perceive as being like ourselves.[14] This has been recognised by decision-makers, such as judges, as limiting their neutrality or objectivity.[15] It is not just that such understanding is so automatic that it goes unnoticed by the empathiser, but that literature offers opportunities for contested readings. How one reads may relate to one's own values.

A caveat must be entered to the theory that understanding always leads to morality and justice. For example, understanding the feelings of another may increase cruelty, manipulation and sadism. The bully may use his knowledge of his victims' vulnerability to inflict pain more successfully. Bernard Williams makes this point:

> But one thing that must be true is that the insightful understanding of others' feelings possessed by the sympathetic person is possessed in much the same form by the sadistic or cruel person; that is one way in which the cruel are distinguished from the brutal or the indifferent.[16]

However, this is not an argument against empathy, but rather a caution; for as Williams says elsewhere, 'sympathetic identification with others ... [is] basic to ethical experience'.[17] Such experience may be lacking in law students at the beginnings of their working lives, who may nevertheless arrive at some understanding through reading.

Our identities

Working out who and what we are is a major preoccupation in most lives. Some aspects might seem to be given: our genes, our bodies, sex, colour, appearance. Yet doubt has been cast on the extent to which such material aspects of the self are fixed. Geneticists, whilst positing that genes can be mapped and located for physical and mental traits, including criminality, also propose that DNA will enable the elimination of 'undesirable' genes. In other words some scientists argue that the fixedness of genetic inheritance can be changed through science.[18] Significant academic writers also argue fluidity and even plasticity of the self.[19] The relevance of this new 'fluid identity' is that it appears to deny the limitations of our actual identities - limitations to cognition of difference - limitations to empathetic identification with others. The agenda of choice presented includes not only our outward and inward selves, but also the very material, DNA, of which we are made.

I have argued elsewhere that this is a mistaken agenda.[20] Firstly, most people have little or no choice about their genes. Secondly, parental choices about the genetic make-up of their children are largely negative choices. These are choices *not* to reproduce with a particular partner, or at all.[21] Thirdly, the idea of changing genes, because of alleged criminality, for example, pre-supposes current beliefs in genetic essentialism.[22] A debate about change starts from a premise of fixedness. An alternative method of analysis, I suggest, should start from the social interpretations placed on embodiment and external appearances. For the purposes of this paper we must consider how such interpretations construct and limit the possibilities of what a person can be. It may be that empathy, or imaginative sympathy, developed through reading and discussion, can challenge social interpretations which stigmatize and victimize. Whether this is expressed in terms of the 'neighbour principle' or of Kantian universalisability, is of lesser significance. At present, external interpretation allied with internal self-identity limits the possibilities of empathy for, or identification with, others.

I have already suggested that empathy requires a stepping-aside from our own self-interest, emotions, and immediate concerns. This does not necessarily involve leaving our own identities behind; for it is possible to build into our identities a capacity for empathy. I am deliberately presenting this as a social trait, a social choice, rather than as an inherent or genetic trait.

The stepping-aside under discussion here is intended to deal with a different scenario from the mind experiments involved in the Rawlsian social contract.[23] Rawls argues that his principles of justice will be chosen under a veil of ignorance because no one will want to risk ending up poor or oppressed. In a sense, Rawls assumes self-interest, albeit in a highly theoretical scene. This chapter addresses the practicalities of the education of real people who already exist in a world of identities.

What has this to do with legal education?

Dissatisfaction with the current state of legal education has led to Law and Literature courses. There may be disagreement over the concept of justice and what it requires. These are moral arguments. So if a theory concerning the educative possibilities of Law and Literature can be elaborated, its value in teaching may go beyond the undergraduate classroom. However, the criticism may be levelled at existing advocacy of law and literature courses, that specificity of why, how and to what effect, is lacking.[24]

In relation to undergraduate legal education, I see a role for literature and drama in teaching legal ethics. The consultation paper on the initial stage of legal education published by the Lord Chancellor's Advisory Committee on Legal Education and Conduct includes the theme that 'legal education should stress the ethical values upon which law is based'.[25] Later the paper states that to 'understand the law, it is necessary to understand its moral quality'.[26] This is more than professional ethics, which occasionally may provide a cover for unethical actions. It is also more than deconstructing the content of substantive law for its moral content. It is self-evident that study of, for example, criminal law will include a discussion of responsibility. But surely the teaching of legal ethics must go further? The consultation paper recognizes that the lawyers, in the conduct of legal affairs may be open to criticism, but the moral content of the law may also be subjected to critical scrutiny: the ought in addition to the is. Moral dilemmas, of the kind posed regularly in law and medical ethics courses, do not necessarily permit of an absolute answer. Nevertheless classroom discussion is valuable where it permits the expression of plural perspectives, a variety of narratives, and differences. If this comes about it will be a change for law students; in general argument on levels other than the legal is not welcomed in the classroom.

A debate about the values and limits of Law and Literature studies continues in the United States in legal education. Although there is consensus that the 'professional voice' with which students are taught to speak from their earliest days in law school is an impersonal abstract voice, there is disagreement as to the adequacy of this voice. 'The magical moment at which the 'light dawns' and bewildered first-year students are transformed into lawyers occurs when this [the professional] voice becomes the student's own'[27] is seen by some as the moment when the human voice is lost. The professional voice has been criticised as using language which 'removes some of the feeling and empathy that are part of ordinary human discourse'[28] and the argument has been advanced that to 'represent people adequately a lawyer often must use her capacity for empathy'.[29] Participants in this debate are agreed in their dislike of pompous rhetoric, unnecessarily technical language, and elitism.

The doubts expressed concern the undermining of formal justice. The imposition of some form of order on differing claims and diverse voices is advanced by defenders of current legal education as an inherent part of the task of law and lawyers.[30] A consensus about the need for both voices, the human and the professional, emerges. The difficulty is to find appropriate places for each and to allow space for both.

This disagreement, explained above, touches on differing views of priorities in law's functions. Shared ground about the goals of legal education can be discerned. Others see a quite different role for law and literature studies, and offer a communitarian vision of law 'not as a system of rules or bureaucratic mechanisms, but as an activity of mind and language, to the understanding of which parallel activities can be helpful'.[31] This is a vision of law as a set of people talking to each other, using language, a rhetorical activity aided by the study of literature. Yet it can be presented as concerned with legal education. The major divide is between those who see literature as improving the present model of legal education and those who see such studies as providing a place from which to mount a critique of law.[32] There may be possibilities to do both.

Thus far it has been argued that empathy is an important capacity to be developed in legal education, as basic to ethical experience, and as improving legal skills. The examination of empathy as providing a basis for critique will now be made. If a further step is made of understanding those whose perspectives and voices are excluded by law, whose subjectivity and experiences are not included in legal imaginings of how things should be, then this may provide an understanding from which to be critical. It is difficult to provide an external critique from an insider's perspective. Law has its own internal viewpoint, its own order, a relatively autonomous coherence. Pointing out internal inconsistency is a different activity to pointing out injustice.

The Consultation Paper on Legal Education assumes that legal ethics can be learnt from law, that law is moral by definition.[33] If this is so, it becomes difficult to criticise law from the moral point of view, since the law itself is taken to be moral. Where can a place be found outside the law from which to be sceptical or critical? One answer offered is the analytic methodologies of the humanities of writing, reading and responding to narrative texts.[34] It is in this response that an empathic understanding of others may develop.

Limits to identification: adjudication

Thus far it has been argued that personal identity may limit identification. There may be many reasons why this happens, including the tragic example of Peter Van Daan.[35] In order to empathize, particularly with those others whom we see as different from ourselves, we have to stand back from our own personal interests, identities, fears, emotions. This is what lawyers and judges claim to do in handling and judging law cases. Yet is it so easy for us to leave our identities behind when we don a particular garb? That garb marks us externally as 'lawyer' or 'judge'. That particular identity is part of our larger identities, but does the larger identity disappear?

This essay argues that it is not possible for us to abandon our larger identities by putting on one aspect of our identities. Furthermore our identities may limit the possibilities of empathetic identification as we listen or read. Nevertheless reading can involve some entry into the experiences of the characters or *dramatis personae* depicted. Many possible examples to illustrate this are available, involving persons differentiated from the reader (or judge) by class, gender, race, religion, ethnicity. Given that hitherto, most members of the higher judiciary have been men with a particular background and training, questions of empathy unawares with persons identified as similar arise. Where future decision-makers are being educated the enhancement of their abilities to listen to others, to understand alternative viewpoints, to appreciate the human meanings of legal rules and processes is desirable. However the judicial role requires that a decision be made. It is unlikely therefore that the judge can move very far from his judicial identity. Judges know this and have particular ways of explaining this to themselves and others, a story about the judicial function.

Stories about the role of the judge can be told from a number of viewpoints. Of these the internal and the external dominate. From the internal point of view the process of adjudication is 'entirely predicated upon the assumption that the judge's task is to find the right answer'.[36] This is how judges think about what they are doing. In this story, the sources of the right answer are limited to principles which can plausibly be derived from earlier cases and from statutes. From the external vantage point things look rather different. Firstly, there are cases in which, by implication, judges admit that they were wrong in the past. Secondly, there are cases in which the result is dictated by public policy, in which impartiality cannot be claimed. Thirdly, there are cases which may find the right answer from an internal viewpoint, but which are perceived as wrong externally.[37] In the latter two cases it may be possible to say, 'I am stating what the law actually is'. However the first case is harder to account for.

An example of a series of cases in which the answer was wrong externally, if not internally, is the marital rape saga. A change in the law, recognising a wife's autonomy in decisions about her sexual relations with her husband, was covered in the bland phrase 'changed social conditions'.[38] Although the judges involved in previous decisions denying autonomy to wives might have claimed that they were trying to find the right answer, or even that, from an internal view the answer was right, such claims are problematic from an external point of view. Not to recognize this, and to claim that the insights of the external view 'are trivial and unhelpful',[39] is a failure of empathy. It is also a narrow definition of the judicial role. It cannot be denied that the very nature of judicial decision making as conceived of internally, involves exclusion.[40] But this may be overlooked on the inside. Whether the internal viewpoint is distinguishable from the institutional viewpoint is open to question. The trouble for law is that external viewpoints have justice as their referent.

Each person's life is a story. Each trial, or law case, tells a story. Who is the narrator? Who is the interpreter? Who chooses between competing stories? Who is in command of language, definition and decision? These are questions about power.

The literary account of law can be about resistance. It can tell us what the coercive theory leaves out - how it feels to suffer under law. It offers a critique of law's injustice. It offers an external view. But literary works are themselves the creatures of a particular time and place. Textual representations of those silenced or excluded by law may enable an interrogation and cross-examination of law, but they are themselves limited. Nevertheless, in drawing attention to inequities arising from law's exclusions, they are a valuable supplement to legal texts.[41]

Identification unawares

In a characterisation of feminist work in law as motivated by love and rage, Robin West makes a distinction between the 'cognitive' position and the 'moral' position. The cognitive position is 'that an empathic understanding of the differences of others ... constitutes an important source of *information* about the totality of persons who will be affected by a legal decision'.[42] The moral position is 'that empathic understanding of and sensitivity to the context in which differently situated others find themselves is but one aspect of a truly caring relationship with those others ...'.[43] West advocates the latter position as reclaiming love as the root of morality, going beyond understanding to lessening a burden. 'Sensitivity to difference is part of the work of sympathizing with the pain of others to work towards lessening that pain'.[44]

There is much to admire in this advocacy. But it is directed to feminists working and writing in law. It does not confront the reality that most legal decisions are made by persons with a particular kind of embodiment and identity. If such decision-makers can be persuaded of the cognitive position, this will be a gain. But how is this to be done? Some writers have entered doubts on this question. Maria Aristodemou raises the question whether morality can be taught at all and, if so how?[45] As she points out such questions bring us to contested views of human nature, of knowledge and learning, of the ideology of education, which is itself part of society.

For her literature's service to legal studies may lie in providing a base from which to challenge the dominant ideology. In this the possibilities of subjective and contingent values are to be welcomed.[46]

Thus far it has been argued that each person is limited by her or his own identity and may thus be precluded from identifying with others. Furthermore, faced with an opportunity of empathetic understanding we may refuse. Classroom discussion will not necessarily overcome resistance. Nevertheless, I want to argue that conscious refusal to identify with particular characters - perhaps precisely *because* they are victims - can be analytically distinguished from those identifications which we make unawares. It is these latter identifications which can be confronted and made explicit in successful discussion of literature. It is not necessary to make over-general claims about the beneficial effects of literature. I am aware that an academic assumption that reading teaches the reader is naive. Literary scholars deplore such a use of texts. Yet the idea that personal limitations of identity can be expanded in shared discussion of a text does have relevance to teaching of legal ethics. The multiplicity of readings adds to the possibilities, rather than hindering them.

It has become a truism of feminist and of critical legal scholarship to state that legal decision-makers are not objective or neutral - in the sense that such a way of being is superhuman. The judiciary itself admits as much. Thus, Lord MacMillan has said that the lofty judicial duty of neutrality is not easy of attainment.

> The ordinary human mind is a mass of prepossessions inherited and acquired, often, none the less dangerous because unrecognised by their possessors. Few minds are as neutral as a sheet of plate glass, and indeed a mind of that quality may actually fail in judicial efficiency, for the warmer tints of imagination and sympathy are needed to temper the cold light of reason if human justice is to be done.[47]

Embedded values, assumptions, beliefs based on experience form part of the identity of adult human beings. For most people this is part of their personality and poses few, if any, problems. But for the judiciary this is another matter. To maintain its legitimacy law must retain the confidence of those whose lives it governs. This argument is not confined to judges. Lawyers too need to see their clients as human beings, and to be able to present them and their stories as such to the judge.

Conclusion

Arguments have been advanced in this paper that empathy is basic to ethical experience, that empathy can be developed by reading imaginative literature, and that such readings can create a space outside legal texts from which to critique law. It is hardly a surprise that not everyone accepts such arguments. Some believe that interpretation of a literary text which draws support for ethical or political positions is invalid.[48] This seems to be motivated by concern for the principle of freedom of speech, rather than as clarificatory of *which* texts, if any, may legitimately be called upon in support of a moral point of view. That legal texts, such as statutes and precedent cases may be so drawn upon is not in doubt. But the exclusion of literary texts as imaginary seems both arbitrary and ignorant of the effect that such texts have had in the past on changing the law.[49]

Analytically, claims about ethical aspects of law may be internal or external. If law is seen by those internal to the legal system as coextensive with morality, that is an internal viewpoint. But if a law is seen and felt by those who suffer its attentions as unjust, those outsiders must be calling on another standard, external to this law itself. Such an external viewpoint may draw on many sources, including other aspects of law. The need to dispute the legitimacy of sources must depend on the forum in which they are cited. It is self-evident that literary works cannot be authorities in legal argument. Their role is supplementary. What they can do is to draw attention to law's exclusions, and thereby develop empathetic understanding. This is an adequate justification for giving a place to literature in legal education.

Notes

1. Toibin (1992).
2. Toibin (1992), p. 90.
3. Toibin (1992), p. 90.
4. Toibin (1992), p. 92. For similar thoughts about a different dilemma for English judges see n. 5, below.
5. For example, in *Airedale NHS Trust v Bland* [1993] 1 All E.R. 821 Lord Mustill deals with the ethical aspects of the question of whether a patient in a persistent vegetative state should have his treatment withdrawn. In so doing he acknowledges that the line between law and morals is unclear and that the law is in an imperfect state. Lord Browne-Wilkinson reflects that the moral, social and legal issues raised in the case are more suitable for Parliament than for the courts:

   > The judges' function in this area of the law should be to apply the principles which society, through the democratic process, adopts, not to impose their standards on society. If Parliament fails to act, then judge-made law will of necessity through a gradual and uncertain process provide a legal answer to each new question as it arises. But in my judgment that is not the best way to proceed (p. 879).

6. See for example, West (1988), p. 129. Weisberg (1992) makes a claim for law and literature in teaching ethics.

7. This chapter makes a distinction between instrumental legal skills and the development of a capacity for empathy. Although it is tempting to define the latter, but not the former, as ethical, skills can serve the interests of clients and justice.

8. This was the approach of Prime Minister Paul Keating in asking Australians to understand and empathise with the history, experiences and feelings of the descendants of the original inhabitants of Australia.

9. Henderson (1987), p. 1574.

10. Frug (1992).

11. Henderson (1987), pp. 1574-5.

12. McGahern (1974), pp. 120-4.

13. *The Diary of Anne Frank* (1954), p. 133.

14. Henderson (1987), p. 1584.

15. Scrutton (1921), p. 8 (1921); Winters (1975); Wilson (1990) p. 507.

16. Williams (1985), cited in Henderson (1987) p. 1585.

17. Williams, cited in Henderson (1987) p. 1585.

18. Hamer and Copeland (1994).

19. Giddens (1991).

20. O'Donovan (forthcoming, 1996).

21. As a result of genetic screening, the choice may be to have children only through donated genes or adoption.

22. Murray and Hernstein (1994).

23. Rawls (1973); Okin (1989).

24. Some academics offer lists of 'recommended books'. Very often these are for 'law in literature' courses, as opposed to 'law and literature' courses. For this distinction see Lee (1990), p. 252. Franz Kafka, *The Hunger Artist*, and most of Kafka's other short stories and novels are extolled. Dickens, *Bleak House* is an obvious choice, as are: Melville, *Billy Budd*; Shakespeare, *The Merchant of Venice*; Sophocles, *Antigone*; Miller, *The Crucible* and *A View from the Bridge;* Camus, *L'Etranger*. The communitarian strand of the law and literature movement looks to Twain, *Huckleberry Finn*, Jane Austen, *Emma*.

    Then there are the commentaries: Ward (1993), p. 323; Aristodemou (1993), p. 157 makes a distinction between law *in* literature and law *as* literature, and Literature: Ward (1994), p. 133.

25. Lord Chancellor's Committee (1994), para. 1.25.

26. Lord Chancellor's Committee (1994), para. 4.14.

27. Getman (1988), p. 577.
28. Getman (1988), p. 578.
29. Getman (1988), p. 583.
30. Yudof (1988), pp. 589-622. For Yudof law 'constitutes a distinct context of human knowing' (p. 590). As a form of order, with a set of principles which transcend individual cases, law is, for Yudof, a means of ordering 'the disparate human voices in any legal controversy' (p. 590). He acknowledges that legal ordering is spun from the human imagination. His disagreement with Getman is over the idea that neglected human voices should be allowed to establish a form of substantive justice for individuals. To him this 'undermines the very idea of formal justice for all' (p. 591).
31. White, (1994).
32. Nussbaum (1994), p. 714; Weisberg (1992); Ward (1994), p. 389.
33 Lord Chancellor's Committee (1994).
34. West (1993).
35. Although the name Van Daan appears in my 1954 edition of Anne Frank's *Diaries*, it is now known that she altered certain names in the course of writing. The definitive edition gives Peter's name as van Pels. See Barnouw and Van der Stroom (1995).
36. Hoffman (1989), p. 142.
37. *R v R* [1991] 4 All E.R. 481. The history of the marital exemption from criminal prosecution for rape undermines the idea that judges seek the right answer through an examination of legal principles. Where one principle such as the autonomy of adult subjects, conflicts with another principle such as the unity of conflicts with another principle such as the unity of spouses, a judge may choose the 'wrong' principle.
38. Hoffman, (1989), p. 142.
39. This point was made to me by participants at a discussion of this paper at Southampton University Law Faculty.
40. Thomas (1991).
41. West (1989), p. 106.
42. West (1989), p. 106.
43. West (1989), p. 106.
44. Aristodemou (1993), p. 157.
45. Aristodemou (1993), p. 157. See further Hirshman (1988), p. 177.

46. Lord MacMillan, cited by Madame Justice B. Wilson (1990), from Yankwich, 'The Art of Being a Judge', in Winter's *Handbook for Judges* (1975).
47. Posner (1988). For disagreement, see Nussbaum (1994), p. 714.
48. For example, works of literature such as Beecher Stowe's *Uncle Tom's Cabin,* helped to change attitudes to slavery. The short stories of Nadine Gordimer gave a voice to oppressed South Africans. There is a long Irish tradition of poetry and song of resistance. Tennyson Jesse's novel *A Pin to See the Peepshow* challenged the conviction and capital sentence for homicide of Edith Thompson. Many writers, including Judge Posner, have used Susan Glaspell's short story, *A Jury of Her Peers* to bring out alternative conceptions of justice.

References

Aristodemou, M. (1993), 'Studies in Law and Literature: Directions and Concerns', *Anglo American Law Review,* Vol. 22, pp. 157-193.

Barnouw, D. and Van der Stroom, G. (1995), *The Diary of Anne Frank: The Critical Edition*, Viking, London.

Frank, A. (1954), *The Diary of Anne Frank*, Pan Books, London.

Frug, M.J. (1992), *Postmodern Legal Feminism*, Routledge, London.

Getman, J.G. (1988), 'Colloquy: Human Voice in Legal Discourse', *Texas Law Review*, Vol. 66, pp. 577-588.

Giddens, A. (1991), *Modernity and Self Identity*, Polity Press, Oxford.

Hamer, D. and Copeland, P. (1994), *The Science of Desire*, Simon and Shuster, New York.

Henderson, L.N. (1987), 'Legality and Empathy', *Michigan Law Review*, Vol. 85, pp. 1574-1653.

Hirshman, L.R. (1988), 'Bronte, Bloom and Bork: An Essay on the Moral Education of Judges', *University of Pennsylvania Law Review*, Vol. 137, pp. 177-231.

Hoffman, L.H. (1989), 'Review of Simon Lee, *Judging Judges*', *Law Quarterly Review*, Vol. 105, pp. 140-145.

Lee, S. (1990), 'Law and Literature: Goodbye Austin, Hello Austen', *Oxford Journal of Legal Studies*, Vol. 10, pp. 252-259.

Lord Chancellor's Committee (1994), Lord Chancellor's Advisory Committee on Legal Education and Conduct (June 1994), *Review of Legal Education: Consultation Paper*.

McGahern, John (1974), *The Leavetaking*, Little, Brown and Co., Boston.

Morgan, R. And Lee, S. (Eds.), *Designer Babies? Legal and Social Dimensions*, Dartmouth, Aldershot.

Murray, C. and Heirnstein, R. (1994) *The Bell Curve*, Free Press, New York.

Nussbaum, M. (1994), 'Skepticism about Practical Reason in Literature and the Law', *Harvard Law Review*, Vol. 107, pp. 714-744.

O'Donovan, K. (forthcoming, 1996), 'Genes or Jeans: Who Am I?' in Morgan, D. and Lee, G.R. *Designer Babies*, Dartmouth Press, Aldershot.

Okin, S. (1989), *Justice, Gender and the Family*, Basic Books, New York.

Posner, R. (1988), *Law and Literature: A Misunderstood Relation*, Harvard University Press, Cambridge, Mass.

Rawls, J. (1973), *A Theory of Justice*, Harvard University Press, Cambridge, Mass.

Scrutton, L.J. (1921), 'The Work of the Commercial Courts', *Cambridge Law Journal*, Vol. 1, pp. 6-20.

Thomas, Brook (1991), 'Reflections on the Law and Literature Revival', *Critical Enquiry*, Vol 17, pp. 510-539.

Toibin, Colm (1991), *The Heather Blazing*, Picador, London.

Ward, I. (1993), 'The Educative Ambition of Law and Literature', *Legal Studies*, Vol. 13, pp. 323-331.

Ward, I. (1994/i), 'From Literature to Ethics: The Strategies and Ambitions of Law and Literature', *Oxford Journal of Legal Studies*, Vol. 14, pp. 389-400.

Ward, I. (1994/ii), 'Law and Literature; A Feminist Perspective', *Feminist Legal Studies*, Vol. 2, pp. 133-158.

Weisberg, Richard (1992), *Poethics and Other Strategies of Law and Literature*, Columbia University Press, New York.

West, R. (1988), 'Communities, Texts and Law: Reflections on the Law and Literature Movement', *Yale Journal of Law and the Humanities*, Vol. 1, pp. 129-156.

West, R. (1989), 'Love, Rage and Legal Theory', *Yale Journal of Law and Feminism*, Vol. 1(101), pp. 101-114.

West, R. (1993), *Narrative, Authority and Law*, University of Michigan Press, Michigan.

White, J.B. (1994), 'Teaching Law and Literature', *Mosaic*, Vol. 27, pp. 1-13.

Wilson, M.J. (1990), 'Will Women Judges Really Make a Difference?', *Osgoode Hall Law Journal*, Vol. 28, pp. 507-522.

Winters, G.R. (1974), *Handbook for Judges*, The American Judicature Society, Washington D.C.

Yudof, M.G. (1988), 'Tea at the Palaz of Hoon: The Human Voice in Legal Rules', *Texas Law Review*, Vol. 66, pp. 589-620.

3 Bursting Binary Bubbles: Law, Literature and the Sexed Body

THÉRÈSE MURPHY

Once upon a time...

If Disney World is a place where dreams come true, then law's world is the stuff of nightmares. It is a place full of facts, stripped of fantasy, fun and feeling. A place where the professional voice overwhelms all others and the virtues of precedent blithely trump those of justice. However, whether despite or because of this, law's public face retains an unassailable vibrancy. Its triumph is such that non-law or 'law and' disciplines emerge as for the also-rans. Their hyphenated worlds appear dingy when compared with the forthrightness of law. They are also beset by a grubby earnestness. We sense that these 'other' disciplines seek empathy and, unlike law, have no stomach for absolute truth. With them, there are no certainties, there will be no resolution. This makes the choice between law and non-law an uninspiring one. In part, that is the nature of oppositional or binary pairs; they tend to be unforgiving, unrelenting and violently lop-sided. This makes the capacity of such pairs to insinuate themselves everywhere rather worrying. Law is not the only discipline to trade in such binarisms: philosophy, literary theory and medicine all perpetuate the stranglehold grip of Cartesian-style dualisms by trading in uneven oppositions around the mind and the body, the real and the romantic, the scientific and the fantastic.

A further key binary pair in contemporary thought has been provided by feminism's use of the sex/gender axis. Anglo-American feminism's challenge to law erected itself upon this sex/gender binary pair by challenging the inevitability, naturalness or fixed characteristics of gender. The choice was, in large part, a happy one and, in step-by-step fashion, it facilitated the exposure of law's partisan nature. A volley of powerful charges - first, law as sexist, and then, law as male - cut through law's public face, securing feminism's challenge.[1] Many layers were peeled back, discarded forever, even in denial. Accepted 'truths' were exposed as partial and exclusionary. New 'feminine' values, purportedly garnered from women's real experiences, were substituted and argued to be essential to a better future.

Recently, however, feminism's progress in and with law has been halted by the joker in the *fin de siècle* theory pack: postmodernism. This joker is

57

often hard to pin down, but when shorn of its penchant for jargon and distanced from relativism, it becomes compelling. For feminism - or at least Anglo-American legal feminism - it has also become perilous because of the questions which it throws up about the rigidity of binary understandings of identity, about the use of 'experiences' by new social movements in their constructions of supposedly new and challenging, political subjects, and about the possibility of absolute truth. Feminism is being sorely tested by these postmodern questions. We watch as its favourite political subject - Woman - which is meant to represent the voices of all women becomes not, as expected, a non-essential, but instead a liability. This Woman now stands accused: she has repressed differences between women; she has given an immutable, or essential, essence to gender because of her craving for a universal female nature; and, because of her obsession with gendering or construction, she has ignored the sexed and sexual body. Postmodernism, allied with 'queer theory' and black feminist scholarship, has made us face real women. Not surprisingly, there are millions of them and, although intuitively this path seems more appropriate, it creates a whopping political headache. Anglo-American feminism's Woman had become familiar, if not entirely reliable; women, by contrast, are unruly and seem impossible to represent. Women's heterogeneity is overwhelming and it seems as if we might never clawback from relativism and recover a feminist 'subject'. Meanwhile, men's studies and the New Right are fast infecting vast tranches of the public mind.

Some feminists have found safe passage in the realm of the symbolic: Drucilla Cornell, for example, shifts our focus from Woman to the feminine, deploying the power of myth to escape the problem of differences between women.[2] In fact, the proliferation of the symbolic makes it difficult to escape the feeling that today it is France, not the United Kingdom, the United States nor Canada, that is 'the scene of feminisms'.[3] But the French feminist solution - *l'écriture féminine* or the constructing of a new language by writing Woman - can be mystifying to the outsider. In particular, it has no easy fit with Anglo-American legal feminism and we skulk around it, embarrassed by inevitable admissions of inaccessibility. This generates frustration because feminism is already a world where one has 'to run to keep up with the publication of relevant texts'.[4] Moreover, too much of the symbolic is distasteful to the consciously political and pragmatic feminism of the Anglo-American: it lacks the combative concreteness and scientificity of women's 'experience' and therefore seems unable to compete with dominant theories of knowledge as a 'politically sound truth'.[5]

Recently however, the postmodern has begun to sap the vitality from 'experience' and this bedrock of feminism's assault on law is being rendered unsafe and unsound.[6] Postmodernism has been problematizing the homogenizing tendencies in feminism and other new social movements which claim to recount people's experiences. It has also been challenging known truths and accepted identities. If these are unhinged by the postmodern, the question must be: how are alternative feminist truths based on 'experience' to succeed? The damage to Anglo-American legal feminism looks as if it will be immense: both its critical and constructive projects seem likely to be implicated because both are already struggling to cope with the displacement of Woman by the unruly reality of women's lives and the seeming loss of a collective, gendered feminist subject.

In this chapter, I will be sketching out my version of Anglo-American legal feminism's 'postmodern problem' and offering one way around it. For me, much of the trouble stems from this feminism's failure to engage with the stranglehold grip of identity binarisms - such as mind/body, nature/nurture, sex/gender - on modern thought, including feminism itself. I am concerned that by clinging to an unevenly-crafted understanding of the sex/gender binary pairing in the construction of its political subject, 'Woman', through which it purports to represent the experiences of real women, Anglo-American legal feminism has distorted the relationship between sex and gender. In particular, because of its preoccupation with gendering or social construction, it has rendered the sexed, or 'biologically female', body as either inert, or mechanical, or completely culturally porous. Part I will explain further my concerns about the sexed body within this feminism.

In thinking about ways out of the impending sex/gender-mind/body feminist dead-end, I became concerned not to 'blame' feminism alone for encouraging a warping of identity binarisms. It seemed to me that other disciplines peddled even more violently lop-sided binarisms in their constructions of individual identities. Thus, I became taken with the idea of challenging medicine and literature, both of which seemed to me to be getting away with trading in particularly ugly binarisms around the sexed body. When taken together, medicine and literature seemed to me to be able to encase the sexed body within problematic social representations *and* scientific facts. However, 'righting' the worlds of medicine, literature and feminism all at once seemed foolish and out-of-reach. Fortunately, working in a law school meant that Medical Law and Law and Literature were available and they seemed to offer perfect target practice before a move on to their better-armoured siblings. In Part II, I will be introducing you to Medical

Law and Law and Literature as relative newcomers to our law school curriculum and law review volumes and despairing over the many distortions and closures that have already manifested themselves within these subjects. Part III is a lament for these closures, which is rendered extra poignant by the dormant potential for a 'special relationship' between legal feminism, Medical Law and Law and Literature. Next, in Part IV, I resume the investigation of closures within Medical Law and Law and Literature by zooming in on the particular closures to feminist insights, as well as the ongoing feminist 'mistakes', within these disciplines. I label and challenge the female subjects represented in these disciplines, alleging that Medical Law Woman languishes in a reproduction ghetto and that Law and Literature Woman is generally nowhere to be seen. On scratching the surface, however, I am forced to admit that Anglo-American legal feminism has to take some blame for these ugly constructs of Medical Law Woman and Law and Literature Woman. This feminism has failed to see the potential in the latter and been too easily cornered, and then wrong-footed, by the former. Part V, in closing the chapter, goes on to urge a take-up of interest in the suggested 'special relationship' between legal feminism, Medical Law and Law and Literature as one way out of the impending impasse of existing identity binarisms.

Bursting binary bubbles: feminism and the sexed body

How is Anglo-American feminism negotiating the power of the postmodern insight? The answer is, in general, it is not. It is in retreat or, more commonly, still holding tight to what it knows: an understanding of the sex/gender binary pair that is so obsessed with the gendering of the mind of some supposedly universal female subject that it not only represses differences among women, but renders their sexed bodies either a counter-intuitive irrelevance, or an inexplicable, already-constructed or natural entity. The overwhelming emphasis is on our sense of ourselves as women being inscribed on our minds by social and cultural patterns; our bodies are taken as already sexed female, as already differently determined by nature and thus, as irrelevant to our feminist 'gender' politics.

Judith Butler[7] numbers among the few who do not fit this pattern. She has called for a rethink on the sex/gender feminist frontier, exploring its replication of a plethora of binary pairs, particularly the mind/body variant. There is an urgency to Butler's inquiries around the mind/body binarism:

'[b]ut what establishes this dualism for us?'[8] She also does not shirk from naming the problem as ours:

> With respect to gender discourse, to what extent do these problematic dualisms still operate within the very descriptions that are supposed to lead us out of that binarism and its implicit hierarchy? How are the contours of the body clearly marked as the taken-for-granted ground or surface upon which gender significations are inscribed, a mere facticity devoid of value, prior to significance?[9]

Despite the power of Butler's inquiries, she continues to number among the exceptions in Anglo-American feminist discourse. We persist in ignoring her exposé of the limitations of, and contradictions within, dominant feminist understandings of the relationship of sex to gender which leave the role of the sexed body in social construction largely unexplained and under-theorised. Behind the scenes of all the gender talk that has taken place (and probably because of it), we seem always to have hung onto our own, individual, lived bodies; never truly 'extricating [them] from the mire of biologism in which [they have] been entrenched'.[10] Our heroes have done the same: Butler notes the 'many occasions in Beauvoir's work where "the body" is figured as a mute facticity, anticipating some meaning that can be attributed only by a transcendent consciousness'.[11] Similar observations are made by Grosz who establishes three 'by no means hard and fast' feminist positions on the body: egalitarian feminism, social constructionism and sexual difference.[12] The last of these - sexual difference - is the most recent, the least common and the only one that is overtly suspicious of feminism's traditional sex/gender frontier. Grosz identifies Luce Irigaray, Monique Wittig, Moira Gatens, Hélène Cixous and Judith Butler as among the adherents to this position who are 'concerned with the *lived* body', a body that is 'neither brute nor passive' but instead, 'interwoven with and constitutive of systems of meaning, signification, and representation'.[13] Within this position, pre-ordained binary pairings are actively refused or transgressed. There is a hunger for a new awareness of the interaction of supposedly fixed categories like nature and nurture, mind and body, or sex and gender. Current assumptions are cast aside such that a category like the sexed female body, which traditionally has been contrasted with the gendered woman's mind, emerges as potentially inscribed by culture *and* determined by nature. In particular, we are warned against treating the female body as natural, as troublesome, or as always dominated: it may be a surface that is capable of resistance, one plays an active part in accruing gender rather than being replaced or passively inscribed by it.[14]

Neither of the other two positions identified by Grosz share the sexual difference understanding of the body. The first listed, egalitarian feminism, comprises a scattered group including de Beauvoir, Shulamith Firestone, and 'other liberal, conservative, and humanist feminists, even ecofeminists'.[15] This grouping is connected by its common acceptance of 'patriarchal and misogynist assumptions about the female body as somehow more natural, less detached, more engaged with and directly related to its "objects" than male bodies'.[16] They argue that it is the 'real vulnerability and fragility' of the reproductive female body that straps women to a secondary, non-productive position and thus, it is 'biology itself that requires modification and transformation' by means of scientific or medical resourcefulness.[17] Social constructionist feminism is equally committed to the mind/body variant on the sex/gender opposition, accepting the body as 'biologically determined, fixed, and ahistorical'.[18] However, it differs from egalitarian feminism in that it sees no need to overcome, control or engage biology. For the social constructionist, the essential shift must occur at the level of gender, with the knock-on effect that the body and its functions will have different meanings. She has no need to think the body, rethink it, or, in postmodern fashion, transgress it: for her, the body is a straightforward biological reality which offers up its passive surface to gender inscription.

Much though I admire many adherents to both the egalitarian and social constructionist positions, I now suspect that Butler, Grosz and others are right: thinking the body outside known binary pairs is the future for feminism. It really does seem to promise new understandings. Unfortunately, it also carries a threat; it threatens accepted ideas of identity and, in postmodern times, it is tempting to see this threat as more powerful than the promise. Feminism may have used Woman as gendered subject to shatter certain taken-for-granted particularities of identity, but it is the postmodern and 'queer theory' which are now rattling the idea of the self. In such a climate, it makes perfect sense that feminism should crave reassurance and this is what makes the body so tempting. The body offers comforting solidity, blocking the tyranny of complete constructionism. It makes it seem as if there is still a little corner where nature reigns and the essential self is unassailable. Bodies are like anchors in our swirling new postmodern world: here, an individual body can represent one's essential self, different from the male body, different also from other female bodies.

I have no doubt, however, that the security of the body will be breached. For example, the sexual body - homosexual, heterosexual, bisexual - is now much less safe: as noted above, it has been engaged by the postmodern and 'queer theory', losing its (falsely) comforting certainty in the process. But if sexualities are not immutable or natural but instead produced by systems, including law, how long can the sexed body hold out? The answer must be, not long. The power of the feminism's favourite binary pair - sex/gender - is fading fast. Feminism *needs* to think the sexed body outside of this pair and its entourage. Everything points to this. We have reached a time where identity can no longer be forged from the violent imbalance of the sex/gender binary pair, or from its reduction, or from the illusion of harmonious fusion. Questions which we cannot answer are tumbling out, proliferating wildly. Grosz urges us to consider the following:

> [i]s sexual difference [*i.e.,* the sexed female or male body] primary and sexual inscription [*i.e.,* being gendered as a woman or a man] a cultural overlay or rewriting of an ontologically prior differentiation? Or is sexual differentiation a product of the various forms of inscription of culturally specific bodies? Do inscriptions produce sexual differentiation? Or does sexual difference imply a differential mode of inscription?[19]

Not surprisingly, Butler has a similar set of questions for us:

> Is 'the body' or 'the sexed body' the firm foundation on which gender and systems of compulsory sexuality operate? Or is 'the body' itself shaped by political forces with strategic interests in keeping that body bounded and constituted by the markers of sex?[20]

The message is clear and it is growing stronger: postmodernism means that categorical cravings are out for the *fin de siècle* and beyond.[21] To secure the insights of feminism, we must relinquish our craving of an uneven sex/gender opposition. We must also interrogate its accompanying essentialist identity politics which privilege woman's experience and crowd out the sexed body as devoid of significance or always already gendered. Unfortunately, however, even if the fact that feminism needs to think the sexed body is obvious, figuring out how it should do so is not at all clear. French feminists have their way, but it seems inappropriate for the very different intellectual tradition of Anglo-American feminism. Too much of the postmodern too early on might also prove alienating. As noted earlier, in what follows, I will be proposing one starting point. Clearly, there are other, perhaps better, starting points. My choice here is influenced by a strong sense of personal intrigue as well as a recognition of current institutional politics. It centres itself in a fresh feminist engagement with the familiar - Medical Law - and a call for engagement with the newly institutionally-acceptable - Law and Literature. The arrangement isn't intended as a selfish one; the idea is that it should benefit all parties given that all currently play their part in flogging binary thinking and all will thus come to pay the postmodern price. I begin by examining the closures in Medical Law and Law and Literature.

But is it *law* (or *literature*)?

Questions which look short and sound simple are often the most horrible. The strain of questions which commences with the words 'But is it ... ' is particularly vicious. For example, how many law teachers have felt misunderstood and hounded by a 'But is it Law?' variant. It is possible to retort provocatively, 'What is Law?', but it rarely seems worth the hassle, given the irritating inevitability of the ensuing tussle. Thus, faced with the 'But is it Law?' question, real options usually appear slim on the ground and vocal allies few in number. This makes for predictable, and depressing, outcomes. The misunderstood and hounded either retreat, despairingly, to seek out the commiserations of other 'non-lawyers', perhaps to fight another day or they are co-opted by the 'lawyers', comforted by dreams of inside attack or, more realistically, by the enhanced promotion prospects which come as reward for 'hard law' expertise. Sometimes, these skirmishes stir up talk of dangerous supplements, bottom-up theory and outsider jurisprudence, but through it all, law school life goes on much as before.

Teachers of Medical Law once considered themselves the most afflicted by annoying questions about their 'law' credentials. They were regularly accused of promoting a scavenger, not a subject. Medical Law was considered to be dangerously unbounded, preying on, and playing around with, the established 'law subjects' of tort, contract, trusts, family and child law. Medical Law has now grown into a fairly respectable and increasingly hip 'law subject'. However, this legal gentrification did not come cost-free: Medical Law has opted for very closely-defined boundaries which betray an obsession with the professional man of medicine and his patient. The doctor/patient relationship is the great crisis issue of Medical Law; so much so, that the sense of being hemmed in by *Bolam*'s 'reasonable doctor' test[22] is overwhelming. Lawyers' 'hard law' has also proved incredibly resilient within the subject: torts, contracts, and trusts are the language of Medical

Law, even where astoundingly inappropriate as, for example, with surrogacy arrangements or the 'sham' trusts and contracts of the post-1990 National Health Service.[23] Moreover, even where outdated, the common law does not give way: one wonders for how much longer it will insist on dominating medical confidentiality with the idea of the single doctor/single patient dynamic in an era of unprecedented access to health information.[24] One could point to the fact that human rights skirmishes are increasingly intermittent in Medical Law as evidence of change afoot, but these encounters are generally inconclusive or worse, distortive. Furthermore, although principles of non-discrimination have a growing foothold, it is an unstable one which is currently too susceptible to displacement by public health concerns or by ideas of 'natural' differences between the sexes.

The story of Law and Literature is somewhat similar to that of Medical Law. Troubled by annoying 'But is it Law?' queries and yearning for legal gentrification, it also erected closures and the promise of a new hyphenated world which would allow for a slithering across the law/non-law binary pair was forgotten. Law and Literature's closures were somewhat nation-specific. Thus, in the United Kingdom, the closure was to the very idea of Law and Literature as worthy of teaching or research energies in the law school. Aristodemou observes that 'in England ... literature was generally seen as, at best, a pleasant and graceful adjunct to the study of law, little more than a broadening social grace or a civilizing influence on lawyers'.[25] Consideration of appropriate aims - educative, political, ethical or otherwise - for Law and Literature courses and scholarship never arose. Instead, narcissism was the order of the day; there was an 'exclusive concern with offering "playful comments on law in great literary works", enlightening ... literature readers with legal details that might have escaped them but without contemplating (or acknowledging) that literature might hold any lessons in the other direction'.[26] In sum, there was no such pursuit as Law and Literature but instead merely a diversion or amusement for the high-minded, never long dallied over, although guaranteed to preserve, and perhaps enhance, status.

Meanwhile, in the United States, aims talk around Law and Literature had spread like wildfire. It was serious, high-powered stuff: was Law and Literature's ambition 'firstly educative, and only then, secondly, social and political' or not?[27] This aims talk was accompanied by a preoccupation with categorisation. Law and Literature was found to be an umbrella term, shading law in, of, and through literature. Moreover, law school traditionalists, protective of their own intellectual turf and hungry for new conquests, reminded us that there has always been a law *of* literature. The possibility of categorisation facilitated Law and Literature's ascent to respectability. Categorisation came from an honourable tradition which resonated with scholarly virtue and, thus, the Law and Literature enterprise acquired an academic glow and the patronage of the established. Those who had been little more than a scattering of malcontented legal educationalists and status-less interdisciplinarians became a class act. The tenure-hungry cashed in their Law and Literature credentials. Heavyweights - including Richard Posner and Ronald Dworkin - began to stake out the territory, symposia proliferated, and journals were dedicated to the cause. Law and Literature also came by a worthy lineage: acknowledged scholars and jurists of earlier generations - Benjamin Cardozo, Roscoe Pound and Oliver Wendell Holmes amongst others - were found to have shared the commitment to exploring the connections between law and literature. Resonances of Law and Literature were picked up elsewhere and the powerful storytelling scholarship of Derrick Bell[28] and Patricia Williams[29] was brought into the expanding fold. This groundswell culminated in the award of 'movement' status to Law and Literature, and the struggle for ' "the soul" of the academy and ultimately for that of the polity'[30] was enjoined. Suddenly, Law and Literature ranked up there with Law and Economics, Critical Legal Studies and Feminism, together comprising 'the four horsepersons of the apocalypse'.[31]

I take the view, however, that respectability has had its downside for Law and Literature. The original charm has been blunted and the call to 'fun' rings hollow as the preoccupation with categorisation becomes tiresome. Self-conscious 'law in, as, and through literature' labelling gets under the skin in a loathsome manner and the much-vaunted aims talk sometimes sounds like aims squabbling. One could dismiss these as the teething pains of the transition to status in the academy. More pessimistically, one might argue that they are an inevitable and lasting by-product of the 'industrialisation' or co-opting of Law and Literature by law's world.[32] For my part, the most irritating closure within Law and Literature is that which has been effected by yet another variant of the afore-mentioned bad-penny 'But is it ... ?' question. Remember that, as regards Medical Law, I argued that fear of ambush as non-law has provoked closure and obsession. For Law and Literature, the sting has been a little different: with eyebrow cocked, the questioner here need only inquire 'But is it *literature*?' Having earned some measure of legal respectability, and thus, escaped the immediate clutches of the 'But is it Law?' question, Law and Literature afficionados have been careful to close ranks around their sacred texts to stave off further challenge. Dickens, Shakespeare, and Kafka bring credibility to the movement. They are the old reliables who ensure that the 'Great Books Project'[33] can hold its own with the more consciously-intellectual Law as Literature enterprise. They are the 'great masters' who explore the 'great' themes.[34] Thus, in Law and Literature, radical literary criticism is generally ignored. Here, literature is literature: there are no surprises. There is no taste for trumping or trashing notions of canonicity and devotees have no time for engagement with Roland Barthes' a-canonical assertion that 'Literature is what gets taught'.[35] Not surprisingly, feminist literary criticism - whether the *écriture féminine* of the French or the context-engaged politicking of the Anglo-Americans[36] makes no impression whatsoever.

For such a status-conscious Law and Literature, 'trash' fiction ought to be truly risky. It seems, however, that this is not the case or, at least, that the literature/trash dualism is a leaking one because status is being accorded to science fiction and crime genres. My own view of this is that while science fiction and crime may be seen as trashy, the 'true trash' sticker is being reserved for romantic fiction. It seems that even 'trash' has standards to maintain, dualisms to perpetuate, and 'others' to create in order to establish its own norms. In such a climate, romantic fiction is an obvious enemy. It is not the stuff of literature, nor is it just trashy: it is 'women's stuff', of the body/flesh and not of the mind/intellect. With romantic fiction, one is said to sink into the feeling, scaling neither the heights of imagination, as with science fiction, nor those of the intellect, as with realism. Romance cannot then be of concern to the 'literature' of Law and Literature. And, we already know that it is unlikely to be of concern to 'law' with its carefully-tended 'scientific' boundaries.

Intriguingly, a case has recently been made for the romance as the ultimate 'flagrantly anachronistic', and thus keenly postmodern, text.[37] The resemblance is erected upon the romance's uncanny and non-modernist capacity to defy boundaries of genre and time. The accepted void between the romantic works of Emily Brontë, Barbara Cartland and Kathy Acker pinpoints the argument that 'the term "romance" is ... neither [a] fixed generic prescription nor [an] abstract transhistorical category'.[38] Elam is not the first to testify to the genre-bashing capacities of the romance. Henry James, in the preface to *The American* (1878), pushed a similar point, declaring that the only general characteristic of the romance that he could find grew from the unknowability, immeasurability, and liberation of experience which it alone could provide. Elam echoes this and, in studies of Umberto Eco, George

Eliot, Sir Walter Scott, Jacques Derrida and others, she shows that 'what the genre of romance is remains an uncertainty: each text must in some way redefine what it means by "romance," must in the process of this redefinition create a meaning for the genre of romance to which it addresses itself, at the same time as it loses older, perhaps more established, meanings'.[39]   Elam also labels the romance as capable of blurring manifold other literary binarisms, including high and low culture, via its illogical status as both high art - courtesy of Emily Brontë *et al.* - *and* mass-market, through the machinations of Mills and Boon and Harlequin. Ideas of the real and the imagined, past and present are also up for grabs because of the romance's capacity to replicate both our day-to-day living and our fantasies. Moreover, in common with postmodernity, one finds a 'constant difficulty in calculating [the] politics' of the romance: is it 'the radical reinvention of a freer world? Is postmodernism the subversion of existing cultural orthodoxy?   *Or* is romance merely escapist fantasy, postmodernism merely ineffectual playfulness?'[40]

Feminism and knights in shining armour

For feminism, the closures of Medical Law and Law and Literature sketched out in the last section are tragic. There are surely overwhelming affinities between Medical Law and feminism, between Law and Literature and feminism, and between all three together. The affinity between Law and Literature and feminism seems to me to be especially powerful. They are like a predestined pair:

> [The former's] ambitions are two-fold; to better educate the lawyer, and to better reveal the politics of law. Feminist literary criticism ... enjoys essentially the same ambitions. There is, if nothing else, a coincidence of ambition.[41]

There is much more to trumpet here, however, than a Law and Literature/feminism 'special relationship'. All three subjects aspire to, and can, 'transform the legal mask into a living face'.[42]   Each one can captivate audiences, illuminating with the power of stories. Emotions also intrude noisily in all three. Law and Literature and legal feminism take this in less self-conscious manner: both are determinedly upbeat, aware enterprises. Medical Law presents itself as more sombre, but its professional voice is constantly mediated by the immediacy of the personal in life and death decision-making. All three also temper the excesses of law's discipline.

They are subjects of 'eclectic elasticity ... insolently, urgently meaningful in [their] failure to respect generic boundaries'.[43]   Law and Literature, for example, has never been captivated by law's quest for certainty and final resolutions: instead, 'as tends to be the case in specifically interdisciplinary studies [it] has simply attempted to reveal the possibilities presented by alternative approaches to the study and the teaching of law'.[44]   Legal feminism and Medical Law share this immunity.   Respect for generic boundaries would amount to political suicide for the former, whereas concentration on ethical outcomes, and more recently, on human rights dimensions, restrains the trend to aggrandizement in the latter. Thus, there is much that points to a special relationship between these three, but is there, in fact, any evidence of its presence? Has feminism actually got a foothold, or perhaps more, in these new corners of the law school curriculum?

The ugly sisters? Medical Law Woman meets Law and Literature Woman

Exploring newcomer subjects to law school curricula and law review pages is fascinating; their boundaries are particularly telling, all the more so if one sets oneself the particular task of asking where and why women have been allowed in and where and why they have not. My own conclusion is that, when Medical Law Woman meets Law and Literature Woman (if she can be found), there are currently few real women present. Unfortunately, feminism itself must take some of the blame for this; it has wasted opportunities, attacked false enemies, and misused its intellectual weaponery. In what follows, Medicine's idea of the female body - the ultimate challenge for science's control over nature - is unrecognisable to most of us. Its 'expert' and 'scientific' body management renders our individual bodies 'more useful, more powerful and more docile'.[45]   Feminism has been alert to this, cautioning over-reliance on medicalisation as a guarantor of, or ally as regards, abortion access[46] and re-writing the history of the medicalisation of childbirth.[47] It is reassuring then that Medical Law is less 'body-conscious' and more holistic than medicine, in that it sets out to conduct itself as concerned with the dignity of the individual. However, when the rhetoric is stripped back, and the 'individual' who engages with Medical Law is a woman, the depressing tradition of confinement to the body is still in evidence. Thus, although it is true that the 'Woman' of Medical Law has been permitted a corner of the Medical Law syllabus and encouraged to call it her own, that which is of concern there is predictably narrow: the troubled and troubling female body as reflected in pregnancy, abortion, assisted reproduction, sterilization and anorexia. Terminology used elsewhere in law discourages direct association with the female body of Medical Law Woman: for example, in employment law, pregnancy has either been akin to a sickness in the male body or without a comparison, thereby trapping the woman within a needy female body that requires stigmatic 'special treatment'. The terminology of Medical Law can be equally alienating: body parts and bodily functions - egg donor, sperm donor, genetic mother, surrogate mother - submerge the persons involved whilst property language cloaks sperm, eggs, embryos and genetic material. There is also, of course, the confounding nature of the actual phrase 'surrogate mother' and, more generally, the contractual web that is enclosing thinking around surrogacy arrangements.

Recently, even this reproduction ghetto of Medical Law Woman has come under threat: increasingly, she is having to share her space with the state's interest in the foetus, the best interests of children, and the rights of male partners. Ultimately, she may be edged out and although feminism is doing much to problematise this encroachment, I suspect that a continued addiction to its sex/gender weapons, will leave feminist 'successes' wrong-footed on increasingly treacherous terrain. For example, feminist talk of the body as private, as property and as inviolable has clearly helped to reinforce abortion rights in liberal minds, but, what is less often acknowledged is that this feminist strategy submerges the porous boundaries of the 'natural' body by refusing the intensity of cultural inscription and further bolstering mind/body dualisms. It can also fail to capture the pregnant body and, as such, it rings hollow for many women who have never felt (and do not name a desire to feel) such armour around their bodies. Such talk is also dated by medical 'viewing' technology, like foetal scanning, which makes the private interior of the pregnant female body available to expert spectators (the medical profession) as well as enemy audiences (foetal rights campaigners).

Working in opposition to this idea of the natural, inviolable female body is an equally-flawed feminist social constructionist account which tends to ascribe a counter-intuitive passivity to the female body:

> The body is typically regarded as passive and reproductive but largely unproductive, an object over which struggles between its 'inhabitant' and others/exploiters may be possible. Whatever agency or will it has is the direct consequence of animating, psychical intentions. Its inertia means that it is capable of being acted on, coerced, or constrained by external forces.[48]

Other social constructionist accounts have also come under attack. Sawicki[49] has exposed an excess of mothering theory in some cultural feminisms, noting that while a celebration of maternal experience may provide audience-friendly justification for women's 'true' perspectives on reproductive issues, the 'mother' of this feminist discourse can be frighteningly ahistoric, acultural, naturalistic and universal. Sometimes, she is just plain unrecognisable. Her blanking out of presumptions and stereotypes about race and class is also startlingly naive. Where, for example, would Toni Morrison's slave mother, Sethe, from her novel *Beloved* (1987), find a place in this mothering utopia? Sethe's mothering experience was all about responsibility without any of the corresponding rights: she was the slave mother 'whose responsibility was to produce the commodity of slaves, but whose right to a relationship with her own children was deemed irrelevant, or, at least, secondary'.[50] Sethe had to destroy her beloved child in order to wrench not only the child's, but also her own, humanity from the ownership of the master and to claim the mother/child relationship. Sethe's story of mothering is a confusing one, wherein child destruction emerges as an act of maternal love. Our confusion should remind us that maternal experience can be a tool for feminist struggle only if it is also a site of acknowledged differences: we must not presume to know the maternal experience. Ambiguity and paradox may be legal offences; they need not be legal feminist ones.

Elsewhere within the reproduction ghetto of Medical Law, other feminisms have been guilty of overdoing the demons. Sawicki[51] details the targetting of reproductive technologies by Gena Corea[52] and other members of the Feminist International Network on Resistance to Reproductive and Genetic Engineering (FINRRAGE). She credits them with the necessary politicisation of reproductive technologies but cautions against the 'too pessimistic, moralistic and one-dimensional'[53] character of their discourse:

> Their anti-technology stance sometimes lapses into utopian romantic appeals to a pre-modern era and is therefore not helpful to the majority of women facing decisions about childbirth ... today. More adequate analyses would make clearer why many women regard them as beneficial. They would also highlight the different positions that women occupy in relation to the new technologies in order to identify multiple sites of potential resistance.[54]

Feminism also needs to be more focused on the lacking as regards men's bodies, particularly for example around assumptions about infertility. Elsewhere - as for example around AIDS discourses - where the male body is all-pervasive, feminism must commit to the entirely different task of pushing the needs of the female body, in opposition to popular conceptions of the woman as carer, child-bearer or contraceptive custodian in these discourses.[55]

The female body ghetto in Medical Law rebounds on feminism in other ways too. Consider, for example, why feminism has impinged so narrowly in Medical Law. Women generally don't feature in Medical Law and neither does feminism; it is only women's troubled and troubling bodies that perform at centre-stage in the reproduction ghetto. Medical Law doesn't seem to discuss women as carers who are affected by resource allocation decisions. Women also go unheard in the euthanasia debate although they live longest, as well as being the most frequent carers. And the nurse is, in the main, absent, although we agonize over the professional man of medicine.[56]

The silence in Law and Literature is even more bizarre than the ghettoization in Medical Law. We know that legal institutions have been heavily battered by feminism. Literary institutions have also felt its impact.[57] Yet, together, in Law and Literature, there is little trace of this hard-won legacy. Gemmette, writing in 1989, found Law and Literature courses at thirty-eight American Bar Association-approved law schools, but thirty-seven of the course reading lists made no mention of feminism.[58] Feminism fares no better in legal writing around Law and Literature. Reviewing a testament to the 'vitality' of the Law and Literature movement - the Levinson and Mailloux-edited collection *Interpreting Law and Literature: A Hermeneutic Reader* - Koffler finds that it 'omits some of the most stimulating contributions in the area; it ignores almost entirely, but perhaps all too predictably, feminist contributions to the debate and indeed excludes any serious self-doubt about the patriarchal concepts underlying "community", "conversation" or "convention"'.[59] None of Robin West's work is included in the collection. Also missing is any trace of 'the flood of feminist writings that address the [jurisprudential] debates raised in the book'.[60] Most callously of all, Clare Dalton's article 'An Essay in the Deconstruction of Contract Doctrine', which assessed how feminist theory might expose the hollow objectivity in principles of contract law, is included but 'radically unsexed, with editorial amputations mutilating its feminist arguments'.[61]

Feminism has failed to counter these closures within Law and Literature. Heilbrun and Resnik complain that '[l]iterature, as it has so far been discussed by lawyers in law journals, rarely is considered as a source by which readers may come to understand the sufferings of women'.[62] Their theme is picked up by Ward.[63] He also notices the overwhelming negativity of the little feminist engagement with Law and Literature that is present, although he himself goes on to offer a vibrant example of the available opportunities. I find legal feminism's neglect of this intellectual terrain startling and hard to explain. Feminist literary criticism offers it almost pre-packaged guides to 'law as literature' and 'law in literature' materials. Moreover, the promise of engagement with French feminism would surely be closer in a living feminist Law and Literature culture. I also think that fiction can offer feminism a means by which to challenge law's truths. We know that law uses renderings of facts to secure its truths, but feminism has opened our eyes and allowed us to see that the 'facts as interpreted by the court may not render the truth of women's lives'.[64] Because it is a gateway to the imagination which in turn 'challenges thought and recreates the boundaries of what is recognized as truth',[65] fiction might allow us to upset the fact/fiction-truth/lies fixations of the law.

There is some temptation to call up Robin West's juxtaposition of 'literary woman' with 'economic man'[66] as a counter to this alleged feminist non-engagement with Law and Literature. West contrasts the literary analysis of law with its 'closest interdisciplinary cousin',[67] economic analysis of law by picking out the salient features of both approaches. The contrast is a striking one from which 'economic man' emerges as a scruffy undesirable and 'literary woman' as that to which we should all aspire. 'Literary woman' is special because '[s]he represents not just our cultural heritage, but more importantly (and relatedly) she represents our potential for moral growth'.[68] West's 'literary woman' and that for which she stands - the literary analysis of law - are argued to deepen our understanding and enhance our communication and problem-solving capacities. Literature, it seems, can open many doors for us. West's creation of these two characters is fascinating and very readable, but my own view is that this sort of juxtapositioning should be resisted, at least while there is such little other feminist engagement with Law and Literature. Although West is careful to ascribe no fixed gender to 'literary woman', I am concerned that without other forms of feminist engagement, West's 'literary woman/economic man' approach to Law and Literature may shore up the world of binary pairs from which the postmodern insists that we escape. I have also insisted throughout this chapter that this is a world whose intellectual energy is fast being used up by Anglo-American legal feminism and I see no lasting safe haven in a new feminist celebration of 'literary woman', without a probing of the Law and Literature enterprise as a whole, as well as feminism's own methodology.

My preference is for promoting the special place of the romance in a feminist Law and Literature. Elam's text sends out a call for a feminist 'romancing' of the postmodern by means of an overt and sustained inquiry into the postmodern features of the romance, thereby occasioning a new challenge to the 'historical, epistemological, and aesthetic assumptions that continue to erase and devalue the feminine'.[69] This all seems to me to raise the stakes for a key positioning of the romance within a prised-open and newly feminist Law and Literature. Those who would ridicule us for delving into the romance can be bought off with a lesson on its 'respectable' history. The links between the feminine and romance have only recently been forged: '[i]t was written and read by aristocrats of both sexes until the eighteenth century; only then did it begin to be mocked as a feminine occupation'.[70] In postmodern times, however, there is probably little to be gained from any traditional, straightforward gendering of the romance genre. It is more important that we cash in on the genre's enviable irrepressibility and popularity to surge forward within Law and Literature and to kickstart the feminist rethink on sex/gender. However, it is worth noting that even the modern mockery of romance as a 'feminine' pursuit may be misinformed; feminist analyses of romance, such as that by Janice Radway,[71] portray its readers not as mockable objects - passive, escapist victims, who want only to sink into the feeling - but as active, discerning readers who have an 'ability to see that the romance is an alterable set of generic conventions rather than a natural and immutable form'.[72] Radway's women are active, skilled readers who ferret out preferred romances, reject 'substandard' ones, and share their knowledge with others in their romance-reading community. But, Radway's analysis, while compelling, also has an intriguingly, counter-intuitive feel to it. Liberation through a happy ending or being swept off one's feet seems awkwardly non-feminist. A striking example of this uneasiness is offered by Rosalind Coward's 1985 study of female desires which closes with the reminder that 'women do acquire power in these [romantic] fantasies ... this power, however, is always familial, always regressive'.[73] Others fight back against Coward's cynicism, claiming that even the 'contemporary mass-produced narratives for women contain elements of protest and resistance underneath highly "orthodox" plots'.[74] It seems that there is no one feminist line on the romance; it persists as an un-'boxed' genre, ever-tempting, ever-disturbing in its unknowability and thus, perfectly suited to fuzzing feminism's sex/gender-mind/body binarisms.

I am convinced that, for a feminist Law and Literature which is concerned to excavate the sexed body from the 'natural' or the ignominy of complete construction, the romance is truly brimful with possibilities. How often do our law reports replicate the romantic narrative which 'leads to resolution through heterosexual union, which closes down the possibility of other desires and other narratives, and relegates women to a position beyond culture and history, firmly placed in the realm of "nature" and "eternal truth"'?[75] To what extent did the 'literature' of our girlhood - the teenage romance - inscribe our sense of our female bodies, their beauty and their sexuality?[76] How has the modern, mass-produced romance negotiated feminism? The romance may help expose and shift the 'vanilla quality'[77] of our writing on the sexual body, igniting a 'politics of personal transformation'[78] for the sexed body, by making us confront the pleasures of identifying with happy endings and the restoration of 'natural' order.[79]

Happy ever after?

There is much work to be done: most importantly, the body must appear anew within Anglo-American legal feminism, but also feminism must claim its place within Law and Literature and review its standing within Medical Law, if a transgression of sex/gender and mind/body dualisms is to be realised and the postmodern de-problematised. Knowing that these are battles which feminism must join - that neutrality is a sham and retreat is not a lasting option - helps to stiffen resolve but makes the path no clearer. For example, why call, as I have, for a re-engagement with Medical Law and an assault on Law and Literature in order to shift sex/gender frontiers to better describe the sexed body? Clearly, I do not want to claim that this is the only way forward; it is but one potential way. I choose it, and have sought to push it here, for three particular reasons. First, because '[b]oth "law" and "literature" share the activity of generating narratives that illuminate, create, and reflect normative worlds, that bring experiences that might otherwise be invisible and silent into public view'.[80] Further, as Heilbrun and Resnik imply, both law and literature reflect and replicate the stranglehold grip of binary pairings on our ways of thinking, seeing and living.[81] Law, for example, clearly aligns itself with the mind. Judgment, reason, rationality, knowledge are what help keep it distinct. 'Body' traits - unknowability, uncontrollability, seepage, the inevitability of frailty - are alien to the law's avowed prowess. Embodiment would muddy the mind of law. Literature is also mined in the mind/body dualism, in that it inhabits the territory of the intellect and the imagination, free from the mere corporeality of the body.

This distaste for the body is also evidence in its repression of the romance and preference for realism.

The second reason motivating my call for a feminist engagement with Medical Law and Law and Literature is less imaginative and more about self-preservation. Both Medical Law and Law and Literature can offer safe passage to Anglo-American feminism, such that space for regrouping can be carved out in the face of the postmodern. There is much that can be mined during such a regrouping: Law and Literature is almost entirely uncolonised and Medical Law can be counted on as a perpetual source of dilemmas. However, the most important reason behind my urging of this feminist engagement grows from my belief that both Medical Law and Law and Literature harbour the potential for a vigorous feminist engagement with the postmodern, particularly the latter's liberation from binary pairings and their accompanying essentialism. I see Medical Law and Law and Literature as ripe for a re-reading of the body and view this as a happy coincidence for Anglo-American legal feminism which, in the face of the postmodern, must simultaneously wrench the body from the scientific *and* the cultural. The former has dominated it for too long and the latter appropriates it too readily.[82] There are also grounds for suspicion that feminism itself has been complicit in all of this because of the manner in which it has shored up the sex/gender binary pair.

As regards Medical Law, I have tried to sketch some feminist starting points in my criticisms of the status quo. My argument has been that, given the need to redraw the sex/gender divide, a feminist refocusing on the body must unsteady cultural constructionism, scientific realities and feminist 'truths'. The body is both culturally inscribed and naturally determined while also resisting both. Medical Law offers Anglo-American legal feminism the opportunity to challenge science, law, and our own ambivalence. Law and Literature, by contrast, will be new terrain for feminism. I take the view that it is terrain which feminism has been foolish in not cultivating. Here, a general feminist engagement would mean that '[t]he texts would be different texts and the same texts would be read differently'.[83] These texts will function 'both as a representation and simultaneously as a critique of the processes of representation'.[84] This must be tackled immediately; there is little enough feminist-friendly terrain in the law school and feminist literary criticism offers an established 'literature' if tickets to respectability are deemed necessary. However, as regards my primary task - that of re-orienting the sex/gender-mind/body divide and other dangerous binary oppositions - and the utility of Law and Literature therein, I have been particularly concerned in this essay to nominate the 'true trash' genre of the romance as our salvation. The romance as 'true trash' can rescue the body from its conscription by the natural sciences. It can also resuscitate the body within the humanities by imperilling the part played by that discipline in the spread of mind/body dualisms by its privileging of realism over romance. Moreover, it also should expose the violence of 'literature's' edging out its own supposed binary opposite, 'popular culture'.

It is time for Anglo-American legal feminism to make amends and to plough a new course for the new century. We must neither entrench nor melt the sex/gender binary pair and its terrible entourage: we need simply to fuzz them a bit and wait for the sparks to fly. Using Medical Law and Law and Literature, I think that we might be able to create just the right degree of controlled chaos.

Notes

1. Smart (1992).
2. Cornell (1991).
3. Jones (1985), p. 361.
4. Bell (1993), p. ix.
5. Smart (1990), p. 199.
6. Smart (1990).
7. Butler (1990, 1993).
8. Butler (1990), p. 129.
9. Butler (1990), p. 129.
10. Grosz (1994), p. 188.
11. Butler (1990), p. 129.
12. Grosz (1990), p. 15.
13. Grosz (1990), p. 18.
14. Butler (1995), p. 5.
15. Butler (1995), p. 15.
16. Butler (1995), p. 15.
17. Butler (1995), p. 16.
18. Butler (1995), p. 16.
19. Grosz (1994), p. 189.
20. Butler (1990), p. 129.
21. This steals from and adapts Carl Stychin's (1995) fascinating intervention in the debates surrounding human rights and sexual

orientation, focusing on categorical thinking in Canadian anti-discrimination law and essentialist conceptions of identity. Stychin concludes that the promise of human rights law will only be secured if we relinquish our craving for analytical tools that categorize, compartmentalize, and ultimately contain us as subjects of law.

22. *Bolam v. Friern Hospital Management Committee* [1957] 2 ALL E.R. 118.
23. Hughes (1991).
24. Gostin (1995).
25. Aristodemou (1993), p. 164.
26. Aristodomou (1993), p. 164.
27. Ward (1993), p. 323.
28. Bell (1987).
29. Williams (1991).
30. Koffler (1989), p. 1387.
31. Koffler (1989), n. 31.
32. Koffler (1989), p. 1376.
33. Cohen (1990), p. 352.
34. Aristodemou (1992), p. 167.
35. Cohen (1992), pp. 352-3.
36. Writing in 1985, Elaine Showalter described the difference in terms which associated Anglo-American feminist criticism with the recovery of women's historical experiences both as readers and as writers whereas the French *l'écriture féminine* represented an *avant garde* writing style which sought to subvert the patterns of Western narrative by 'writing in the feminine' and thereby overpower the silencing of feminine difference within current discourses.
37. Elam (1992), p. 12.
38. Parker (1979), p. 5.
39. Elam (1992), pp. 6-7.
40. Elam (1992), p. 19 (emphasis added).
41. Ward (1994), p. 134.
42. Camilleri (1990), p. 563.
43. Cohen (1990), p. 347.
44. Ward (1993), p. 323.
45. Sawicki (1991), p. 83.
46. Sheldon (1995).
47. Witz (1992).

48. Grosz (1994), p. 9.
49. Sawicki (1991).
50. Tobin (1993), p. 240.
51. Sawicki (1991).
52. Corea (1985).
53. Sawicki (1991), p. 70.
54. Sawicki (1991), p. 70.
55. Gruskin (1995).
56. Montgomery (1992).
57. Showalter (1985); Moi (1985).
58. Heilbrun and Resnik (1990), pp. 1913-4.
59. Koffer (1989).
60. Koffer (1989), p. 1388.
61. Koffer (1989), p. 1388.
62. Heilbrun and Resnik (1990), p. 1927.
63. Ward (1994).
64. Tobin (1993), p. 238.
65. Tobin (1993), p. 238.
66. West (1989).
67. West (1989), p. 868.
68. West (1989), p. 878.
69. Sawicki (1995), p. 741.
70. Jones (1986), p. 198.
71. Radway (1983).
72. Radway (1983), p. 152.
73. Coward (1985), p. 196.
74. Modleski (1982), p. 25.
75. Bridgewood (1986), p. 167.
76. Christian-Smith (1990).
77. Kennedy (1994).
78. Bartky (1986).
79. Barrett (1980).
80. Heilbrun and Resnik (1990), p. 1914.
81. Heilbrun and Resnik (1990), p. 1914.
82. Grosz (1994).
83. Heilbrun and Resnik (1990), p. 1942.
84. Tobin (1993), p. 2424.

References

Aristodemou, M. (1993), 'Studies in Law and Literature: Directions and Concerns', *Anglo-American Law Review*, Vol. 20, pp. 157-193.

Barrett, M. (1980), *Women's Oppression Today*, Verso, London.

Bartky, S.L. (1988). 'Feminine Masochism and the Politics of Personal Transformation' *Hypatia*, Vol. 7(5), pp. 323-334.

Bell, D. (1987), *And We Are Not Saved: The Elusive Quest for Racial Justice*, Basic Books, New York.

Bell, V. (1993), *Interrogating Incest: Feminism, Foucault and the Law*, Routledge, London.

Bridgwood, C. (1986), 'Family Romances: The Contemporary Popular Family Saga', in Radford, J. (Ed.) *The Progress of Romance: The Politics of Popular Fiction*, Routledge, London.

Butler, J. (1990), *Gender Trouble: Feminism and the Subversion of Identity*, Routledge, London.

Butler, J. (1993), *Bodies That Matter: On the Discursive Limits of 'Sex'*, Routledge, London.

Camilleri, M. (1990), 'Comment, Lessons in Law from Literature: A Look at the Movement and a Peer at Her Jury', *Catholic University Law Review*, Vol. 39, pp. 557.

Christian-Smith, L.K. (1990), *Becoming a Woman Through Romance*, Routledge, London.

Cohen, J.M. (1990), 'The Arrival of the Bee Box: Feminism, Law, and Literature', *Harvard Women's Law Journal*, Vol. 13, pp. 345-361.

Corea, G. (1985), *The Mother Machine: Reproductive Technologies from Artificial Insemination to Artificial Wombs*, Harper and Row, New York.

Cornell, D. (1991), *Beyond Accommodation: Ethical Feminism, Deconstruction and the Law*, Routledge, London.

Coward, R. (1985), *Female Desires: How They Are Sought, Bought and Packaged*, Grove Press, New York.

Elam, D. (1992), *Romancing the Postmodern*, Routledge, London and New York.

Gostin, L. *et al.* (1995), 'Privacy and Security of Health Information in the Emerging Health Care System', *Health Matrix: Journal of Law-Medicine*, Vol. 5(1), pp. 1-37.

Grosz, E. (1994), *Volatile Bodies: Toward a Corporeal Feminism*, Indiana University Press, Bloomington and Indianapolis.

Gruskin, S. (1995), 'Negotiating the Relationship of HIV/AIDS to Reproductive Health and Reproductive Rights', *The American University Law Review*, Vol. 44, pp. 1191-1206.

Heilbrun, C. and Resnik, J. (1990), 'Convergences: Law, Literature, and Feminism', *Yale Law Journal*, Vol. 99, pp. 1913-1953.

Hughes, D. (1991), 'The Re-organisation of the National Health Service: the rhetoric and reality of the internal market', *Modern Law Review*, Vol. 54, pp. 88-103.

Koffler, J.S. (1989), 'Forged Alliance: Law and Literature', *Columbia Law Review*, Vol. 89, pp. 1374-1393.

Jones, A.R. (1985), 'Writing the Body: Toward an Understanding of l'Écriture féminine', in Showalter, E. (Ed.), *The New Feminist Criticism: Essays on Women, Literature and Theory*, Panthcon Books, New York.

Jones, A.R. (1986), 'Mills and Boon meets feminism', in Radford, J. (Ed.) *The Progress of Romance: The Politics of Popular Fiction*, Routledge, London.

Kennedy, D. (1993), *Sexy Dressing Etc.*, Harvard University Press, Cambridge, Mass.

Modleski, T. (1982), *Loving With a Vengeance*, Archon Books, Hamden.

Moi, T. (1985), *Sexual/Textual Politics*, Routledge, London.

Montgomery, J. (1992), 'Doctors' Handmaidens: The Legal Contribution', in McVeigh, S. and Wheeler, S. (Eds.), *Law, Health and Medical Regulation*, Dartmouth, Aldershot.

Parker, P. (1979), *Inescapable Romance: Studies in the Poetics of a Mode*, Princeton University Press, Princeton.

Radway, J. (1984), *Reading the Romance: Women, Patriarchy, and Popular Culture*, University of North Carolina Press, Chapel Hill, North Carolina.

Sanger, C. (1989), 'Seasoned to the Use', *Michigan Law Review*, Vol. 87, pp. 1338-1365.

Sawicki, J. (1991), *Disciplining Foucault: Feminism, Power, and the Body*, Routledge, New York and London.

Sawicki, J. (1995), 'Book Review', *Signs, Journal of Women in Culture and Society*, pp. 738-741.

Sheldon, S. (1995), 'The Law of Abortion and the Politics of Medicalisation', in Bridgeman, J. and Millns, S. (Eds.) *Law and Body Politics: Regulating the Female Body*, Dartmouth, Aldershot.

Showalter, E. (1985), 'Introduction: The Feminist Critical Revolution', in Showalter, E. (Ed.) *The New Feminist Criticism: Essays on Women, Literature and Theory*, Pantheon Books, New York.

Smart, C. (1990), 'Law's Power, the Sexed Body, and Feminist Discourse', *Journal of Law and Society*, Vol. 17, pp. 194-210.

Smart, C. (1992), 'The Woman of Legal Discourse', *Social and Legal Studies*, Vol. 1, pp. 29-44.

Stychin, C.F. (1995), 'Essential Rights and Contested Identities: Sexual Orientation and Equality Rights Jurisprudence in Canada', *Canadian Journal of Law and Jurisprudence*, Vol. 8(1), pp. 49-66.

Tobin, E. (1993), 'Imagining the Mother's Text: Toni Morrison's Beloved and Contemporary Law', *Harvard Women's Law Journal*, Vol. 16, pp. 233-273.

Ward, I. (1993), 'The Educative Ambition of Law and Literature', *Legal Studies*, Vol. 13(3), pp. 323-331.

Ward, I. (1994), 'Law and Literature: A Feminist Perspective', *Feminist Legal Studies*, Vol. 2(2), pp. 133-157.

West, R. (1988), 'Economic Man and Literary Woman: One Contrast', *Mercer Law Review*, Vol. 39 (3), pp. 867-878.

Williams, P. (1991), *The Alchemy of Race and Rights*, Harvard University Press, Cambridge, MA.

Witz, A. (1992), *Professions and Patriarchy*, Routledge, London.

4 The Unpardonable Sin

RAY GEARY

Introduction

Glanville Williams has described the case of *R v. Dudley and Stephens*[1] as being a dramatic illustration of the difference between utilitarian and deontological ethics.[2] The case involved four English seamen who were adrift in an open boat in the Atlantic with neither food nor water. Eventually one of them, Richard Parker, was killed and parts of his body and blood consumed, in order to sustain the others until they could be rescued. The two seamen who were tried and convicted of the murder, Dudley and Stephens, did not consider that they had done anything wrong; they had carried out an established custom of the sea when compelled to do so by necessity. If none of them had been killed and eaten in this way then they would all have died. In an exhaustive study of the subject Simpson has contended that, 'the whole point of the prosecution was to reject the barbarous practices of seamen'.[3] Procedural irregularities were resorted to that are dealt with in Simpson's book,[4] and are not to be considered in this essay, that resulted in the legal questions being referred to five judges of the Queen's Bench Division of the High Court of Justice. The opinion of that court was delivered by the Lord Chief Justice of England, Lord Coleridge.

As to the question of necessity, Lord Coleridge considered that, '[d]ecided cases there are none'.[5] He then proceeded to consider various legal authorities as to whether necessity could be an answer to a charge of murder. The cannibalism was not itself, of course, a criminal offence, but it lay at the centre of the case; there was no suggestion that Parker would have been killed it if had not been intended to eat him. There was a literature that was available to Lord Coleridge, some of which he referred to when he invoked the duty of dying for others, but on which he remained silent as to the problem of cannibalism. This literature is vast and can only be touched upon in this essay, but its importance lies in the fact that it also provides an alternative discourse to the one delivered by Lord Coleridge, and one of which he would have been to a considerable extent aware. He was a classical scholar and had an interest in literature, and has been described as, 'a good scholar and of literary taste ... as a judge he was, though not learned, a lucid expositor of law'.[6]

The purpose of this essay is to consider that literature as it developed through the classical writings of the Greeks and Romans to the depiction of cannibalism in novels, in order to see how it may have influenced Lord Coleridge's views, and how it may provide an alternative to them. For throughout the literature there is a dual representation of the cannibal as monster and as an unfortunate to be understood or pitied. In his review of Simpson's book Chase is consequently wrong when he says that, '[I]n the late-Victorian era, the perception of cannibalism changed'.[7] Cultural and social anxieties may have resulted in one of the aspects of cannibalism being stressed at that time, but its two aspects had always existed and were always available depending on the use to which the cannibalistic image was to be employed. Finally it is considered whether Lord Coleridge could have adopted a more relative approach by considering his review of Charles Kingsley's *Yeast* and the notion of sin and redemption. It is possible to compare the function of the judge in pronouncing on human conduct, with that of a reviewer delivering a verdict on the moral behaviour of fictional characters. References to ritualistic cannibalism should not infer belief or disbelief about the veracity of the subject or its extent. That debate belongs elsewhere[8] and this essay is concerned with the representation of cannibalism rather than its actuality.

The importation of cannibalism

The representation of cannibalism, whether in literature or as reportage, is constrained by conventions dating back to ancient Greece and Rome. These conventions emerged in classical literature and have continued through the centuries to determine how we view the cannibal and cannibalism, or anthropophagy as it was originally termed. It has also been suggested that later accounts of ritualistic cannibalism among the Amerindians were themselves the products of these conventions. Pagden, in commenting on Arens, has concluded that,

> I, at least, have not found a single eye-witness account of a cannibal feast nor, indeed a single description which does not rely on elements taken from classical accounts of anthropophagy.[9]

Those ascriptions of cannibalism had followed a traditional route, of attempting to impute the act to some 'other', the savage or the foreigner or to the gods themselves, and thereby achieved a dissociation between the act and human, or at least civilized culpability.

In *The Odyssey* the terror is not of human eating human, but of monsters eating human flesh. Odysseus is confronted by Scylla,[10] a six-headed monster, by giants in the Land of the Laestrygonians[11] and most memorably by Polyphemus,[12] the giant one-eyed cyclops. The vividness of the depiction of the cannibalism varies, however, in proportion to the degree of monstrosity of the culprit, and of their distance from the Greek's home. Rawson has noted:

> The more unreal the context, the more enabling an environment it is for the portrayal of the cannibal scene. In this Homer belongs to what became a long narrative tradition. Whether deliberately or by an instinct which seems to be common among story-tellers at all periods, the Homeric poet shows a reticence which suggests that the cannibal elements in the Laestrygonian episode are not so much kept brief because they are unreal as made brief because they risked becoming too real.[13]

This approach can be contrasted with the later treatment of the story of the Cyclops by Euripides. Here the horror is muted by comic farce that enables the details of the cannibalism to be dealt with in gloating detail, resembling in many ways the depiction of cannibalism in later fairy stories, and as one of the devices employed by Charles Dickens to mitigate the horrors of cannibalism in at least some of his works. Thus Euripedes can allow his Cyclops to utter:

> Be as good as to go and sharpen the cleavers and the carvers and get a nice big fire going. Then I can slit their throats and barbecue the best bits to take the edge off my appetite. Stew the rest. I'm fed up with mountain-meat. And, if I ever have to face boiled lion again ... or stag ... Time for man-chop.[14]

Farce and monstrosity masked the proximity of cannibalism to Greek society, but its presence is apparent in their writings. According to Plato[15] cannibalism was the lot of humans and animals before the appearance of vines and olives. Those appetites, he argued, may still lie dormant, requiring to be controlled by laws and reason. To illustrate this Plato referred to the bestial and savage desires that are released in drink and sleep:

You know how in such a state it will dare everything, as though it were freed and released from all shame or discernment. It does not shrink from attempting incestual intercourse, in its dream, with a mother or with any man or god or beast. It is ready for any deed of blood, and there is no unhallowed food it will not eat. In a word, it falls short of no extreme of folly or shamelessness.[16]

This shamelessness, the exhibition of unrestrained desires in their animal savagery, is the fate of both the cannibal and the cruel tyrant. Just as 'he who tasted the human flesh ... must of necessity become a wolf, so also must the ruler of the people who cruelly abuses his power have a fateful necessity thrust upon him, either to be slain by his enemies or to be a tyrant, and become a wolf instead of a man'.[17]

This connection between cannibalism and animal behaviour is a recurrent theme in classical literature. Hesiod argued that men differed from animals because of their belief in justice:

For this law hath the son of Cronus ordained for men, for fishes indeed and beasts, and winged fowls to eat each other, since justice is not among them: but to men hath he given justice, which is far best.[18]

Juvenal was later to argue that in contrast to animals it was only humans who ate one another,[19] but the association between cannibalism and primitive, animal behaviour, has continued to the present day. Dudley himself was later to describe his and his companions' behaviour as being 'like mad wolfs (*sic*)'.[20] Cannibalism though, was generally restricted to the unnatural pleasures of barbarians.

Aristotle wrote of

bestial characters, ... savage tribes of the coasts of the Black Sea, who are alleged to delight in raw meat or in human flesh, and others among whom each in turn provides a child for the common banquet.[21]

Polybius in his description of the Carthaginian Mercenary War emphasises the barbarian nature of the mercenaries; the contrast of 'the difference of character between a confused herd of barbarians and men who have been brought up in an educated, law-abiding, and civilised community'.[22] Eventually the mercenaries are besieged and resort to cannibalism, 'a fitting retribution at the hands of Providence for their violation of all law human and divine'.[23]

The representation of the cannibal was thus established by the classical writers, determining the conventions by which later writers were to portray the subject, and the manner in which Lord Coleridge was to later view Dudley and Stephens. These conventions were carried through the imaginative literature of the late middle ages, providing an impression of the unknown world, 'a cluster of images which were thought to constitute a real world of nature in the remoter parts of the world where, precisely because they were remote, the unusual and the fantastic were thought to be the norm'.[24]

Thus Mandeville can describe a people amongst whom there is

> a wekkede custome amongys hem, for they wele gladly etyn manys flesch more than ony othir flesch. Neuertheles the lond is replenyshid with flesch and fisch and gold and syluer and othir good inow. Theydr marchauntys bryngn childeryn to selle, and the men of that contre beyen hem. And yif they ben fatte, they etyn hem anon; and if they bene lene, they fedyn hem tyl they ben fatte and etyn hem thanne.[25]

Consequently when Columbus sailed, supposedly, for Asia in 1492 he carried with him both physical and mental maps of what he might encounter, including the image of the cannibal. In the latter at least, he was not to be disappointed. His journal entry of Friday, 23rd November, 1492, contains a description by the Arawak Indians that he was carrying of a land

> which they said was very large and that on it there were people who had one eye in their foreheads, and others that were called canibales, of whom they showed great fear ... because these people would eat them, and are well armed.[26]

On his voyage home Columbus also wrote a letter mentioning Carib cannibals.[27] The validity of the attribution of cannibalism to the Island Caribs, and to the Amerindians generally, has been fiercely debated.[28] What is not in doubt is the effect that such an allegation had for the Caribs and Amerindians generally. From the first employment of the term in Columbus' journal, cannibal[29] began to replace the description of anthropophagi in western writings and by the early seventeenth century had largely replaced it.[30] It was not, however, a simple substitution of one word for another; for the term cannibalism contained connotations far stronger than that contained in its predecessor, invoking the ferocious consumption of human flesh. Hulme has argued:

> Cannibalism is a term that has no application outside the discourse of European colonialism: it is never available as a neutral word. Confirmation for this argument could be found in the usual absence in discussions of cannibalism of the Christian communion. Even to have cannibalism and Christian communion in the same sentence seems indecorous.[31]

Reports emanating from the Americas as to the prevalence of cannibalism provoked the question as to why it should be regarded as being against all natural law, a question that was discussed by the sixteenth century theologians, Vitoria and Acosta. Vitoria declared that, '[e]ating human flesh is abominable to all nations which live civilised and not inhuman lives'. This is supported by the historical writings and if all men 'have held this custom to be a vile one this is because it is so according to natural law'.[32]

He went on to argue that cannibalism involves homicide, which is a violation of the sixth commandment, and denies the victim the opportunity of a proper burial. More importantly, however, cannibalism involves a breach of the natural order.

> When eating one another cannibals were not only committing the sin of ferocity (peccatum ferocitas) by breaking the law of nature which forbade the killing of innocent men; they were also violating the hierarchical divisions of the creation.[33]

Cannibalism was also to be equated with the category of unnatural crimes, particularly those relating to sexual deviances such as onanism and sodomy.[34] Acosta argued that the eating of any inappropriate foods was an act of self-defilement, but the worst pollutant was human flesh. Cannibals were given up 'to uncleanness through the lusts of their own hearts, to dishonour their own bodies between themselves'.[35] Consequently

> [c]annibalism, onanism and sodomy were, Acosta argued, prohibited at all times, though the failure to eat will result in death through starvation and the failure, for a man, to have sexual intercourse may result in a serious disturbance of the humours.[36]

These cannibalistic images were at first only gradually introduced into England, and then at an accelerated rate as the Elizabethans became increasingly involved with the Americas.[37]

It was against this background that Montaigne produced his essay *On the Cannibals* in 1580. In contrast to the prevailing representations of cannibalism, Montaigne found much to praise about their society (but not in the cannibalism itself). He contended that 'there is nothing savage or barbarous about those peoples, but that every man calls barbarous anything he is not accustomed to'.[38] This cultural relativism allowed him to contrast the reported iniquities of the cannibals with the barbarities exhibited by his own countrymen in the endemic civil wars in France:

> I think there is more barbarity in eating a man alive than in eating him dead; more barbarity in lacerating by rack and torture a body still fully able to feel things, in roasting him little by little and having him bruised and bitten by pigs and dogs (as we have not only read about but seen in recent memory, not among enemies in antiquity but among our fellow-citizens and neighbours - and, what is worse, in the name of duty and religion) than in roasting him and eating him after his death.[39]

Montaigne evokes the spirit of the stoic school of Zeno and Chrysippus, that it is permissible to use carcasses for whatever purpose was needed, including using them for food.[40] He cites the example of medical men utilizing cadavers and of how when the Gaulish town of Alesia was besieged by Julius Caesar it was proposed that those who were unable to fight because of their age should be eaten in order to sustain the besieged.[41] Juvenal described a similar scene and asked:

> What man, what deity
> But would pardon these famished victims, after all the horrors
> They'd suffered, for such an act? The very souls of the dead
> Bodies that gave them sustenance might condone it. Zeno offers
> Us better advice - there is much that's permissible, within limits,
> For the saving of human life.[42]

Thus there was an alternative viewing of the cannibal, not simply denouncing but attempting to come to an understanding of the motives and context of cannibalism, and at the same time raising the cannibal from being a brute beast to being a human being. These images, derived from the classical writers, travellers' fantastic tales and the representations emanating from the Americas, combined in various forms to produce an English impression of cannibalism. At the very moment that England were expanding outwards in the form of Elizabethan colonialism, she was also importing the image of the cannibal into the public and private imagination.

No longer were cannibals the inhabitant of the unknown world, they now formed part of English private fears and English public life.

The English cannibal

The English, however, could already point to cannibal neighbours. Gibbon was later to write that the Scottish included 'a valiant tribe of Calidonia' who 'are accused, by an eye-witness of delighting in the taste of human flesh'.[43] More pertinent, however, is the accusation of cannibalism that has been levelled against the Irish. Two thousand years ago the Greek geographer Strabo wrote:

> Concerning this island I have nothing certain to tell, except that its inhabitants are more savage than the Britons, since they are man-eaters as well as heavy eaters, and since, further, they count it an honourable thing, when their fathers die, to devour them, and openly to have intercourse, not only with the other women, but also with their mothers and sisters; but I am saying this only with the understanding that I have no trustworthy witnesses for it.[44]

Strabo goes on to say that man-eating is said to be a custom of the Scythians, who originally inhabited a region north of the Black Sea, and who are 'deemed by a tendentious etymology to be the ancestors of the modern ... Irish'.[45] Such an association was to become a common refrain. Sir William Petty was to refer to it in his analysis of *The Political Anatomy of Ireland*,[46] and Swift was to incorporate it into both his *A Modest Proposal* and *Gulliver's Travels*.[47]

The association of classical antecedents and contemporary examples of cannibalism have constantly been used to render a people to the literal level of beasts; cannibalism is the epitome of savage, beast-like behaviour and so justifies colonial intervention, whether it be to redeem or enslave the indigenous population. Edmund Spenser served as secretary to the Lord Deputy of Ireland and described his experiences in Ireland, of

> a most populous and plentifull Countrye sodenlye lefte voide of man or beaste, yeat sure in all that warr theare perished not manie by the sworde but all by the extreamitye of famine which they themselves had wroughte.[48]

The effect of this was to reduce the populace to eating carrion and one another, and Spenser proposed measures to quell the rebellion so that 'by this harde restrainte they woulde quicklye consume themselves and devour one another'.[49] It has been debated though, whether this was 'a terrible proposal, uttered with cold deliberateness' or a recognition of an inevitable horror emanating from the manner in which the war was being fought.[50] The imagery of the savagery that he encountered in Ireland was also to find echoes in his depictions of the wild man in *The Faerie Queene*.[51]

The litany of Irish cannibalism continued with Fynes Moryson's *An Itinerary*, published in 1617, which contained a description of the famine that occurred during Tyrone's rebellion in 1602, with 'poore people dead with their mouthes all coloured greene by eating nettles, docks, and all things they could rend up above ground'.[52] The Irish were reduced to the level of the beasts of the field and it was therefore only to be expected that cannibalism would have occurred; Moryson duly provides his evidence. He cites examples of children eating their mother in Newry and of old women murdering and eating children.[53] These examples were later quoted by Thomas Sheridan in the *Intelligencer*, a periodical that he wrote with Jonathan Swift. No.18 contains the references to Moryson and to a 'very horrible Fact; too horrible indeed to mention!'[54] This reticence is then immediately followed by a narration of the facts, although in a somewhat muted form. Whether Swift was aware of Moryson's narrative before his friend's publication is not known, but he certainly knew of it from that publication and it foreshadows his own *A Modest Proposal* published in the following year, 1729. In that ironical work Swift gave the assurance that

a young healthy child, well nursed, is, at a Year old, a most delicious, nourishing, and wholesome food; whether stewed, roasted, baked, or boiled; and I make no doubt, that it will equally serve in a Fricasie, or Ragoust.[55]

He therefore proposed that of his estimated one hundred and twenty thousand children born to the poor every year, twenty thousand should be reserved for breeding purposes and one hundred thousand offered up for sale for human consumption.[56] Rawson has contended that:

The cannibal imputation has been a staple of ethnic defamation since as far back as Homer ... Swift's fable, showing the Irish to be fit for a cannibal economy, is perhaps the most uncompromising use of the cannibal slur ever directed at them in modern times. There is no sign of a desire to moderate or soften the attack, but although the evidence of literal enactment offered obvious reinforcement to the fable, Swift made sure that the metaphorical boundaries were not crossed.[57]

These descriptions of Irish cannibalism offered the English a ready proximity to cannibalism, both literally and metaphorically, that reinforced the natural tendency to incorporate the cannibal image into private and public life. Whilst retaining monsterous images from Mandeville, the cannibal was also becoming part of the natural world. Shakespeare has numerous cannibal references in his works, but the most sustained reference, although no cannibalism actually occurs, is to be found though in the depiction of Caliban in *The Tempest*. His name itself is probably an anagram of 'can[n]ibal',[58] and his representation is as 'a monstrous symbol of man's savage state'.[59] Exhibiting a lack of repentence, ungrateful and sexually aggressive, Caliban is the epitome of the savage, although Shakespeare may have been influenced by Montaigne to soften the image by allowing the monster some dignity and sensitivity. Certainly it is accepted that Gonzalo's speech in Act II is derived from a reading of Montaigne.[60] Whilst Shakespeare could confidently write of the gulf that separated Prospero from Caliban, later writers began to draw attention to the relevance of the cannibal to their own society.

Just as external colonialism was discovering the cannibal, so the natural philosophers and medical dissectors were discovering our own cannibalism; our bodies, alien to the sensitivities that inhabit them, devour themselves. In his thoughts on religion, *Religio Medici*, published in 1642, Sir Thomas Browne wrote:

> all those creatures [which] we behold, are but the herbs of the field, digested into flesh in them, or more remotely carnified in our selves. Nay further, we are what we all abhorre, Antropophagi and Cannibals, devourers not only of men, but of ourselves.[61]

Sawday has noted that

> the trope of the body as innately cannibalistic, meshing with puritan conceptions of the body's voracious hunger for physical satisfaction, engendered the peculiarly apposite conceit of the natural philosopher as a colonising, and thus civilising, force within the boundaries of the natural (and, by analogy, political) body.[62]

Nine years after the publication of *Religio Medici*, Thomas Hobbes published *Leviathan*. In this work the state of man during a time of war is 'solitary, poore, nasty, brutish, and short',[63] and this is exemplified by 'the savage people in many places of America [who] ... live at this day in that brutish manner.'[64] He argued that in such a place 'The notions of Right and Wrong, Justice and Injustice have there no place'.[65] Hobbes' knowledge of the Americas was sparse, particularly compared to that of John Locke, but even the latter was to write that 'The Caribes were wont to geld their Children, on purpose to fat and eat them'.[66] Thus the cannibals made their contribution to the development of the English political sciences, the past being used to confirm current beliefs of cannibalism.

Defoe and Dickens

The image of the cannibal as a monstrous entity has been sustained through the development of the modern realist novel, but, as with its depiction in other forms of writing, that is only one aspect of the dualism of cannibalism. The monstrous image is invoked to deny the possibility of understanding or sympathy; its counterpoint evokes a more human image, rendering the cannibal as fallible and deserving of compassion. In terms of the novel this dichotomy is no more vividly represented than in the respective approaches to cannibalism taken by Defoe and Dickens.

In Defoe's *Robinson Crusoe*, first published in 1719, Crusoe is confronted by cannibals. Initially he proposes to kill them, but then he has second thoughts, reasoning that they do not know any better. He therefore decides to leave them alone unless he is forced to confront them in self-defence. This neutrality is maintained until he decides to intervene and rescue one of the cannibals' prisoners, the man who subsequently becomes Friday. Friday, however, is also a cannibal and consequently must be taught the rudiments of civilization and Christianity if he is to be a worthy companion and servant for Crusoe. When they come across the remains of a cannibal feast 'Crusoe threatens murder to make his savage civil'.[67] He finds that Friday:

> was still a cannibal in his nature; but I [showed] as much abhorrence at the very thoughts of it, and at the least appearance of it, that he durst not [exhibit] it; for I had, by some means, let him know that I would kill him if he offered it.[68]

Defoe's dilemma is that he wishes to retain the image of the threat of their unmitigated ferocity whilst at the same time, as with Montaigne, presenting them in human form. Defoe's, or rather Crusoe's, ignorance is later corrected by his servant when Friday describes his former life amongst his own people, the Caribs, and mentions that there are white men amongst them whom the cannibals had saved from drowning and then given shelter to. Crusoe asks why they had not been eaten only to receive the rebuke that the cannibals only eat those who offer violence against them in war.[69] This approach is shattered, however, when Crusoe comes across the cannibals preparing to eat a European. Crusoe resolves to massacre the cannibals in order to save the prisoner,[70] marking a 'pardigmatic transformation' in the cannibal 'for all future colonial adventure stories, from a moral problem of some importance to merely a mass of dreadful wretches'.[71]

Crusoe had had his doubts resolved by Providence through the sight of the European prisoner, but there was still the question of European cannibalism, and as regards that Defoe was unequivocal. When a group of English mutineers land on the island with some prisoners Friday is convinced that the prisoners will be eaten just as if they had been captured by savages. '"No, No" says I, "Friday, I am afraid that they will murder them, but you may be sure that they will not eat them"'.[72] That eventuality, for a European, could only occur under more dire circumstances. Earlier in the novel Crusoe had come across the wreck of a ship but could find no trace of its crew. He had concluded that they had gone off in one of their boats and had been 'carried out into the great ocean, where there was nothing but misery and perishing; and that perhaps they might by this time think of starving and of being in a condition to eat one another'.[73] This Defoe could understand, for 'Hunger knows no Friend, no Relation, no Justice, no Right, and therefore is remorseless, and capable of no Compassion'.[74] This was a theme that Defoe constantly returned to, that the necessity for self-preservation obviated every other consideration.[75] Later he was to pose the question whether the most honest of men, if he were drowning in the Thames, would not grab hold of his neighbour in case he might drown him.

> Nay, will you not pull him down by the Hair of his Head, tread on him with your feet, tho' you sink him to the bottom, to get your self out? ... I tell you all, Gentlemen, in your Poverty, the best of you all will rob your Neighbour; nay, to go farther ... you will not only rob your Neighbour but if in distress, you will EAT your Neighbour, ay, and say Grace to your Meat too - Distress removes from the Soul, all Relation, Affection, Sense of Justice, and all the Obligations, either Moral or Religious, that secure one Man against another.[76]

Such a situation had been contemplated by Grotius and Pufendorf, two leading commentators on the natural law. Grotius agreed with Lactantius, the early Christian theologian, that a man 'does not do amiss who abstains to thrust a drowning man from a plank, or a wounded man from his horse, even for the sake of his own preservation'.[77] Lactantius had been objecting to the opinions of the Greek philosopher Carneades. This 'Hobbist of antiquity'[78] had argued that 'if a just man does not take away a horse from a wounded man or a plank from one shipwrecked in order to save his own life, he is a fool',[79] particularly 'since there is no witness in the middle of the sea'.[80] For Lactantius such a view denies consideration of the afterlife; for Grotius it also denies Cicero's dictum that '[t]he greatest necessity is that of doing what is honourable'.[81]

In contrast to this approach Pufendorf quotes the example of the seven Englishmen who were driven out to sea in the Caribbean in 1641, and after days of being without food or water chose one of their number, by lot, to kill and eat. The remaining six thereby survived and although subsequently tried for homicide they were acquitted. Pufendorf considered that by such an action 'they needed to fear no peril to their souls', and that:

> Nor can it be called cruelty when he who dies for the safety of all, suffers less agony in bowing his neck to the sword than the other does in giving the stroke.[82]

Defoe repeats the story but comes to the same conclusion for different reasons, namely, 'all that can be said is, that necessity makes the highest crimes lawful, and things evil in their own nature are made practicable by it'.[83] Dickens was certainly conversant with Defoe, and in *Nurse's Stories* he recounts, 'I never was in Robinson Crusoe's Island, yet I frequently return there ... the sandy beach on which the memorable footstep was impressed, and where the savages hauled up their canoes when they came ashore for those dreadful public dinners, which led to a dancing worse than speech-making'.[84] He was also though, diametrically opposed to Defoe's position on cannibalism in general, and his views on survival cannibalism in particular. For Dickens shared his contemporaries' fascination and horror with cannibalism and also imbued the subject at a deeper level.[85] As Stone has noted,

> [f]or cannibalism, however disciplined and transformed by Dickens' mature art, continued to harbor, for him, elements of unresolved anxiety and unshriven guilt.[86]

In 1853 Dickens published *The Long Voyage*, in which he reminisces about various travels and the travails that they involve, including 'a fearful story of travel derived from that unpromising narrator of such stories, a parliamentary blue-book'.[87] This is probably a reference to the confessions of Alexander Pierce contained in the Report of the Select Committee on Transportation in 1838.[88] In that Report and in Dickens' narrative a prisoner escapes twice from a prison settlement in Van Dieman's Land. On each occasion he murders and eats his companions, only to be captured a second time and taken back to be hanged. Dickens felt that he should 'never see that sea-beach on the wall or in the fire, without him, solitary monster, eating as he prowls along, while the sea rages and rises at him'.[89] The image of the cannibal convict was to be returned to later in *Great Expectations* (1861), when Magwitch threatens Pip, 'and your heart and your liver shall be tore out, roasted, and ate'.[90] Such imagery, either literal or allegorical, was to be constantly used by Dickens throughout his works, 'a paradigm of supreme degradation and inhumanity'.[91]

For Dickens it was not only the fear of being eaten, but also the fear of himself indulging in human flesh, of succumbing as a last resort. Hence his consternation when it was reported in 1854 that the last Artic expedition led by Sir John Franklin had before their deaths resorted to cannibalism. Dickens vehemently rejected the notion and in a letter to Mrs Richard Watson stated,

> In famous cases of Shipwreck, it is very rare indeed that any person of any humanizing education or refinement, resorts to this dreadful means of prolonging life. In open boats, the coarsest and commonest men of the shipwrecked party have done such things; but I don't remember more than one instance in which an officer has overcome the loathing that the idea has inspired.[92]

Dickens went on to write three articles in *Household Words*[93] defending Franklin against the allegation of cannibalism. He stressed Franklin's fortitude, the character of his carefully selected crew and ascribed other instances of survival cannibalism to the fact that the participants were foreigners or had been members of 'an inferior class'.[94] The theme was also to reappear in *The Wreck of the Golden Mary*. In this story a ship runs into an iceberg and the crew behave stoically, the only panic being shown by one of the passengers whose behaviour threatens the smooth evacuation of the ship. The captain threatens him with a pistol: 'I won't murder forty-four people to humour you, but I'll shoot you to save them'.[95]

Later when they are at sea in an open boat the Captain tells the survivors the story of Captain Bligh following the mutiny on the Bounty. He concludes the tale by saying that:

> Bligh, who was no delicate man either, had solemnly placed it on record ... that he was sure and certain that under no conceivable circumstances whatever would that emaciated party, who had gone through all the pains of famine, have preyed on one another. I cannot describe the visible relief which this spread through the boat, and how the tears stood in every eye.[96]

Dickens was not alone in the nineteenth century in invoking the image of the cannibal, but he was probably the most articulate and persistent employer of the image. As with earlier descriptions of Irish cannibalism, however, literary portrayals largely followed the Empire, stressing the need to bring civilization, and particularly Christianity, to the savage. The South Seas featured in both R.M. Ballantyne's *The Coral Island* and Harriet Martineau's *Dawn Island*. It was only with the increasing imperial involvement in Africa from the mid-century onwards that African cannibalism began to be stressed in reports and literature.[97] Cannibalism was the ultimate sign of depravity and was therefore a justification for British expansionism.[98] Coinciding with this, however, was a developing fear of degeneration,[99] that Europeans, rather than constantly progressing, were in fact facing decline, possibly back to the level of the savages that they were ostensibly civilizing. Hence the fear to be later expressed in Joseph Conrad's *Heart of Darkness* that 'The Horror! The Horror!',[100] that lies at the end of the novel resides in Mr Kurtz having resorted to cannibalism. It is against the background of this literature of cannibalism that Lord Coleridge's judgment can be considered.

The judgment of Lord Coleridge

Lord Coleridge commenced his judgment by reading out the special verdict of the jury at the trial of Dudley and Stephens at Exeter. In it the jury stated that they were ignorant of whether in the circumstances as established, the killing of Richard Parker was murder and that they had therefore referred the matter for the Court's determination. The prisoners' dilemma is admitted but then immediately diluted by emphasising the offence to Richard Parker:

> But nevertheless this is clear, that the prisoners put to death a weak and unoffending boy upon the *chance* of preserving their own lives by feeding upon his flesh and blood after he was killed, and with the *certainty* of depriving him of any possible chance of survival.[101]

The jury had found that if the surviving sailors had not eaten Parker they would 'probably' have died before being rescued, and that Parker, being the weakest, was likely to have died before the others. Simpson has shown that this was not the jury's intention and that it was the wording of Baron Huddleston, who had presided at the trial and drafted the special verdict, which changed the certainty of the sailor's deaths if they had not eaten Parker, to a mere chance.[102]

Glazebrook[103] has also criticised Lord Coleridge for his use of the words 'chance' and 'certainty'. For Parker there was only a very slight chance of survival; whilst for the others, who already had a greater chance of survival, their chances of survival would be increased by killing and eating him. It was a balancing of chances rather than comparing a certainty with a chance, and Dudley and Stephens firmly believed that if they had not killed Parker when they did, then they would all have died, which is the conclusion that the jury had originally wished to be entered in the special verdict.

Lord Coleridge then considers the various legal authorities that had been argued before him. Bracton is held not to support the contention that it is lawful to kill an innocent party to save one's own life, and that the inevitable necessity of which he was writing related to physical danger.[104] It is then contended that this position receives even stronger support from Lord Hale.

Lord Coleridge quotes Lord Hale to the effect that the only necessity justifying taking someone's life is that which amounts to self-defence, the protection of one's own life or property.[105] Equally if the only means of escaping from a murderous assault necessitates someone killing an innocent party, then it is still murder, 'for he ought rather to die himself than kill an innocent'.[106] Further support is then derived from Lord Hale's discussion of the position adopted by Grotius and Pufendorf that in cases of extreme necessity, either of hunger and clothing, then 'theft is no theft'. Lord Coleridge then quotes from Lord Hale:

'But', says Lord Hale, 'I take it that here in England, that rule, at least by the laws of England, is false' ... If, therefore, Lord Hale is clear - as he is - that extreme necessity of hunger does not justify Larceny, what would he have said to the doctrine that it justified murder?[107]

That is, in fact, a totally misleading quotation, ignoring the qualifications and justifications provided by Lord Hale. The full quotation is: 'I do therefore take it, that, where persons live under the same civil government, as here in England, that rule, at least by the laws of England, is false.' Extreme circumstances do not pertain in England,

> [b]ecause by the laws of this kingdom sufficient provision is made for the supply of such necessities by collections for the poor, and by the power of the civil magistrate.[108]

Lord Hale then goes on to consider circumstances more apposite to the plight faced by Dudley and Stephens, although again in the context of theft. By Rhodian law[109] and common maritime custom it was permissible for a ship's master to seize the goods of mariners and passengers if it was for the preservation of the ship's company. Equally it was accepted custom that if a ship required necessaries and the inhabitants of any land would not supply them, then those necessaries could be taken by force and compensation paid. This was lawful because it was necessitated by the extremity and,

> because there are no other means to obtain it by an application to superiors; but were this done by English mariners upon the English shore, where both are under the same civil magistrate, the case would be otherwise, because capable of another remedy.[110]

Lord Coleridge has, as in his previous review of *Yeast*, taken passages out of context in order to support his own contentions. Having dealt with these matters, Lord Coleridge still had to contend with the analogy of the plank that was unable to support the two shipwrecked sailors. Lord Bacon had contended that it was justifiable for the one sailor to thrust the other off in order to save his own life.[111] Various authorities are considered by Lord Coleridge in order to see whether they would support Lord Bacon, but he finds the evidence inconclusive and concludes that whatever the position was in the past, 'it certainly is not law at the present day'.[112] One authority that he omitted to consider is Blackstone, who had been quoted by Dudley and Stephens' counsel at their trial.[113] Blackstone wrote:

> There is one species of homicide *se defendendo*, where the party slain is equally innocent as he who occasions his death: and yet this homicide is also excusable from the great universal principle of self-preservation, which prompts every man to save his own life preferably to that of another, where one of them must inevitably perish. As, among others, in that case mentioned by Lord Bacon ...[114]

Lord Coleridge did not wish any evidence to be adduced that could lead to the case being considered on utility grounds. Chase has pointed out

> what Coleridge wishes to bury: the argument that the drowning man may keep hold of the plank, not merely to save himself, but because it is better that one rather than two should die. Coleridge's analysis obscures the fact that Parker's death may have saved the lives of three men.[115]

Pufendorf's case of the seven English sailors in the Caribbean suffers a similar fate, as it is only mentioned in a medical treatise and so cannot be of any authority in an English court.

Lord Coleridge in conclusion discusses Justice Stephen's treatment of necessity in his *Digest* and *History of the Criminal Law*. Justice Stephen's analysis was not considered to cover the case in point and it is considered that 'it is satisfactory to know that we have, probably at least, arrived at no conclusion in which if he had been a member of the Court he would have been unable to agree'.[116] Later Justice Stephen was to write that he would have agreed with the Court had he been a member of it

> though not in all of the reasoning of the judgment. I should have based my judgment on the fact that the special verdict found only that if the boy had not been killed and eaten the survivors would probably not have survived.[117]

The effects of Baron Huddleston's draughtsmanship consequently continued to cast their influence.

Lord Coleridge then closed his judgment by invoking morality and the duty that we owe one to another:

> The duty, in case of shipwreck, of a captain to his crew, of the crew to the passengers, of soldiers to women and children, as in the noble case *of The Birkenhead*; these duties impose on men the moral necessity, not of the preservation, but of the sacrifice of their lives for others, from which in no country, least of all, it is to be hoped, in England, will men ever shrink, as indeed, they have not shrunk.[118]

The Birkenhead had sunk in 1852, with troops drawn up upon the deck in order to allow the insufficient lifeboats to be allocated to the women and children. Once the ship had gone down, however, the advice of Defoe appeared pertinent to at least some of the survivors. One survivor wrote to his father that he had stayed on the ship until she went down and, 'the suction took me down some way, and a man got hold of my leg, but I managed to kick him off and come up, and struck off for some pieces of wood'.[119] It is tempting to consider whether in invoking the image of *The Birkenhead*, Lord Coleridge was, consciously or otherwise, contrasting it with the wreck of the French ship *Medusa* in 1816. In that case the officers abandoned their crew, and the crew and passengers adrift on a raft resorted to cannibalism, later to be portrayed in Géricault's painting of the *Raft of the Medusa*.[120]

Lord Coleridge continues that it would be too easy to quote from Greek and Roman authors, Horace, Juvenal, Cicero and Euripides, who had stressed the duty of dying for others. In a Christian country, the example of Christ should be enough, and Milton's *Paradise Lost* is evoked to show the alternative: 'So spake the fiend, and with necessity / The tyrant's plea, excus'd his devlish deeds'.[121] The court's verdict of murder was then announced and Dudley and Stephens were sentenced to death, although the sentence was later commuted by the Crown to six months' imprisonment.

Conclusion

Lord Coleridge came from an intellectual and literary background and would certainly have known many, if not all, of the classical and literary references to cannibalism. Certainly it would have been strange if during his deliberations he had not thought of the writings of his great-uncle, Samuel Taylor Coleridge, who in *The Rime of the Ancient Mariner* had penned the lines: 'Water, water, everywhere, / Nor any drop to drink'.[122] In 1795 Samuel Coleridge had delivered a lecture against the slave trade and asked his audience to abandon the products of West Indian slavery, sugar and rum as exploiting humans and therefore essentially cannibalistic:

> Gracious Heaven! at your meals you rise up and pressing your hands to your bosom ye lift up your eyes to God and say O Lord bless the Food which thou hast given us! A part of that Food among most of you is sweetened with the Blood of the Murdered. Bless the food which thou hast given us! O Blasphemy! Did God give Food mingled with Brothers blood! Will the Father

of all men bless the Food of Cannibals - the food which is polluted with the blood of his own innocent children?[123]

Lord Coleridge was sitting in judgment on a case of literal cannibalism, however, and would not have wanted his thoughts to be distracted by notions of the links that existed between the cannibal act and himself. It would not be possible to pronounce on sin if he were himself tainted, and offering a judgment on sin was what he was essentially doing.

He was later to write that, 'in criminal courts men are punished, not for sins, but for crimes; some sins, amongst the worst men can commit, are unpunished and unpunishable by human tribunals'.[124] The case of Dudley and Stephens was a unique opportunity to ensure that at least one sin was in some measure punished. Nor would he have been swayed by utilitarian arguments; if the act was itself sinful then that was the end of the matter. Lord Coleridge had earlier written an article against vivisection, in which he had declared:

> even if it be admitted to be a means of gaining scientific knowledge, such knowledge is unlawful knowledge if it is pursued by means which are immoral; and that a disregard of all proportion between means and ends often makes both alike unlawful and indefensible.[125]

He never deviated from that attitude and one of its earliest manifestations can be found in a review of Charles Kingsley's *Yeast* written for *The Guardian* in 1851:

> It is the countenance the writer gives to the worst tendencies of the day, and the manner in which he conceals loose morality in a dress of high-sounding and philosophical phraseology, which call for plain and decided condemnation ... Of all the miserable delusions of a hollow and unreal age, none is more utterly delusive than the pursuit of a nominal reality, by the neglect, on principle, of the only possible means by which sinful men can attain to being real ... But the instincts of mankind are higher than their reasons, and in the long run, in spite of argument, they have ever done honour to spotless purity, and refused to believe self-indulgence to be nobler than self-restraint.[126]

For Lord Coleridge sin had to be condemned and punished, even if the punishment were to be later mitigated. He had commenced that review by describing the beginning of the novel, of how:

Lancelot, a healthy animalist, who has gone through that course of profligacy which is considered necessary to develop the nature and impart breadth and manliness to the intellect of the apostles of the latest and most philosophical phase of Christianity ...[127]

Towards the end of the novel Lancelot is asked what it is that he wants; he replies simply 'Be Pardoned'.[128] That, however Lord Coleridge could not allow.

In a letter to *The Guardian* Kingsley rejected the allegations made against him and the contentious manner in which they were made.[129] He concludes each of his points by quoting Pascal: *'Mentiris impudentissime'*, (He lies most impudently).[130]

In his review and in his judgment Lord Coleridge had done what he considered to be his duty, but in order to achieve the result that he desired he had been tendentious and one-sided in his criticisms. Other discourses had been open to him but he failed to consider them. Cannibalism was a sin and therefore had to be condemned.

In contrast to that conclusion there is the one offered by Conrad, who knew of the case of Dudley and Stephens[131] and developed it in his short story *Falk*. There, when a man expresses revulsion on being told that a companion had eaten man, he is rebuked, 'You are too squeamish, Hermann'.[132]

Notes

1.   [1884] 14 Q.B.D. 273.
2.   Williams (1977), p. 94.
3.   Simpson (1986), p. 234.
4.   For a summary see Chase (1985).
5.   [1884] 14 Q.B.D. 284.
6.   Walker (1980), p. 241.
7.   Chase (1985), p. 1253.
8.   See Arens (1979) and for example Sanday (1986).
9.   Pagden (1982), p. 216, n.154.
10.   *The Odyssey*, 12: 223-61.
11.   *The Odyssey*, 10:82-199.
12.   *The Odyssey*, 9: 89-460.
13.   Rawson (1984), p.1161.
14.   *Cyclops*, lines 241-49.

15. *Laws*, VI.782 B-C.
16. *Republic*, IX.571
17. *Republic*, VIII.565-66.
18. Hesiod, lines 275-79.
19. *Satire* 15.
20. Public Records Office, HO144/141/A36934.
21. *Ethics*, VII.V.2.
22. *The Histories*, I.65.7-8.
23. *The Histories*, I.84.9-10.
24. Pagden (1982), p. 10.
25. Mandeville (1963), p. 97.
26. Quoted in Hulme and Whitehead (1992), p. 18.
27. Quoted in Hulme and Whitehead (1992), pp. 14-5.
28. See Hulme (1986); Boucher (1992); Harris (1977) and Pagden (1982).
29. For a description of the derivation of the term see Taylor (1958).
30. Vaughan and Vaughan (1991), p. 28.
31. Hulme (1986), p. 84.
32. Quoted in Pagden (1982), p. 85.
33. Pagden (1982), p. 86.
34. *Summa Theologica*, Q.142, Art 4.
35. Eden (1885).
36. Pagden (1982), p. 177.
37. Eden (1885), pp. 29-30.
38. Montaigne (1993), p. 82.
39. Montaigne (1993), pp. 86-7.
40. Montaigne (1993), p. 87.
41. Gallic War, VII.77.
42. *Satire* 15, lines 103-7.
43. Gibbon (1836), pp. 282-83.
44. *Geography*, 4.5.4.
45. Rawson (1992), p. 20.
46. Petty (1691), p. 103
47. Rawson (1984), p. 1184.
48. Spenser (1949), p. 158.
49. Spenser (1949), p. 381
50. Spenser (1949), p. 381.
51. See Pearce (1945).

52. Moryson (1908), ii, p. 283.
53. Moryson (1908), ii, pp. 282-3.
54. Wooley (1992), p. 198
55. Swift (1975), p. 257.
56. See generally Rawson (1978).
57. Rawson (1992), p. 20.
58. See Vaughan and Vaughan (1991); Hulme (1986), Chap. 3; Hogden (1952) and Orgel (1987).
59. Boucher (1992), p. 28.
60. Act II, Scene 1, 143-68.
61. Browne (1968), p. 48.
62. Sawday (1995), p. 25.
63. Hobbes (1968), p. 186.
64. Hobbes (1968), p. 187.
65. Hobbes (1968), p. 188.
66. Locke (1975), p. 71.
67. Flynn (1990), p. 155.
68. Defoe (1994), p. 204.
69. Defoe (1994), p. 219.
70. Defoe (1994), p. 230.
71. Hulme (1986), p. 211.
72. Defoe (1986), p. 246.
73. Defoe (1986), p. 184.
74. Defoe (1927), p. 142.
75. Defoe (1938), iii, p. 109.
76. Defoe (1938), viii, p. 302.
77. Grotius, II.ii.8.
78. Novak (1963), p. 70.
79. Lactantius (1964), p. 370.
80. Lactantius (1964), p. 368.
81. De Inventione, II.58.
82. Pufendorf, II.vi.3.
83. Defoe (1925), p. 39.
84. Dickens (1880), p. 149.
85. For a general discussion of this subject see Marlow (1983) and Stone (1994), pp. 1-26.
86. Stone (1994), pp. 267-8.
87. Dickens (1858), p. 203.

88. Transportation (1968).
89. Dickens (1858), p. 204.
90. Dickens (1994), p. 8.
91. Stone (1994), pp. 255-6.
92. Dickens (1993), p. 456.
93. Household Words (2nd, 9th and 23rd December, 1854).
94. Stone (1987).
95. Dickens (1956), p. 145.
96. Dickens (1956), p. 152.
97. Hammond and Jablow (1970), p. 94.
98. See Street (1975); Bratlinger (1988) and MacDonald (1994).
99. See Pick (1989) and Greenslade (1994).
100. Conrad (1973), p. 117.
101. [1884] 14 QBD 273 at 279 (emphasis added).
102. Simpson (1986), p. 214.
103. Glazebrook (1972), p. 115
104. Bracton (1879), Vol. 11, p. 277.
105. [1884] 14 QBD 273 at 282.
106. [1884] 14 QBD 273 at 283.
107. [1884] 14 QBD 273 at 283.
108. Hale (1736), p. 54.
109. Ashburner (1909).
110. Hale (1736), p. 55.
111. Bacon (1859), Vol. VII, p. 344.
112. [1884] 14 QBD 273 at 286.
113. 1 T.L.R. 118 at 121.
114. Blackstone (1769), Book 4, p. 186.
115. Chase (1985), p. 1265.
116. [1884] 14 QBD 273 at 286.
117. Stephen (1887), p. 25.
118. [1884] 14 QBD 273 at 287.
119. *The Times*, 15th April 1852.
120. Eitner (1972), pp. 7-11.
121. Milton (1992), Book IV, lines 393-94.
122. Coleridge (1957), p. 41, lines 121-122.
123. Coleridge (1971), p. 248.
124. Coleridge (1890), p. 803.
125. Coleridge (1882), p. 231.

126. *The Guardian*, 7th May, 1851.
127. *The Guardian*, 7th May, 1851.
128. Kingsley (1884), p. 299.
129. Kingsley (1877), pp. 283-4.
130. Pascal (1967), p. 234.
131. Boyer (1986).
132. Conrad (1986), p. 182.

References

Abbot, G. (1970), *A Brief Description of the Whole World*, Da Capo Press, Amsterdam.
Aquinas, T. (1942), *The Summa Theologica of St.Thomas Aquinas*, Burns, Oates and Washbourne, London.
Arens, W. (1979), *The Man-Eating Myth*, Oxford University Press, Oxford.
Aristotle (1976), *Ethics*, Penguin, Harmondsworth.
Aristotle (1962), *The Politics*, Penguin, Harmondsworth.
Ashburner, W. (1909), *The Rhodian Sea-Law*, Clarendon Press, Oxford.
Bacon, F. (1859), *The Works of Francis Bacon*, Longman, Green, London.
Ballantyne, R.M. (1990), *The Coral Island*, Oxford University Press, Oxford.
Blackstone, W. (1769), *Commentaries on the Laws of England*, Clarendon Press, Oxford.
Boucher, P. (1992), *Cannibal Encounters*, John Hopkins University Press, Baltimore.
Boyer, A. (1986), 'Crime, Cannibalism and Joseph Conrad', *Loyola of Los Angeles Law Report*, Vol. 20, p. 9.
Bracton, H. (1879), *De Legibus et Consuetudinibus Anglieae*, Longman, London.
Brantlinger, P. (1988), *Rule of Darkness*, Cornell University Press, Ithaca.
Browne, T. (1964), *The Works of Sir Thomas Browne*, Faber, London.
Caesar, J. (1898), *Caesar's Commentaries on the Gallic and Civil Wars*,George Bell, London.
Chase, A. (1985), 'Fear Eats the Soul', *Yale Law Journal*, Vol. 94, p. 1253.
Cicero (1949), *De Inventione*, Loeb, London.
Coleridge, J. (1890), 'The Law in 1847 and the Law in 1889', *The Contemporary Review*, p. 797.

Coleridge, J. (1882), 'The Nineteenth Century Defenders of Vivisection', *Fortnightly Review*, p. 225.

Coleridge, J. (1851), 'Review of Yeast', *The Guardian*, 7th May.

Coleridge, S. (1971), *The Collected Works of Samuel Taylor Coleridge*, Routledge, London.

Coleridge, S. (1957), *Samuel Taylor Coleridge: Selected Poetry and Prose*, Penguin, Harmondsworth.

Conrad, J. (1986), 'Falk', in Conrad J., *Typhoon and Other Tales*, Oxford University Press, Oxford.

Conrad, J. (1983), *Heart of Darkness*, Penguin, Harmondsworth.

Defoe, D. (1994), *Robinson Crusoe*, Penguin, Harmondsworth.

Defoe, D. (1927), *Further Adventures of Robinson Crusoe*, Basil Blackwell, Oxford.

Defoe, D. (1925), *Serious Reflections of Robinson Crusoe*, Constable, London.

Defoe, D. (1938), *Defoe's Review*, Columbia University Press, New York.

Dickens, C. (1994), *Great Expectations*, Penguin, Harmondsworth.

Dickens, C. (1993), *The Letters of Charles Dickens*, Clarendon Press, Oxford.

Dickens, C., 'The Long Voyage', in *Edwin Drood and Reprinted Pieces*, Chapman and Hall, London.

Dickens, C. (1854), 'The Lost Artic Voyagers', *Household Words*, Vol. 10, pp. 361-65, 385-93, 433-37.

Dickens, C. (1956), 'The Wreck of the Golden Mary', in *Christmas Stories*, Oxford University Press, Oxford.

Eden, R. (1971), *The First Three English Books on America*, Kraus Reprint, New York.

Eitner, L. (1972), *Géricault's Raft of the Medusa*, Phaidon, London.

Euripides (1991), *'Cyclops'* in *Plays: Two*, Methuen, London.

Flynn, C. (1990), *The Body in Swift and Defoe*, Cambridge University Press, Cambridge.

Gibbon, E. (1838), *The History of the Decline and Fall of the Roman Empire*, John Murray, London.

Glazebrook, P. (1972), 'The Necessity Plea in English Criminal Law' *Cambridge Law Journal*, Vol. 30, p. 87.

Greenslade, W. (1994), *Degeneration, Culture and the Novel*, Cambridge University Press, Cambridge.

Grotius, H. (1853), *De Jure et Pucis*, Cambridge University Press, Cambridge.

Hale, M. (1736), *The History of the Pleas of the Crown*, London.

Hammond, D. and Jablow, A (1970), *The Africa that Never Was*, Twayne, New York.

Harris, M. (1977), *Cannibals and Kings*, Random House, New York.

Herodotus (1972), *The Histories*, Penguin, Harmondsworth.

Hesiod (1856), *The Works of Hesiod,Callimachus and Theognics*, Henry G. Bohn, London.

Hobbes, T. (1968), *Leviathan*, Penguin, Harmondsworth.

Homer (1987), *The Iliad*, Penguin, Harmondsworth.

Homer (1991), *The Odyssey*, Penguin, Harmondsworth.

Hogden, M. (1952), 'Montaigne and Shakespeare Again', *Huntington Library Quarterly*, Vol. 16, p. 23.

Hulme, P. (1986), *Colonial Encounters*, Methuen, London.

Hulme, P. and Whitehead, N. (1992), *Wild Majesty*, Clarendon Press, Oxford.

Juvenal (1974), *Sixteen Satires*, Penguin, Harmondsworth.

Kingsley, C. (1884), *Yeast*, Macmillan, London.

Kingsley, F. (1877), *Charles Kingsley*, Henry S. King, London.

Lactantius (1964), *The Divine Institutes*, Catholic University of America Press, Washington.

Locke, J. (1975), *An Essay Concerning Human Understanding*, Clarendon Press, Oxford.

MacDonald, R. (1994), *The Language of Empire*, Manchester University Press, Manchester.

Mandeville (1963), *The Bodley Version of Mandeville's Travels*, Oxford University Press, Oxford.

Marlow, J. (1983), 'English Cannibalism: Dickens After 1859', *Studies in English Literature, 1500-1900*, Vol. 23, p. 647.

Martineau, H. (1845), *Dawn Island*, J. Gadsby, Manchester.

Milton, J. (1992), *John Milton*, Routledge, London.

Montaigne, M. (1993), *The Essays: A Selection*, Penguin, Harmondsworth.

Moryson, F. (1908), *An Itinerary*, James MacLehose, Glasgow.

Novak, M. (1963), *Defoe and the Nature of Man*, Oxford University Press, Oxford.

Orgel, S. (1987), 'Shakespeare and the Cannibals', in Garber, M. (Ed.) *Cannibals. Witches, and Divorce,* Johns Hopkins University Press: Baltimore.

Pagden, A. (1982), *The Fall of Natural Man,* Cambridge University Press, Cambridge.

Pascal, B. (1967), *The Provincial Letters,* Penguin, Harmondsworth.

Pearce, R. (1945), 'Primitivistic Ideas in *The Faerie Queene'*, *Journal of English and German Philology,* Vol. 64, p. 139.

Petty, W. (1970), *The Political Anatomy of Ireland,* Irish University Press, Shannon.

Pick, D. (1989), *Faces of Degeneration,* Cambridge University Press, Cambridge.

Plato (1926), *The Laws,* Loeb, London.

Plato (1976), *The Republic,* J.M. Dent, London.

Polybius (1922), *The Histories,* Loeb, London.

Pope, A. (1967), *The Odyssey of Homer,* Methuen, London.

Pufendorf, S. (1934), *On the Law of Nature and Nations,* Clarendon Press, Oxford.

Rawson, C. (1984), 'Narrative and the Proscribed Act', in Strelka, J. (Ed.), *Literary Theory and Criticism,* Peter Lang, New York.

Rawson, C. (1992), 'Stewed, roasted, baked or boiled', *London Review of Books,* 6th August.

Rawson, C. 1978), 'A Reading of A Modest Proposal', in Hibson, J. *et al* (Eds.), *Augustan Worlds,* Leicester University Press, Leicester.

Report from the Select Committee on Transportation (1968), British Parliamentary Papers, Irish University Press, Shannon.

Sanday, P. (1986), *Divine Hunger,* Cambridge University Press, Cambridge.

Sawday, J. (1995), *The Body Emblazoned,* Routledge, London.

Simpson, A. (1986), *Cannibalism and the Common Law,* Penguin, Harmondsworth.

Spenser, E. (1978), *The Faerie Queene,* Penguin, Harmondsworth.

Spenser, E. (1949), *The Works of Edmund Spenser,* Johns Hopkins Press, Baltimore.

Stephen, J. (1887), *A Digest of the Criminal Law,* Macmillan, London.

Strabo (1969), *The Geography of Strabo,* Loeb, London.

Street, B. (1975), *The Savage in Literature,* Routledge, London.

Stone, H. (1994), *The Night Side of Dickens,* Ohio State University Press, Columbus.

Stone, H. (1987), 'The Contents of the Kettles', *The Dickensian*, Vol. 83, p. 7.

Swift, J. (1975), 'A Modest Proposal', in *A Tale of a Tub and other Satires*, Dent, London.

Taylor, D. (1958), 'Carib, Caliban, Cannibal', *International Journal of American Linguistics*, Vol. 25, p. 156.

Vaughan, A. and Vaughan, V. (1993), *Shakespeare's Caliban*, Cambridge University Press, Cambridge.

Walker, D. (1980), *The Oxford Companion to Law*, Clarendon Press, Oxford.

Williams, G. (1977), 'A Commentary on R v Dudley and Stephens', *Cambrian Law Review*, Vol. 8, p. 94.

Woolley, J. (1992), *The Intelligence*, Clarendon Press, Oxford.

5 Stories for Good Children

JOHN MORISON

Introduction

This chapter seeks to make what at first sight must seem a rather unlikely connection between children's literature and the study of law, order and discipline. Children's literature is an increasingly important area of study within a variety of disciplines.[1] However, the insights that examination of such work can bring to legal and criminological studies are largely unexplored. This is unfortunate as children's literature exists within the context of the wider society in which it is produced and stands out as a cultural product capable of bearing understandings about the particular circumstances in which it is created and consumed. Indeed, children's literature is perhaps uniquely placed to help us understand how our concepts of right and wrong, of safety and dangerousness, of consensus or otherness are created, transmitted and policed.

The critic Jacqueline Rose observes that a gift of a book from an adult to a child lies 'somewhere between a bribe and a demand'.[2] This can be interpreted as perhaps capturing the essence of the importance of children's literature in this inquiry. It is argued here that children's books exist as cultural artefacts capable of being interpreted to give an understanding of the wider society which produced them and in which they are consumed. Children's literature is a commodity produced by adults within particular artistic, social and economic contexts. It is also largely chosen by adults and so contains a reflection of their ideas about its function, the views it should be representing and what adults want from children. Although children's literature is laden with adult burdens it is shaped by children too. Their acceptance of adult choices about what books to produce and give is moulded by their experiences of childhood and by the changing experience of childhood itself. Whether children's literature is designed overtly to improve, instruct or merely entertain it still carries with it culturally encoded messages from the wider society. It matters not whether children read a particular title or are demonstrably influenced by it: children's literature exists as a tangible and reasonably accessible imprint of the child-adult relationship. Children's literature is a reflection of (as well as actually a small part of) a wider socialization process. It is a distillation of how adults see the world, what adults want for children and how children themselves are constituted in that world. The literature of childhood is like an essence of childhood - a process of shaping, controlling, preparing and disciplining as well as, more actively, growing into the wider culture. It is this that gives us a particular opportunity to read this literature and attempt to come to grips with how ideas of right and wrong, acceptability and deviance, insiders and outsiders are reflected there as information necessary for joining the wider adult culture and making the appropriate responses and choices there.

One legal theorist who does consider children's literature within a straightforward law and literature approach is Ian Ward.[3] His account, made within the context of a general survey of the possibilities and perspectives for law and literature is an important one. However, it is different from the argument advanced here. Ward stresses the importance of psychology, and in particular Piaget's ideas about the evolution of children's ability to form moral judgments, as he examines 'pre-adolescent' and 'adolescent' books. He suggests that we read these as 'jurisprudential texts'.[4] For Ward books such as *The Tales of Beatrix Potter*, *Alice's Adventures in Wonderland* and *The Jungle Book* are essentially covering similar themes to those in dealt with in works of jurisprudence. For example, Ward suggests that Beatrix Potter's *Tale of Ginger and Pickles*, concerning two animals who attempt to run a shop without requiring payment in cash, 'is as jurisprudential a tale as Posner's *Economic Analysis of Law*'.[5] Indeed, he maintains that such works may be more important because they are more widely read than orthodox jurisprudential works: 'only a tiny minority of the community will ever study law ... but the vast majority who encounter a reasonably wide spectrum of children's literature will already have engaged in jurisprudential debate'.[6] I am not sure if the simple fact that both types of work make reference to broadly similar issues is enough by itself to render children's books into works of legal theory any more than a menu, which offers a choice between beef, fish and the vegetarian alternative, can therefore be seen as a treatise on ethics or moral philosophy. The argument offered here is a different one.

This account suggests that the cultural context which produces a work and in which it is consumed, can be seen reflected in the work. It looks at the dynamics surrounding the production and consumption of children's books, along with the evolution and history of the idea of childhood itself, to suggest that children's literature can be looked at as a reflection of the child-adult relationship and as a distilled inscription of socialization messages which seeks to discipline children into productive adults. Children's literature is seen as presenting a unique opportunity to unpick the messages of order from the wider culture that are contained there. Margaret Meek, an educationalist, tells us that even inexperienced readers are aware of 'something that lies behind the words, embedded in the sense'.[7] Watson suggests that

> what lies behind the words is culture, that vast and volatile language which the story belongs to. Culture is not laid out like a microfiche to be learned or scanned; it is a shifting social pattern of shared understandings and sanctioned responses of such necessary complexity that becoming a member of the culture involves knowing the choices, recognizing the known predicaments and permitted reactions.[8]

In what follows it will be argued that children's literature offers us an important way of exploring these messages of order, censure and difference from the wider culture.

Children's literature and childhood

Children's literature here refers to books or stories produced for and read by or told to children. It is distinct from adult literature or books aimed at adolescents. It is discrete also from fables and legends although it does overlap with folk and fairy stories. Although originally consumed by all ages, these have in the relatively recent past been oriented towards children. Also, the definition of what is being considered here could be extended to cover stories as told: not only oral culture and games but also television and cinema. Even toys can be read as texts which carry with them messages and instructions about how to carry out sex roles and power relationships. Rather like books, which are produced and purchased mainly by adults within a particular context,[9] toys too are subject to adult influence and contain messages from the wider adult culture.[10] The focus is on well-known or 'classic' works, rather than say comics or other more ephemeral forms. This is because the argument here does not depend on the impact of any particular book on any individual reader. 'Effects' research, which seeks to establish through empirical investigation the impact of material on the behaviour and attitudes of the young has a long historical pedigree.[11] Originally concerned with the suspected deleterious effect of penny dreadfuls and comics it is nowadays centred on television, cinema and video recordings and games. While this may be a highly developed specialism its value remains inconclusive and of little assistance here where the emphasis is on children's books as cultural artefacts: as products of the particular circumstances that surround them as they are created and consumed. Indeed it is these circumstances, this context, that supplies our interest in them as well as our hold on them. By understanding better the processes by which a book comes into existence and 'works' as an item of communication for the writer, publisher, purchaser and various consumers it can be seen how it relates to the wider world that produces it.

The 'myths' of childhood

It is clear that historically children's literature awaited not just the development of literacy and a technology for exploiting this but, more fundamentally, a concept of childhood itself. Such an idea is not as unproblematic as might first appear. It can be argued that we have a very culturally and historically specific idea of what it is to be a child and that it owes little to any idea of Nature predetermining an inevitable stage. The 'myth' of childhood that we currently live with is not completely settled but, basically, it sees children as apolitical, asexual and thoroughly dependent on adults. The family and home is centred around children. Childhood is regarded as a time for idyllic carefree play rather than work. (Childhood in our culture is now typified perhaps by the Christmas extravaganza of sentimentality over children where they are celebrated as playthings and recipients of toys.) This stage is only gradually superseded by school and the discipline of adult world whereby the growing child is made ready for the adult world of work, responsibility and the production of children in turn.

As in the third world now, it was not always like this in Europe. The social historian Philippe Ariès was among the first to argue in his *Centuries of Childhood* that the invention of childhood as a separate status corresponds with transition from feudalism to capitalism and that in the early modern world 'the idea of childhood did not exist'. Other historians have followed this up in a broadly similar vein.[12] As recently as the seventeenth century, argues Ariès, children from the moment they cast off their swaddling bands, were not only dressed like small adults of their class but lived much the same life. Ariès maintains that children drank wine and beer like adults, gambled for money at cards and enjoyed similar games and pastimes. Adults played pinwheel and ran after hoops. All ages listened to fairy tales and recited what we know as nursery rhymes.

Social position and economic class were greater determinants of status than age. As Ivan Illich has put it, 'the worker's child, the peasant's child and nobleman's child all dressed the way their fathers dressed, played the way their fathers played and were hanged by the neck as were their fathers'.[13] Children were not only morally responsible but were rational miniature adults. Education was not a phase unique to childhood and work was something experienced by even very young children.[14] Until at least the seventeenth century the home was primarily an economic entity rather than an emotional centre and this was reflected in family relationships which helped to constitute the child in a very different way to that we know of presently. The household was not a private place of the family but a public place where people were seldom left alone. Ariès describes how from the fifteenth to the seventeenth century in the greater part of Europe the houses of the rich sheltered, apart from the family proper, a whole population of servants, employees, clerics, apprentices etc.[15] Smaller houses of the poor may have had fewer people in them but they were not centres of warm family relations. Several historians even maintain that parent-child relationships were different and less warm by modern standards.[16] The discovery and suppression of children's sexuality,[17] along with the reorganization of so many other aspects of social life that was required in order to yield up something like our present view of childhood, was not completed until at least the Victorian era.

The short-term historicity of childhood suggested at here should alert us to the possibility that childhood (and thus certainly children's literature) is a socially constructed phenomenon carrying with it the mark of the circumstances which created it, rather than a simple fact of life.

The development of a literature for children

Children's literature needs the idea of a child. The history of the changing nature of childhood has a parallel history of the changing nature of children's books. This is a different story and one that is fully told elsewhere.[18] Prior to the invention of printing in the later part of the fifteenth century books were exceedingly rare and precious. As Townsend points out, the writing of books to amuse children would have been an 'economic as well as psychological impossibility'.[19] There were some manuscripts in the fifteenth century such as *Symon's Lesson of Wisdom for All Manner Children* which sought to provide instruction although not entertainment. The first English printer, William Caxton, produced *The Fables of Aesop* in 1484 but this, in common with nearly all the very few books produced until the end of the seventeenth century, was used as a school book or book of manners and morals. The Puritan influence of the late seventeenth century yielded works, such as James Janeway's *A Token for Children, Being an Exact Account of the Conversion, Holy and Exemplary Lives, and Joyful Deaths of Several Young Children* in 1671 which were stories of saintly children who died young in a rapture of prayer and clearly designed exclusively for religious edification. Indeed, when John Locke produced his radical *Thoughts Concerning Education* in 1689, introducing something approaching the modern idea of education, he bemoaned the shortage of easy and pleasant books beyond the scriptures and Aesop with which to instruct the child. Indeed it was not until the 1740s, the decade in which the English novel is generally thought to have been born, that books clearly designed for children began to appear. It was of course this period that Ariès and others see as the time when the modern idea of childhood started to emerge. Iona and Peter Opie maintain in their authoritative *Oxford Dictionary of Nursery Rhymes*[20] that no rhyme composed before the eighteenth century was for children exclusively and that the earliest example of marketing of books exclusively for children can be traced to John Newberry in 1744 who produced a series of juvenile works.

From this point the development of children's literature grew apace with the evolution of the idea of childhood. Both histories received a substantial imperative from the influence of Jean-Jacques Rousseau's important work *Emile* (1762). This argued for the innocence of childhood and the importance of controlling its development. This case was made against the prevailing view of childhood as akin to a state of original sin. Paradoxically, although Rousseau was opposed to books being introduced to children at too young an age for fear of their corrupting influence, widespread acceptance of his views produced a spate of, mainly didactic, writing with strongly religious overtones.[21] This didactic strain in children's literature continues even yet, although in a much reduced form. It was, however, dominant in various manifestations for about one hundred and 50 years, indeed right up until almost the end of the 'golden age' of children's literature which ended with the first world war. The purely religious motif which marked the earlier works was gradually superseded in the Victorian era by a more moralistic one which, although equally didactic, worked on themes such as obedience, industry and purity as well as religion. As the critic Maria Tatar sees it:

> from its inception with ABC primers that proclaimed 'In Adam's Fall, we sinned all,' children's literature moved in theological/redemptive mode only to shift gradually, with the introduction of discipline through instruction, into the didactic/moralistic mode. The nineteenth-century, which witnessed the great flowering of children's literature, placed, with some notable Victorian exceptions, an unprecedented premium on sending messages to children through literature even as it nervously sought to preserve the notion of childhood as a wide-eyed, innocent, uncontaminated stage of life.[22]

Thus the books of the mid nineteenth century and later were generally wider in their scope. Indeed the narrative may be linked broadly to particular historical concerns affecting Britain in its new role in the world. Yarns, such as J.D. Wyss's *Swiss Family Robinson* (1814), Captain Marryat's *Masterman Ready* (1841) and R.M. Ballantyne's *The Coral Island* (1857) detailing the adventures of their plucky heroes in all four corners of the globe, no doubt provided a suitable background of moral uplift for a generation of Empire builders. Victorian girls were at the same time catered for by a different genre of domestic dramas of which Louisa May Alcott's *Little Women* (1868) remains the best known in Britain as well as its native North America. Despite its promising start, with its heroine Jo eschewing the stereotyped gender role pre-ordained for her, she eventually embraces her stultifying destiny as an impeccably virtuous and conscientious Victorian woman of good works. The same fate awaits even the heroine of Susan Coolidge's *What Katy Did* (1872) when her career as a mischief maker is finally brought down to earth by her contented marriage to a tall, good looking naval officer in *What Katy Did Next* (1886). Again we may speculate if such a fate befalling the heroines of girls' books made more glamorous or more acceptable the circumscribed role that awaited most virtuous Victorian girls in womanhood.

It would be possible to continue with this tracking of how particular historical concerns surface within children's literature.[23] Modern children's books continue to reflect the preoccupations of their time. (For example, there is a strong environmental theme to a great deal of modern children's fiction.) However, nowadays children's books are able to display a greater range of styles. Imagination, fantasy, folk and fairy tales, various forms of anthropomorphic tale, picture books, verse, gritty realism etc. have all had their moments as a dominant trend in children's literature before settling down to occupy their place as just one of the many genres in the continuing story of children's books. Today all these genres exist both as extant titles available in the bookshops and libraries and as styles that may be adopted by new writers.

Making children's books

So far it has been argued that children's literature exists within the context of an idea of childhood and, as this has changed so too has the style and content of children's literature. There is, however, clearly another aspect to the context within which we must view children's literature. This relates to the processes by which books are produced, sold and consumed.

The adult is central to the production of children's books. Indeed, children's literature is a territory controlled by adults. This straightforward truth has prompted Jacqueline Rose to develop a sophisticated argument about children's literature defining and controlling the idea of childhood and relations between adult and child. In subtitling her book on Peter Pan *The Impossibility of Children's Fiction*, Rose is arguing that

> children's fiction sets up a world in which the adult comes first (author, maker, giver) and the child comes after (reader, product, receiver), but neither of them enter the space in between ... Children's fiction builds an image of the child inside the book [and] it does so in order to secure the child who is outside the book, the one who does not come so easily within its grasp.[24]

In other words, a basic function of children's books is to construct a way of articulating the problematic distinction between adult and child. It does this by projecting a fantasy of what it is to be a child and securing this within a literature designed for children. In this way adult ideas about what it is to be a child can be projected on to children obliterating their experience by silencing it with the eloquence of fiction. This notion that children's literature is not simply for children but rather that it contains within it all sorts of indications of what the adult demands and expects of the child is the source of much of its interest to us here. The idea is that the adult world is connected to children's literature and that thus it is there possible to see in sharp relief all sorts of expectations and understandings about the child and the world beyond childhood. But how exactly are adult perspectives transmitted into children's books?

Watson has pointed out that 'children's literature is not a tranquil backwater where Ratty and Mole, Benjamin Bunny and Pooh Bear go about their innocent business. Their business is their author's business'.[25] Authors and illustrators are, obviously, in a prime position to represent their view of the world to children through their work. Sometimes, as with didactic writers, particularly those from the last century, the objective lying behind the production of a book is clear. Education, especially moral instruction, is intended. However, since the beginning of this century children's books have been less obviously didactic and the messages in them rather more complex and indeterminate. Of course that is not to say that more recent books are without a disciplinary agenda, although often now there is room for speculation about the motives of an author who re-works their imaginative experiences for others through books containing fantasy. From the literary criticism perspective, for example, detailed textual evidence can be produced arguing for various interpretations of children's literature as expressions of the human condition - or at least the author's condition. Thus, for example, there is work explaining J.M. Barrie as the boy who would not grow up, a Peter Pan replaying his unhappy childhood and early life in a never never land of fiction.[26] There is the interpretation of Beatrix Potter escaping with Norman Warne, her publisher and fiancé, from her stiffly formal and unhappy home in South Kennsington like the two bad mice - Tom Thumb and Hunca Munca - who smashed the fancy plaster food and vandalized the pretentious doll's house in her *Tale of Two Bad Mice* (1904).[27]

There is also, as mentioned above, the situation where adult concerns about particular debates at a given time surface in work for children. As Briggs[28] recounts, there is critical work interpreting *The Wind in the Willows* (1908) as a fable of class struggle where the weasels and stoats can be seen as the grubby and envious proletariat invading the rural greenness of the Thames valley in opposition to the traditionalist's rural idyll of the respectable Rat and Mole and the playboy, aristocratic Toad. Works such as Anna Sewell's *Black Beauty* (1877) or, more recently, Richard Adam's *Watership Down* (1972) clearly contain much about the author's view of how society is organized and attitudes to nature and to animals. Newer titles such as Colin McNaughton's *Watch Out for the Giant Killers* (1992) and Jan Needle's *The Bogeymen* (1992) - concerned with ecological awareness and anti-racism respectively - are overtly vehicles for proselytising.

Clearly there is an artistic context to such books. There is also a commercial one.[29] Here again adults are central. There is the whole world of producing and marketing a literary commodity. Understanding this would require an appreciation of the processes by which a book is commissioned or accepted, put on a particular list, entered for one of the increasing number of literary prizes and marketed through either bookshops, libraries or educational institutions. The details of a sociology of the production and distribution of children's literature is clearly beyond the scope of this work. Here we need only take away an appreciation that children's literature comes into existence in a complex process and is dependent on many factors. This means that it can not be simply read as a direct result of any particular, specific agenda to educate, socialise, make money or whatever. Books for children come into existence as a result of a whole series of largely unfathomable artistic, economic and educative imperatives. While there is certainly a wider function of shaping and controlling childhood by representing it, there is no one simple aim - hegemonic or otherwise - that *explains* children's literature.

The consumption of children's literature

It is generally adults - parents mainly, but other family members and friends as well as librarians, teachers etc. - who buy books. Indeed, this aspect of adult involvement is here even more important than the influence of authors and publishers, not least because it is more tangible and more commonplace. Undoubtedly choices are made by adults for a whole variety of motives and reasons. Sometimes perhaps adults buy books, or pass on their old books, in order to recapture their own childhood or some ideal of childhood. There is also an increasing trend for books to be prescribed to perform particular jobs in childrearing. Often books are bought by adults because of what they want children to be or to do. Books are bought to entertain, to distract children, but at the same time to instruct them or to 'discipline' them in the widest sense of that word. As Roald Dahl has pointed out, adults have a relentless need to civilise 'this thing that when it is born is an animal with no manners, no moral sense at all'.[30] Even if this is not done directly, as in the didactic books that appeared in the early days of children's literature and reached their height in the nineteenth century, it is still carried out indirectly. Clearly parents (or at least some parents, this role being abandoned to teachers and others in many cases) see books as important. Almost everyone, especially the book buying middle classes, want their children to share their moral beliefs and attitudes. It is not necessary to accept that each new generation is a barbarian invasion to believe in the need to civilise children. Rather than simply bowing to superior strength or social pressure, children are to be persuaded into shape. Stories, from the cautionary tales and fables of an earlier, oral tradition to the films and videos of now, are very much an important part of this process. Children's literature thus gives an adult's view of what children want and of what they, the adults, want children to be. Stories encode information, or cultural messages, about the child's place in society. The images in children's books provide concentrated versions of the discourses of order in wider adult society.

Of course children come into this too. There is no doubt that children's literature addresses two very different interpretative constituencies and that adults and children may have very different readings of the same text. Children's developing sense of self, the sort of issues that they want to know about, are reflected in what is bought for them - or least read by them - and what they take from it. Books that are too obviously about moral improvement are unlikely to be any more appealing to children than novels about heroic tractors drivers exceeding production quotas would be to us.[31] The books that children read, and importantly re-read, as well as the messages they take from books, express something of the child's world and the difficulties about fitting in with the perplexing rules and relationships of the wider adult world. Children's literature reflects these concerns by being fundamentally occupied with portraying how the world is ordered - both morally and hierarchically. It offers, some times more directly than other times, another representation of the world and, particularly, ideas of right and wrong. Right and wrong may not be defined in terms of crime and punishment but in terms of doing the right thing, being good or bad (naughty), letting down friends, negotiating authority and so on. These issues are often set within a framework that, while not necessarily realistic, will reflect the child's experience. The perplexing rules, relationships and limitations of the wider world are previewed in children's literature.

There is an abiding tradition within children's literature of small creatures, little people and even machines who can stand in for the child coming to terms with mysteries of the adult society.[32] Children also of course want books that will celebrate their developing power as well as reflecting their struggles with the adult world and adult emotions. As one commentator remarks in relation to the heroine's propensity to change her size in *Alice in Wonderland*, 'the mechanism of size change fulfils one of the simplest child-fantasies in which one becomes big enough to get one's own way'.[33] Indeed this feature whereby children take control in their literature caused one reviewer of the ever popular Enid Blyton opus to comment drily 'what chance has a gang of desperate criminals against three small children!'[34] Arthur Ransome's stories of *Swallows and Amazons* started in the 1930s pioneered the sort of work that celebrates the competence of children in a world that is almost completely devoid of grown up interference and this approach has been taken up and developed vigorously.

It is striking that many of the most appealing children's books, and certainly many of those that we regard as classics, will also contain an element of what Briggs has termed 'seductive transgressiveness'.[35] They will look around dangerous corners and explore the boundaries of what is proper. Alison Lurie describes such books as 'subversive children's literature'.[36] She regards this as providing a separate, radical and alternative view of the world written for children by those who are in spirit still a part of this alien, partly savage tribe to which we all once belonged. However, what Lurie has really uncovered is simply the change of style that, as we noted earlier, occurred at the end of the 'Golden Age': the movement from the threateningly didactic to the entertaining yet persuasive book that is now usual. All varieties of children's literature - including Lurie's 'subversive' literature - are equally concerned with imposing a vision of what is correct, acceptable or normal. The twentieth century children's writer is in reality no less didactic than the writer of the eighteenth or nineteenth centuries: it is just that the medicine has become more sugar-coated by entertainment values. Since the pioneering books of Mark Twain, Lewis Carroll and others which offered the *frisson* of being mildly subversive, or at least appearing not to take too seriously the more rigid adult strictures, children are not now to be threatened or preached into conformity with an adult view of the world and their place within it. Of course there is nothing really alternative or dangerous in any books for children. There are probably not many, if any, characters in children's literature who are truly evil (as opposed to simply frightening in the bogeyman sense). However, the subject matter of much effective writing for children is badness - or at least naughtiness. Very often the narrative will involve a child, or a character stand-in for a child, surveying what is right and maybe experimenting with what is wrong. Very fine distinctions are here essayed between what may be simply naughty, involving perhaps getting the better of an adult, and what is bad, *stricto sensu,* something which generally is balanced in a fairly overt moral reckoning. Underneath the apparent anarchy of even the most seemingly 'subversive' texts there are still very strong messages about the correct way to live and behave. Indeed the fact that modern children's books very often take as their context (slightly) bad behaviour means simply that they can more winningly and effectively promote their (essentially moral) message.

What children's literature offers then is a representation of the child's and parents' world. Children's writers are not constrained by adult ideas of what is credible and may in fact often provide a simplification of the moral universe in the relatively clear black and white certainties of right and wrong that are deployed in writing designed for the young.[37] This concentrated version of order provides an important and fertile field for study.

Reading children's literature

There is an intricate relationship between a society and the kind of modes of expression that it produces. In the case of children's literature there is a particular dynamic to its production and consumption which places it in a position where it can be read by legal theorists and criminologists to afford understandings of how our culture sees itself and what it wants for, and expects of, its children. There are many voices in children's literature and many messages saying different things. Our interest is in how children's literature simultaneously reflects, and indeed helps to construct, a moral landscape of order within which are reflected adult ideas and expectations from the wider culture as well as children's experience of what it is to learn the appropriate range of responses within that culture.

In the rest of this essay I will consider how a variety of writers, from a number of different disciplines, have approached and interpreted messages about the wider culture that may be contained within writing for children. The concern within some of this work has not been directly with examining how normality, difference and censure are created and controlled. However, some of the work can be bent to our purpose and other aspects are suggestive of what a law and literature approach directed at this subject might look like.

The pedagogy of fear: socialisation and stories

We considered earlier how books for children arose from a didactic project to pass on to children moral tales on uplifting religious themes and how these were gradually superseded by matter-of-fact tales, no less didactic but concerned with a different agenda of useful (moral) knowledge. By the end of the 'Golden Age' these in turn had been supplanted by the whole range of books that have grown up since the first World War where the overt preaching of earlier eras is generally outmoded. Books from the earlier period can perhaps be read fairly straightforwardly as cautionary tales. Indeed, the message from the wider culture that they convey is generally disappointingly simple: obey your parents and those in authority.

Maria Tatar argues that 'from its inception, children's literature had in it an unusual cruel and coercive streak - one which produced books that relied on brutal intimidation to frighten children into complying with parental demands'.[38] This theme can be seen surfacing in literature as early as 1715 when Isaac Watt's *Divine and Moral Songs* asked 'Have you not heard what dreadful plagues\Are threatened by the Lord,\To him that breaks his father's law\Or mocks his mother's word?' However, the cautionary tale flourished most vigorously in what Tatar describes as 'the harsh climate of nineteenth century childrearing practices'.[39] There the intimidation of children took two forms: both made examples of children. There was the cautionary tale proper, which generally killed off its protagonists or made their lives perpetually miserable for acts of disobedience. There were also stories of exemplary children. Both of these conspired to construct the ideal child as the docile child who followed his or her parents' instruction.[40] Within the fairy tale and folktale the moral symmetry is even more relentless but there is at least a little more variety in the lessons offered. According to folklorists there is a whole genre of reward-and-punishment tales with variations ranging across all versions of dutiful/disobedient and into kind/unkind, hard-working/lazy, polite/rude and faithful/treacherous.[41] These are matched to some extent with stories where virtue and hard work receive their just desserts.

One must wonder about the extent to which children accepted and believed the moral messages of such tales. There is, however, some evidence that the tales were reinforced wherever possible with other improving activities such as attending public executions. In late eighteenth century Germany Christian Weisse, a prominent expert on parenting, was writing of the 'pedagogical value of executions' and declaring that in his own family 'the event became the occasion for many edifying discussions among us'.[42] Tartar maintains that the gruesome fairy tales of this period were 'not completely devoid of merit, for they offered children a programme for survival' - lessons about care with fire being important in an era of open fires and flames and so on.[43] However, such simple messages are surely overstated and the medium dwells gratuitously on the torments of failing to heed it. Perhaps the message of these works is better stated more generally as Zipes does where he interprets them as saying that 'to live, a child had to live properly, restraining natural instincts according to rules established by adults. To disobey these rules or to indulge one's sensual drives for pleasure meant death'.[44]

What we can see in this literature are all too obvious and clear messages about the moral imperatives of that society. The overt messages are certainly accessible enough to us by virtue of the didactic nature of the form at that time. There is a genre of criticism that claims that the messages in more modern children's books are no less clear although they may be somewhat less obvious. This type of criticism is focused on what are now regarded as unacceptable class attitudes, sexism and racism as they are reproduced in children's books as part of a process of instilling the new generation with particular values. Much of this work is less concerned with undertaking orthodox sociology relating to themes of socialisation than with advancing an idea of political correctness.[45] Some of it is crude. Often there is an unarticulated assumption that children will inevitably, routinely and uniformly be moulded by reading or viewing certain material and that the effect on their character lasts for ever. The messages taken from books sometimes under-estimate many of the more subtle values and assumptions from the wider culture that are to be found in children's books. This way of reading can only assist us if we are prepared to reject its excesses.

The simplification in children's literature easily reveals the sexist, racist and class snobbery of earlier ages. The so-called 'Golden Age' of children's literature, the period from 1880 to 1914, is a time whose social attitudes have dated badly. Within the staid improving literature of the time the biases are particularly transparent. Even classics that have endured relatively well can be easily read to show what are now dated attitudes. Mark Twain's *Adventures of Huckleberry Finn* (1884) has some references to blacks which, although containing a certain degree of moral irony, are sometimes considered unfortunate today. Kipling's work generally, but *The Jungle Books* (1894-5) in particular, have fairly clear echoes of white supremicism. A work such as Helen Bannerman's *The Story of Little Black Sambo* (1898), although still read now, is clearly from another era. But this is too easy. As we noted earlier, books often reflected wider concerns at the time they were written and simply spotting attitudes from an earlier age, with all the sophistication that a hundred or so years of hindsight can bring, does not reveal very much. Indeed, it is salutary to think that we do not know now what unexpected sins we ourselves may be found guilty of in fifty years time.

A more useful approach is to consider the sort of images, values and hierarchies that are either directly represented in children's stories or lurk behind the assumptions that are made there. Bob Dixon's two part work *Catching Them Young*[46] deserves special mention here for its exhaustive hunt for racist, sexist and class values within children's books. Although it is a little unclear about cause and effect it is redeemed by its collection of examples detailing the sexist horrors in the *Pony Parade* series, Noddy's assault by wicked gollywogs and the snobbery of the Rev. W. Awdry's branch line. Other works within this approach focus too on issues of sex, race and class and argue that much of children's literature has the effect of projecting a view of what is proper and that this view is generally a politically unsound one. Codogan and Craig survey girls' fiction and declare that

> before girls are old enough to go to school they are familiar with Polly Flinders, who is whipped for spoiling her nice, new, feminine clothes, with the other Polly who is encouraged endlessly to put the kettle on and take it off again; they learn that Miss Muffet has an irrational fear of spiders, and see how the little girls who are kissed and reduced to tears by the offensive Georgie-Porgie lack the courage to chase him off, and have to wait until the 'boys' come out to rescue them.[47]

Whether such rhymes are materially responsible for beliefs and behaviours carried into adulthood is certainly debatable. However there is less doubt that much of children's literature can be read to reflect something of the way the world is ordered and sex roles distributed and policed. In fairy tales girls are offered only the limited choice of being a princess or an under-privileged but basically worthy girl who is going to become a princess if she is brave and lucky.[48] Frequently, it is argued, even in more general fiction girls are presented as passive and often the narrative follows boy characters who act upon the world to provide the plot development. Girls are more usually restricted to the home than boys and their role may be more circumscribed or supporting rather than central.[49] Some critics offer a more subtle analysis. Claudia Nelson,[50] examining children's literature from 1857 to 1917, argues that the didactic intentions of Victorian authors can be linked into a project of trying to reform society by shifting the view of human nature towards the selfless and pure ideal associated with the depiction of women in books. She maintains that even in fiction for boys there was during the Victorian period an attempt to promote an essentially feminine ethic which emphasized self-control, selflessness and self-sacrifice.[51] This sort of critical work can be linked further into wider debate about the depiction of women as the 'Angel in House' representing domesticity, nurture and emotion.[52]

Unsatisfactory attitudes to race and class have also been tracked down. Indeed, it is perhaps a measure of the success of such critiques that publishers have felt it necessary to re-edit a number of popular works.[53] Beyond this controversy there remains the accusation that most children's books reflect a middle class view of the world and perpetuate negative attitudes towards the poor and disadvantaged.[54]

There is clearly something of interest for us in this line of analysis. While some of the argument about socialization may not be completely acceptable, the sort of readings offered here should persuade that strong and complex cultural messages are being sent out in much of what young children read. It is important, however, that we should not be restricted to looking only for horrors of sexism, racism or class snobbery in books in order to censor them or whatever. As we approach children's literature we must build upon these insights to see how hierarchies, categories and controls from the wider culture - beyond even those of sex, race and class - are represented and perpetuated.

Folklore and therapy

The idea that stories might contain messages that corroborate the values of society, and that these messages might be in some way be coded to be revealed only in the dynamics of reading, reaches a high point with the psychoanalytical approaches to fairy tales and folklore. These texts, if anything, are over-endowed with interpretation. Indeed, a leading folklorist, Jack Zipes, has complained of *The Trials and Tribulations of Little Red*

Riding Hood (1983ii) referring to the disputes over the origins of this one tale and the arguments concerning its meaning and significance.

There is a whole variety of psychoanalytical approaches to folk and fairy tales which basically argue that such stories contain a complex, symbolic language of fantastic images and motifs that can communicate encoded messages of universal application about how to transcend life's problems and live successfully. Against this general interpretation there is ranged a collection of anthropologists, historians and folklorists. They too believe that folk and fairy stories may contain messages but argue that these are very historically specific and meaningful only within an ethnographic analysis of a particular society. Rather than messages directed at the psyche, such stories reflect only the hardships of peasant life at particular historical times. Thus, for example Darnton[55] finds the stories collected by Perrault as simply detailing peasant life in eighteenth century France with its Malthusian environment of scarce food and high infant mortality. Bottigheimer maintains that the stories produced by the Grimm brothers are historical documents 'well suited to understanding nineteenth century German social and moral values' in all their bleak, misogynist and socially antagonistic detail.[56] Zipes regards the Grimm brothers' stories not as 'primeval narratives reflecting the great folk spirit and universal psyche, and thus containing truths about ourselves' but as in reality 'historical and social creations'.[57]

In opposition to this socio-historical perspective it is argued that folk and fairy tales, far from being culturally specific, are universal multi-cultural documents. Many, if not most, of the classic stories in European culture have their equivalent in other civilizations and historical periods. Indeed, scholars of mythology have contended that, despite the infinite variety of incident, setting and costume, the myths of the world offer only a limited number of responses to the existential predicaments of life.[58] This is the point of departure for a whole range of psychoanalytical approaches which argue that stories contain deeper meanings.[59] The best known exponent of this approach is Bruno Bettleheim. In his *Uses of Enchantment*[60] Bettleheim argues that fairy tales became ever more refined through the centuries of their re-telling until they came to communicate to all levels of the human personality - the conscious, preconscious and unconscious minds - in a way that reaches the uneducated mind of a child as well as that of a sophisticated adult. Bettleheim maintains that there are symbols semiotically encoded in folktales and these can be used as signposts for children to work through traumas of growing up and the basic human problems of growing up, coming to terms with disappointments, relinquishing childhood dependencies and gaining a feeling of selfhood, personal worth and moral obligation. The rules for such reading are based on Freud's *Interpretation of Dreams*.[61] These tales mean more than they appear to. The child reading or hearing them is largely unaware of this directly. The code for interpretation remains unknown to the child: the effect on him or her is largely unconscious. As Bettleheim puts it 'the fairy tale is the primer from which the child learns to read his mind in the language of images, the only language which permits understanding before intellectual maturity has been achieved'.[62] Stories work on the unconscious mind in a way that is not overtly didactic: rather they work by showing indirectly what is right. For Bettleheim fairy stories are vehicles of a 'moral education which subtly, and by implication only, convey [to the child] the advantages of moral behaviour, not through abstract ethical concepts but through that which seems tangibly right and therefore meaningful to him'.[63]

Not only do such tales offer signposts, rather than impose directions, but they put the boundaries of right and wrong and the child's need and capacity to make an effective choice at the centre of the narrative. Bettleheim complains that too often children are shielded from the essential nature of mankind and 'the propensity of all men for acting aggressively, asocially, selfishly, out of anger and anxiety'. While we want our children to believe that people are inherently good, 'children know that *they* are not always good; and often when they are, they would prefer not to be'.[64] The stories take these themes on and are enriched and given authority by doing so. This is very important because it provides a focus on bad/good, normal/deviant dichotomies and the internalized discipline that makes up our controlling ideas of personal responsibility. It is a much more subtle reading of fairy stories than that reviewed earlier which saw them, along with other didactic literature, as primarily, if not exclusively crude cautionary tales. We are provided with a glimpse of how, what Foucault[65] describes as the micro-physics of power, are inscribed in children's books as they are intended to be in children's minds. Within this approach, even if we do not accept the psychoanalytical jargon or the emphasis on Freudian concerns, we still have an important focus on how stories contain coded messages about civil behaviour, good sense, right and wrong, and how to survive. As Lurie maintains from outside the psychoanalytical tradition, such stories prepare children for life as well as to deal with immediate concerns such as perhaps the sort of grandmother who wants to devour her grandchild emotionally or the mother who might envy her daughter for being the fairest of them all. As she complains in relation to such books in her own childhood, 'the simple, pleasant adult society they had prepared us for did not exist. As we had suspected, the fairy tales had been right all along - the world was full of hostile, stupid giants and perilous castles and people who abandoned their children in the nearest forest'.[66]

The disciplining agenda is subtly fulfilled. Within the stories, evil is not without its attractions, symbolised by a mighty giant, the power of a witch or the cunning queen in *Snow White*. Often, indeed, it achieves ascendancy temporarily: the ugly sisters do go to the ball and the wicked fairy is not prevented from ensuring that the princess pricks her finger and falls asleep. However, the moral universe is generally restored to equilibrium in a cathartic resolution where good triumphs. However, the message is not simply 'Beware of being bad as there is punishment'. As Bettleheim remarks, 'in fairy tales, as in life, punishment or fear of it is only a limited deterrent to crime'.[67] The power of the tale lies with the identification that is made with the protagonists who juxtapose opposite characters to allow a positive identification with and sympathy for the hero. Vitally the sympathetic character succeeds. The story offers a vision of the hero getting on, mastering difficulties and acting on the world in a meaningful and rewarding way rather than simply making a series of straightforward choices between good and bad.

Of course there is no reason to limit this to fairy stories or folklore. Modern stories too cover similar ground. As we have seen, at the turn of the century writing for children moved away from the overtly didactic style but even in the new, more child friendly paradigm there is a moral agenda very firmly in place. Personal growth and self understanding rather than moral exhortation are now more central. Indeed, even worldly information sometimes seems secondary to self-knowledge. As Tatar sees this change, 'our own culture has moved into yet another mode of telling children's stories, one that might best be described as empathetic/cathartic, resting as it does on a therapeutic model'.[68] Even as modern authors see themselves primarily entertaining children they can not escape creating new behaviour models and introducing patterns of what is proper from the wider culture. Tatar suggests that, 'in empathizing with children ... they are often at pains to help them work through problems that, in the end, will turn them into 'well-adjusted' (read: 'socialized and productive') adults'.[69] Although modern stories see themselves as stimulating and freeing the child's imagination they are still inundating it with coded messages about what is acceptable. There are very complex cultural understandings being reflected in such work. Although modern stories have a more muted moral lesson, preferring to concentrate on a therapeutic or cathartic effect, and they may be more appealing than the 'dire warning' school of writing of the nineteenth century, they still are almost equally concerned with socialising 'good behaviour'. This must persuade us that a deeper reading of them is important and valuable.

Conclusion

In this chapter I have argued that children's literature should be taken seriously as offering useful insights into the wider culture which both produced it and which it reflects. In particular, it is argued that disciplinary mechanisms penetrate deeply into the culture and run forcefully through its cultural forms. Ideas of right and wrong, praise and censure and consensus and otherness are presented in concentrated form within writing designed for consumption by our children.

This account has not relied on the *effect* that reading books in general or any particular book may have on children. Rather it has sought to argue that children's books are produced within a context and it is this context that gives them their importance. A book for children is a tangible imprint of the child-adult relationship: it provides a distillation of what adults think children to be and what they want them to be. In examining how children's books are produced this account has noted the importance of adults as writers, producers and suppliers but has not neglected the influence of children themselves and the changing concept of childhood. It has argued that children's literature seems almost uniquely placed to provide us with insights about how the wider culture sees itself. Children's books both reflect the order in which they are produced and simultaneously contribute to the production of what Foucault[70] terms 'docile bodies' who create and police their own constraints with little need of force to discipline them. As we examine children's books we should be aware of, and alive to, the coded grammars of individual conscience that are contained there beneath the surface.

This essay (in common with most of the others in this volume) has not prescribed any single, correct way to read these texts. Indeed, there is no standard way to 'do' Law and Literature. What has been suggested here is that we look at a variety of approaches, from sociology to literary criticism to psychoanalysis, in order to see the sorts of ways that insights can be produced relating to how hierarchy and order is represented and communicated within this genre.

G.K. Chesterton was in no doubt that 'my first and last philosophy, that which I believe in with unbroken certainty, I learnt in the nursery'. It is astonishing that so far we have reflected so little on the stories we give to our children. This essay hopes to begin to remedy this but much remains to be done.

Notes

1. Within the field of literary studies there are now courses and conferences, journals and books, and even established chairs in children's literature. Historians, psychologists and sociologists of the family are too beginning to colonise the area. The Opie Collection of children's literature now housed in the Bodleian Library at Oxford would seem to ensure further development of this study.
2. Rose (1984), p. 105.
3. See Ward (1995), chp. 5.
4. See Ward (1995), especially at pp. 98-9.
5. Ward (1995), p. 101.
6. Ward (1995), p. 118.
7. Meeks (1988), p. 20.
8. Watson (1992), p. 13.
9. See further Fraser (1966).
10. For example, the most obvious message of a toy relates to gender roles. It is not true to say that children somehow naturally choose a toy 'appropriate' to their sex. Belotti talks of the 'final pseudo-choice between the choices which have already been made by adults' and claims that 'children have ... learnt to ask for the "right" toy because they know the wrong one will be denied them' (Belotti (1975), p. 79-80). The right toy for girls will very often duplicate the experience of life at home. Housework, child-care and personal appearance are themes covered in many 'girls' toys'. The message transmitted fairly unequivocally in these relates to the future role of the girl as consumer, wife and mother. 'Boys' toys' - vehicles or weapons etc. - perhaps suggest adventure and action and contain a message about

leaving home and going out to work. Indeed, toys that are common to both sexes are often artificially distinguished with, for example, bicycles being characterised as girls' and boys' by colour or in other ways.

11. See for example, England (1977); Barlow and Hill (1986); Signorielli and Gerbner (1988) and Gunter and McAleer (1990).

12. See, for example, Stone (1977) and Plumb (1972) and (1977). There is now even a revision of this revisionist history with, for example, Pollock, (1983) and Houlbrooke (1984) now arguing that the idea of childhood in the past was not really so distant from what we know today.

13. Illich (1973). Indeed, the law did not fully recognise different ages for criminal responsibility: Tudor criminal law permitted hanging for theft at the age of seven and this continued up until the eighteenth century. There are even reports of a child of six who cried for his mother on the scaffold. (See further Hoyles, (1979), p. 20.)

14. Thomas (1989) summarises a number of studies which show how in early modern England work was something started early by even very young children and learned on the job.

15. Ariès (1962), pp. 378-91. He argues that even the design of such houses suggests this. Rooms opened on to each other and generally were not separated by corridors. There were no specialist rooms: people ate, slept, danced, worked and received visitors in the same room.

16. Stone (1977) and Plumb (1977) suggest that Tudor and Stuart parents were reluctant to invest much emotional capital in their children because of the high rate of infant morality. Hoyles (1979), p. 21, claims that up to the eighteenth century figures show that 75 per cent of all children christened were dead before the age of five and in the nineteenth century half the children born died in their first five years.

17. For example, as Foucault comments in relation to the seventeenth century, 'sexual practices had little need of secrecy ... it was a time of direct gestures, shameless discourse, and open transgressions, when anatomies were shown and intermingled at will and knowing children hung about amid the laughter of adults'. Foucault (1981), p. 3.

18. See, for example, Meigs *et al* (1953); Darton (1982) and Townsend (1990).

19.   Townsend (1990), p. 3.
20.   Opie and Opie (1951).
21.   The best known of these may be *The History of the Fairchild Family* (1818) by Mrs Sherwood, with its gruesome threats of hell-fire awaiting the child who did not obey its parents or 'the Great and Dreadful God'.
22.   Tatar (1992), p. 88.
23.   See further for example, Avery (1965); Eyre (1971) and Bratton, (1981).
24.   Rose (1984), pp. 1-2.
25.   Watson (1992), p. 13.
26.   See further Dunbar (1970); Geduld (1971) and Rose (1984).
27.   See Rahn (1984).
28.   Briggs (1989).
29.   See further Marshall (1982), chp. 4.
30.   Quoted in Tatar (1992), p. xvi.
31.   Lurie recalls some of the less inspiring books of her childhood where 'the children and parents in these stories were exactly like the ones I knew, only more boring. They never did anything really wrong, and nothing dangerous or surprising ever happened to them'. Lurie (1990), p. 17.
32.   Jill Barklem's *Brambley Hedge* series from the 1980s demonstrates the attraction of mouse societies and the value of placing ordinary childhood adventures such as disobeying parents, teasing siblings and getting lost within the cosy confines of a mouse's world. Michael Bond's *Paddington*, Rev. W Awdry's *Railway* series and Mary Norton's *Borrowers* provide obvious and well-known examples of this sub genre for the very young.
33.   Batchelor (1989), p. 182.
34.   Quoted in Eyre (1971), p. 89.
35.   Briggs (1989), p. 14.
36.   Lurie (1990). Her classic example is Mark Twain's *Tom Sawyer* (1876) written in irritable reaction to what Twain regarded as 'goody-goody boys' books', that improving literature that was distributed in tremendous volume in the nineteenth century. Beatrix Potter's *Tale of Peter Rabbit* (1901) provides another example with its 'concealed moral' to the effect that 'disobedience and exploration are more fun than good behaviour and not really all that dangerous,

whatever Mother may say'. (Lurie, 1990, p. 95.) Interestingly, Ward considers this story as one his 'jurisprudential texts' but mistakes the moral as being, more simply, that '[t]respass and theft are offences that should not be committed, either by small rabbits or by small children' (Ward (1995), p. 100).

37. As Briggs puts it, 'even in children's books where there is no evident didactic intention, the necessity to simplify is inclined to reveal the nature of social interaction' (Briggs (1989), p. 9).

38. Tatar (1992), p. 8.

39. Tatar (1992), pp. 8-9.

40. A few examples will illustrate the limited range of the messages contained in this genre. There is Tom Tindall in *Tales Uniting Instruction with Amusement* (c.1810) who commits a fairly mild jape with a firework and kills his father. He is left alive to wish he had 'followed his poor father's advice. If he had done so he might now have been at a genteel boarding school ... instead of being a chimney sweeper blind of one eye'. There is also Mrs Sarah Trimmer's heroine Julie Sandford at the end of the eighteenth century who commits a specifically feminine act of rebellion and disobedience in swallowing the ends of her embroidery threads and dies from strangled intestines.

41. Again it only takes a few examples from the many hundreds to make the point that any misdeeds which contravene the stern ethic of absolute obedience lead directly to grisly retribution. Heinrich Hoffmann's *Struwwelpeter* is a German classic of the nineteenth century which has Little Pauline reduced to ashes for playing with matches, Conrad the thumbsucker with his digits cut off by a manical tailor's shears and Hans Head-in-the-Clouds who never watches his step and plunges into icy waters.

42. Quoted in Tatar (1992), p. 47.

43. Tatar (1992), p. 95.

44. Zipes (1983/i), p. 26 (emphasis in original).

45. This debate originated in the 1970s and spilled over into public controversy with such celebrated rows as that which arose when, for example, an Ipswich librarian banned Frank Richard's *Billy Bunter* stories on the grounds that 'nowadays we ... realise excessive fatness is a physical disability like any other'. (See further Tucker (1981), p. 206.)   The same project of vetting books and arguing over

censorship continues now. There are even new books produced as counter propaganda depicting dad strangely aproned at the sink and mum doing blokish things with the car while the rest of the family save the environment.

46. Dixon (1977/i) and (1977/ii).
47. Cadogan and Craig (1976), p. 10.
48. See further Gilbert and Gubar (1979); Rowe (1986); Bottigheimer (1987) and Barzilai (1990).
49. According to Schram (1979) even children's dictionaries and word books reflect this sexism. Action verbs and end-realizing activities in the outside world are depicted using male examples while more passive words and pursuits are illustrated with female examples. As Dixon puts it, 'girls often just are. Boys do - they invent, plan, think about their future careers and are shown as moving into the world. They are confident, outgoing and give instructions (usually to girls)' (Dixon (1977/i), p. 2, emphasis in original).
50. Nelson (1991).
51. Nelson examines a number of school stories - Farrar's *Eric: Or Little by Little* (1858), Kipling's *Stalky and Co.* (1899) - which move beyond the simple cautionary tale to teach the lesson that 'the acquisition of character precedes the acquisition of status - because if one is to avoid power's corruption, one must know through experience that it is virtue rather than glory that matters'. (Nelson (1991), p. 58.) Beyond the school story, books such as Charles Kingsley's *The Water Babies* (1863) are read as attempts to 'unite masculine energy with feminine unselfishness to build the ideal androgynous Christian' while *Peter Pan* (1911) is seen as marking the end of such endeavours of moral exhortation by authors and as serving as 'a prism separating Victorian constellations of childhood, femininity, and morality into their component parts, leaving them free to recombine at will' (pp. 153 and 172).
52. See further for, example Gilbert and Gubar (1979).
53. For example, since the 1973 edition the Oompa-Loompas in Roald Dahl's *Charlie and the Chocolate Factory*, although still pygmies and presented as rather helpless, are no longer black or from Africa. In Enid Blyton's *The Three Golliwogs* the names have been changed in later editions from Golly, Woggie and Nigger to the more acceptable Wiggie, Waggie and Wollie.

54.   Enid Blyton is again an easy target. For example, Watson (1992) complains how she can not tell a story without enemies and they are mostly the poor. Even a book such as Eve Garnett's (1937) which, although intended to provide a realistic setting with which poorer children could identify, perfectly introduces the idea of the deserving and undeserving poor and everyone knowing their place.

55.   Darnton (1985).

56.   Bottigheimer (1987), p. 94. In particular this critic finds 'an entire text of socially sanctioned gender-skewed violent conclusions' (p. 100) and 'a persistent denial of the female voice' (p. 169).

57.   Zipes (1988), p. 116. Warner (1994) stresses how such stories show that behaviour is 'embedded in material circumstances, in the laws of dowry, land tenure, feudal obedience, domestic hierarchies and marital dispositions' (p. xviii-ix) but also admits that they 'show a way to belong' to a wider culture (p. 101).

58.   See further, for example, Campbell (1988).

59.   For example, Fromm (1951) sees there being a fairly rigid system of codes in the tales and interprets these somewhat mechanistically. Dundes (1965) concentrates on anal practices and products for their explanatory power in regard to German culture generally. See also Zipes, (1988) chp. 7 for a hostile review of readings from 'pop psychology'. Feminist critics such as Gilbert and Gubar (1979) and Barzilai (1990) provide radically different interpretations.

60.   (1978).

61.   For instance, the child can be represented in the narrative by different characters or rather different aspects of the child appear in different guises. Generally brothers and sisters help visualize conflicts in the child with Kind/Unkind divisions being played out in different characters. The power of nature, or the instinctive resources of the child, are often represented by a helpful animal. A younger child or simpleton as a hero in a story stands in for inexperience and his or her eventual triumph for maturation. There is also a more technical symbolism where, for example, birds represent the superego, dogs stand in for the ego and the id appears as a frog.

62.   Bettleheim (1978), p. 161.

63.   Bettleheim (1978) p. 5. For example, in relation to *Snow White* Bettleheim argues that 'by camouflaging the oedipal predicaments, or by only subtly intimating the entanglements, fairy stories permit

us to draw our own conclusions when the time is propitious for our gaining a better understanding of these problems' (p. 201).

64. Bettleheim (1978), p. 7 (emphasis in original).

65. Foucault (1977).

66. Lurie (1989) at p. 18. For example she argues, *Jack the Giant Killer* can be seen as a lesson in how to deal with 'the big, stupid, mean, and ugly people you are going to meet in life ... Jack doesn't just zap the giant with a laser gun, because in real life when you meet a bully or an armed mugger or a boss who wants to push you around you probably won't have a laser gun' (p. 25). Jack needs to use his intelligence and powers of invention.

67. Bettleheim (1978) at p. 9.

68. Tatar (1992), p. 90. Indeed, she comments, the effect of this change is that 'children's stories become miniature Aristotelian dramas that secure a child's identification with their protagonists and promote a cathartic effect' (p. 74).

69. Tatar (1992), p. xvii.

70. Foucault (1977).

References

Ariès, P (1962), *Centuries of Childhood*, Jonathan Cape, London.

Avery, G. (1965), *Nineteenth Century Children*, Hodder and Stoughton, London.

Barlow G. and Hill A. (1986), *Video Violence and Children*, St Martins, New York.

Barzilai, S. (1990), 'Reading Snow White: The Mother's Story', *Signs: Journal of Women in Culture and Society*, Vol. 15(3), pp. 515-34.

Batchelor, J. (1989), 'Dodgson, Carroll, and the Emancipation of Alice', in Avery, G. and Briggs, J. (Eds.), *Children and Their Books: A Celebration of the Work of Iona and Peter Opie*, pp. 181-200, Oxford University Press, Oxford.

Belotti, E. (1975), *Little Girls: Social Conditioning and its Effects on Stereotyped Roles of Women during Infancy*, Writers and Readers Publishing Cooperative, London.

Bettleheim, B. (1978), *The Uses of Enchantment: The Meaning and Importance of Fairly Tales*, Penguin, Harmondsworth.

Bottigheimer, R. (1987), *Grimms' Bad Girls and Bold Boys: The Moral and Social Vision of the Tales*, Yale Univeristy Press, New Haven, Conn.

Bratton, J.S. (1981), *The Impact of Victorian Children's Fiction*, Croom Helm, London.

Briggs, J. (1989), 'Reading Children's Books', *Essays in Criticism*, Vol. 34(1), pp. 1-17.

Cadogan, M and Craig, P. (1976), *You're a Brick Angela! A New Look at Girls' Fiction from 1839 to 1975*, Gollanz, London.

Campbell, J. (1988), *The Hero with a Thousand Faces*, Paladin, London.

Darton, H. (1982), *Children's Books in England*. (Third Edition), Cambridge University Press, Cambridge.

Darnton, R. (1985), 'Peasants Tell Tales: The Meaning of Mother Goose', in *The Great Cat Massacre and Other Episodes in French Cultural History*, Penguin, Harmondsworth.

Dixon, B. (1977/i), *Catching Them Young 1: Sex, Race and Class in Children's Fiction*, Pluto, London.

Dixon, B. (1977/ii), *Catching Them Young 2: Political Ideas in Children's Fiction*, Pluto, London.

Dunbar, J. (1970), *J.M. Barrie: The Man Behind the Mask*, Houghton Mifflin, Boston.

Dundes, A. (1965), *The Study of Folklore*, Prentice Hall, Englewood Cliffs.

England, C. (1977), 'Violence in Literature for Children and Young Adults' in *Report of the Royal Commission on Violence in the Communications Industry*, Vol. 4, pp. 115-160, Violence in Print and Music, Royal Commission, Toronto, Canada.

Eyre, F. (1971), *British Children's Books in the Twentieth Century*, Longman, London.

Foucault M. (1977), *Discipline and Punish: The Birth of the Prison*, Penguin, Harmondsworth.

Foucault, M. (1981), *The History of Sexuality - Volume One: An Introduction*, Penguin, Harmondsworth.

Fraser, A. (1966), *A History of Toys*, Weidenfeld and Nicolson, London.

Fromm, E. (1951), *The Forgotten Language: An Introduction to the Understanding of Dreams, Fairy Tales and Myths*, Grove Atlantic., New York.

Geduld, H.M. (1971), *Sir James M Barrie*, Twayne, New York.

Gilbert, S. and Gubar, S. (1979), *The Madwoman in the Attic: The Woman Writer and the Nineteenth-Century Literary Imagination*, Yale University Press, New Haven, Conn.

Gunter, B. and McAleer, J. (1990), *Children and Television: The One Eyed Monster?* Routledge, London.

Houlbrooke, R. (1984), *The English Family 1450-1700*, Longman, London.

Hoyles, M. (1979), 'Childhood in Historical Perspective' in Hoyles, M. (Ed.), *Changing Childhood*, pp. 16-29, Writers and Readers Cooperative, London.

Illich, I. (1973), *Deschooling Society*, Penguin, Harmondsworth.

Lurie, A. (1990), *Don't Tell the Grown-ups: Subversive Children's Literature*, Bloomsbury, London.

Marshall, M. (1982), *An Introduction to the World of Children's Books*, Gower, Aldershot.

Meek, M. (1988), *How Texts Teach What Readers Learn*, Thimble Press, Stroud, Glos.

Meigs, C., Eaton, A., Nesbitt, E. and Viguers, R. (1953), *A Critical History of Children's Literature*, Macmillan, New York.

Nelson, C. (1991), *Boys Will be Girls: The Feminine Ethic and British Children's Fiction 1857-1917*, Rutgers, New Brunswick.

Opie P. and Opie I. (1951), *The Oxford Dictionary of Nursery Rhymes*, Oxford University Press, Oxford.

Pollock, L. (1983), *Forgotten Children: Parent-child relations from 1500-1900*, Cambridge University Press, Cambridge.

Plumb, J. (1972), *In the Light of History*, Allen Lane, London.

Plumb, J. (1977) 'The New World of Children in Eighteenth Century England', *Past and Present*, Vol. 67, pp. 64-93.

Rahn, S. (1984), 'Tailpiece: The Tale of Two Bad Mice', *Children's Literature*, Vol. 12, pp. 78-91.

Rose, J. (1984) *The Case of Peter Pan or the Impossibility of Children's Fiction*, Macmillan, London.

Rowe, K (1986), 'To Spin a Yarn: The Female Voice in Folklore and Fairy Tale', in Bottigheimer, R. (Ed.), *Fairy Tales and Society: Illusion, Allusion, and Paradigm*, pp. 53-74, University of Pennsylvania Press, Philadelphia.

Schram, B. (1979), 'D is for Dictionary, S is for Stereotyping', in Sinton, J. (Ed.), *Racism and Sexism in Children's Books*, pp. 126-34, Readers and Writers Cooperative, London.

Signorielli, N. and Gerbner, G. (1988), *Violence and Terror in the Mass Media: An Annotated Bibliography*, Greenwood Press, New York.

Stone, L. (1977) *The Family, Sex and Marriage in England 1500-1800*, Weidenfeld and Nicolson, London.

Tatar, M. (1992) *Off With Their Heads: Fairy Tales and the Culture of Childhood*, Princeton University Press, Princeton, New Jersey.

Thomas, K. (1989) 'Children in Early Modern England', in Avery, G. and Briggs, J. (Eds.), *Children and Their Books: A Celebration of the Work of Iona and Peter Opie*, pp. 45-78, Oxford University Press, London.

Townsend, J.R. (1990), *Written for Children*, (Fifth Edition), The Bodley Head, London.

Tucker, N. (1981), *The Child and the Book: A Psychological and Literary Exploration*, Cambridge University Press, Cambridge.

Ward, I. (1995), *Law and Literature: Possibilities and Perspectives,* Cambridge University Press, Cambridge.

Warner, M. (1994), *From the Beast to the Blonde: On Fairytales and their Tellers*, Chatto and Windus, London.

Watson, V. (1992) 'The Possibilities of Children's Fiction', in Styles, M. Bearne, M. and Watson, V. (Eds.), *After Alice: Exploring Children's Literature*, pp. 11-24, Cassell, London.

Zipes, J (1983/i), *Fairy Tales and the Art of Subversion: The Classical Genre for Children and the Process of Civilisation*, Heinemann, London.

Zipes, J. (1983/ii), *The Trials and Tribulations of Little Red Riding Hood: Versions of the Tale in Sociocultural Context*, Bergen Garvery, Mass.

Zipes, J. (1988), *The Brothers Grimm: From Enchanted Forests to the Modern World*, Routledge, London.

6 Crime and Punishment: Representations of Female Killers in Law and Literature

MARIE FOX

Introduction

This article focuses on stories told of female killers in law and literature. Elsewhere, Christine Bell and I have argued for the need to move feminist debate about women killers on from its current focus on women who kill abusive men, and who are thus essentially sympathetic. Outside of this context we argued that there is a dearth of (legal) academic discussion of violent women who kill. No feminist script exists for legal scholars who wish to examine the case of violent women who kill outside the battered woman scenario. Cameron and Fraser have gone further, arguing that no script at all exists for the violent woman who kills. In contrast, it is my contention that the problem in talking about violent women is precisely that our discourse concerning women who kill is pre-scripted. The continued lack of feminist analysis of the phenomenon of the female killer[1] exists alongside a proliferation of other discourses about her, which do provide a powerfully constraining script. The myths and stereotypes on which it is based are derived from a number of disciplines:

> [c]riminal anthropology, sexology, and psychoanalysis shared in the complex historical construction of the female offender. Each in its own way linked criminality with deviant sexualities. These discourses overlapped and sometimes contradicted each other.[2]

In this essay it is my contention that literature also has powerfully shaped our discourse concerning female killers. Thus, the problem for feminists is not writing a new script but confronting and revising the stories which already exist about women who kill. Given the long history of double censure of violent women for defying both the criminal law and the natural law of femininity,[3] the weight of ideological baggage makes it difficult to avoid falling into a well worn mode of reportage. However the process of contesting such discourse can be a empowering one: 'women's power

145

to talk back is enhanced by our self-conscious and strategic revisions of the stories that have been used against us'.[4]

In this paper, I want to examine existing discourse on female killers as it applies to the cases of five British female killers. It is my argument that the dominant discourse which emerged in each case powerfully influenced the punishment imposed, which in each case was considered controversial. Given the difficulties of undermining this discourse in real legal cases, and drawing on the educative ambitions of the Law and Literature movement[5] my aim is to ask whether fictional representations of the woman killer have anything to offer the project of changing the terms on which debate concerning violent women takes place.

The script

Currently discussion of women killers is constrained by two dominant scripts about female criminality which are largely derived from a conjunction of literary and criminological sources. Cameron and Fraser argue that our 'stock stories' about female crime both have literary antecedents rooted in the characters of Lady Macbeth (the evil unsexed monster) and Pygmalion (the dupe who is easily manipulated for love).[6] Similar narratives underpin much criminological debate about female crime. As Smart has argued, modern criminology continues to be plagued by ideologies derived from classical criminologists, in particular Lombroso and Ferraro - founders of the biological-positivist school.[7] Because women were perceived as less congenitally inclined to criminal activity, both 'true' and 'occasional' criminal types were rare amongst women. However the true 'born female criminal was perceived to have all the criminal qualities of the male plus all the worst characteristics of women, namely cunning, spite and deceitfulness'.[8] This depiction dovetails neatly with the Lady Macbeth model of the female offender as more fundamentally evil than any male offender. Just as Lady Macbeth was unsexed by her crime, real female criminals 'must have overcome their constituted nature as conformist women ... those few who are real criminals must have had to be extra deviant to clear the hurdle of conformity'.[9] Similarly, Lombroso's depiction of the 'occasional' female offender resonates with the Pygmalion model. As Smart characterises her,

[s]he was ... held to be weak-willed and easily led into crime, the performance of which was frequently abysmal, leading to instant arrest. Her inadequacy in this field was held to be a reflection of the inferiority of women as a whole and her role in the commission of an offence, generally as an accomplice or someone else's tool, was seen as fitting to her 'natural' role.[10]

Hart contends that Lombroso and Ferraro '[b]oth made huge contributions to the vast project of patrolling the borders of femininity by marking off the normal woman from her deviant sisters'[11] in exactly the way which I would suggest literary representations of female killers do.

Beverley Brown has criticised both the routine feminist denunciation of Lombroso, and the idea that the biologism[12] enshrined in traditional criminology has any real impact on the legal disposition of female offenders. She suggests that the relationship between theory and practice is usually the other way round.[13] However, whilst we currently know too little about how exactly attitudes are transmitted to posit a direct causal relationship, it does seem reasonable to suggest that biologistic notions in criminological theory have been popularised in other contexts and have some influence on judicial and jury decision-making. This may be particularly the case where the media so inflame popular opinion that judicial or political attitudes to sentencing are influenced by public outrage.[14] While criminology may impact within the academy, literature has popularised criminological models of female crime. It has helped give criminological stereotypes of female killers the widespread currency they enjoy and helped define the boundaries of acceptable feminity. The two dominant scripts in literary and criminological discourses are supplemented by the even older script that the criminal woman must be mentally defective.[15] Hence the violent female offender is either inherently bad, mad or not really a criminal at all.

The killers

In this paper I wish to examine how these scripts operate in controlling the stories told of five British female killers whose crimes were committed in the years 1955-1991: Ruth Ellis, Myra Hindley, Sara Thornton, Beverley Allitt and Susan Christie. Kathleen Daly has argued that we

should be sceptical of the research on accused women when it appears they were chosen for their dramatic or celebrated-case qualities ... Such research may bring the words and experience of formerly silenced women to light, but it also contributes to the sensationalizing of crime and punishment.[16]

Although their notoriety was largely my criterion for selecting cases, I would argue that it is a justifiable focus. It is because their stories have been sensationalised in both law, and a now extensive literature, that these women have come to bear the weight of the cultural stereotypes and preconceptions about women who kill. My choice was thus motivated partly by the fact that they have become 'symptomatic' images. Suzanna Walters has defined a 'symptomatic text' as one which speaks to larger cultural anxieties and issues surrounding women, men and representation, citing as examples films like *Fatal Attraction* and *Thelma and Louise*.[17] Following her, I would argue that the stories generated by these five women, and their enduring status as cultural icons speak to our cultural anxiety around dangerous femininities. I agree with Walters that the interesting question is why they *became* symptomatic. The symptomatic texts which she examines plug into current anxieties about sexual difference and the place of women and men in society and trouble the borderlines that contemporary popular critical discourse codes as fragile. Similarly, I would argue that the cultural anxiety and moral panics[18] engendered by these women killers reveal similar anxieties.[19]

I am also interested in these women because, with the possible exception of Sara Thornton, the complexity of their cases has meant that feminist theory, like law, has been unable to adequately accommodate them. My selection also demonstrates how differently they have been served by those who purport to tell their stories, given that opportunities for them to speak on their own behalf are strictly circumscribed. Cameron and Frasers' argument concerning the absence of any script for speaking of female killers is largely based on the fact that we do not know what she herself thinks - there is no way of her own story being told. Of course this is not unique to the female killer, Anne Worrall has suggested that this is a feature common to all female offenders.[20] In court their stories are unable to be told as they are controlled by the lawyers and other experts who may well be unable to transcend the influence of myths about violent women.[21]

The enduring nature of popular stereotypes about violent women which operates in the vacuum created by their silence have a two-fold function. On the one hand they partially determine the fate of the women concerned, in that narratives in both law and literature utilise punishment to effect a closure. However, the second and broader aim of these representations is the policing and containment of all women.[22] The vision of idealised femininity which most of the 'True Crime' stories construct shapes us all - what emerges from them is a typology of the female criminal which has implications not only for how violent women will be tried and sentenced, but for all women.

The literary genealogy of images of women who kill

If the voices of female killers are muted in law, their images have proliferated in books about their cases. Phyllis Chessler has bemoaned the absence of both heroic and villainous female literary characters:

> few pre-feminists have ever dared to imagine the lives of women killers and outlaws. Not one character comes to mind: no female Raskolnikov, Meurseult, or Igger Thomas. How could so many great writers have resisted this temptation.[23]

However, contrary to her assertion, there has in fact been a long-standing literary fascination with the woman killer. The prototypical fictional female killers go back earlier than the Jacobean tragedies, ranging from Greek tragedies, through biblical heroines, Renaissance drama, and then to Gothic romance, Victorian literature and beyond. Throughout the ages images of fallen/criminal women show continuities of meaning between the historical definition of women as witches and contemporary representations of women's deviance.[24]

Given my contention that such representations are essentially about policing women and defining femininity, it is unsurprising that Victorian literature contains the genesis of many of our contemporary concerns about violent women. This is largely due to the conjunction of a number of themes in a Victorian society obsessed by sexual morality, and debates concerning the 'new woman' which seemed to run counter to the strong familial ideology of the era. These themes coincided with a new theoretical interest in crime and its causes, and the linkage of female biology with disease.[25] To some extent they are echoed at the end of the current millennium - in particular the connection between female crime and sexual deviance.[26] As Elaine Showalter argues,

> [w]hat was most alarming to the *fin de siecle* was that sexuality and sex roles might no longer be contained within the neat and permanent borderlines of

gender categories. Men and women were not as clearly identified and separated as they had been.[27]

Once again this is a continuing fear; symptomatic texts like contemporary films are preoccupied with precisely the same concerns. However, in the Victorian era such a realisation was particularly threatening to a society which rigidly differentiated women from men by treating women as morally superior, but intellectually, psychologically and biologically inferior to men.[28]

As Morris argues, no women disturbed such conceptions more than those who murdered; particularly as 'responses to female crime were deeply embedded in an even more complex value structure, at the heart of which was the highly artificial construct of ideal womanhood'.[29] Their crimes 'created a sense of dread out of all proportion to the actual threat that they posed to society'.[30] However, as Hart notes 'these representations reached the peak of their popularity during a period when the eruption of violence by women was perceived as a real threat to the social order'.[31] This threat was heightened by the fact that female readers voraciously consumed narratives of criminal woman and flocked to the courtrooms where they were tried: '"the female element" was showing a supportive identification with women accused of adultery and murder'.[32] Efforts were made to contain this threat by representing these crimes as rooted, not in society, but in the aberrations of the individual woman, a theme which ran through the journal articles, charges to juries and crime histories of the century,[33] a trend which continues to this day

Although there is a complex inter-relationship between novels and the legal fabric of their society,[34] it was the novels which contained more realism about women's circumstances and motivations than the Victorian crime histories.[35] The novels challenged the dominant view of female criminality as rooted in biological explanations,[36] and domesticated crime by portraying female killers as rebelling against the restraints of their male-dominated familial and economic lives - in particular their unhappy marriages.[37] In fact, as Morris notes, almost all female killers in Victorian literature commit more or less justifiable homicide.[38] To this extent the Victorian novelists were remarkably progressive for their times. Yet the fictional woman who kills, despite flouting societal expectations, continues to operate in a way which is oddly feminine. Her violence is located in the home, and she strikes back using non-masculine weapons at a man who has abused her. Again this seems to echo criminological accounts of crimes of violence committed by women, where 'the choice of victim and the *modus operandi* of the offence are still in keeping with the "feminine" stereotype'.[39] Furthermore, feminist legal discourse adopts a similar focus on violence precipitated by domestic abuse. Indeed, as Daly argues, battered women who kill have attracted so much feminist and media attention that one might think they represent the average female defendant.[40] Such accounts often present the woman as 'driven to kill'. Not only is she thus portrayed as lacking agency and intent but her victim is depicted as villainous rather than innocent. Hence our images of women who kill have changed little in the past century.[41] What has eventually changed is our attitude to punishing them. Whereas ultimately in Victorian novels women were unable to escape the shackles of gender-role expectations, so that their murders, but perhaps more importantly their 'flouting of conventional decorum and subservience ... put [them] outside the pale, doubly damned',[42] we are only now beginning to recognise that the actions of women who kill in such circumstances may be viewed as powerful and even rational, rather than deviant or pathological.

The 'True Crime' stories

Such recognition still has to compete with older narratives. In examining narratives about my subjects, I take as my source the 'True Crime' style accounts which each of these women have spawned. 'True Crime' accounts now appear to represent a separate genre of writing,[43] and, at least since the publication of Truman Capote's *In Cold Blood* in 1959, one which has some claims to the status of literature. However its ambit remains difficult to define.[44] Not all true stories about crime fit within the genre. Its content is the biography of the violent criminal, whose actions are presented in an acontextual way. The narrative structure of 'True Crime' accounts thus reflects the individualistic methodology of the criminal law, which is unsurprising given that many of them take the trial transcript as a source. They also draw heavily upon traditional criminological theory concerning women offenders and, given the huge audience for these books, have surely helped to popularise it. Hence, not only are women muted in court, but afterwards their stories are told by men writing their accounts of the 'True Crime'.[45] Aside from Sara Thornton's case which fits uneasily into the genre, virtually all the 'True Crime' accounts of the other four women unquestionably accept some version of the dominant stock stories and appear to have little aim other than sensationalizing the crimes and pathologising the woman in question. They thus have traditionally fallen into the profoundly anti-feminist script which I have argued is already written and contribute to it in a more sustained form than the film and press accounts which also draw on it.

In 'True Crime' stories, as in Victorian times, women are contained by being marked off as different and labelled sadistic much more readily than men.[46] This is particularly true of Myra Hindley. More than any criminal this century she has been singled out for vilification and represented as the embodiment of evil.[47] Hindley was convicted in 1966, along with her lover, Ian Brady, of the murders of a ten year old girl and of a 17 year old youth. In addition she was convicted of harbouring Brady knowing he had killed a twelve year old boy. One of the most shocking aspects of the case was photographic evidence depicting the girl - Lesley Ann Downey - in pornographic poses, and a tape recording in which she is heard pleading to be released. Brady also photographed Hindley on the graves of the two children. As Goodman contends they were '*voyeurs, ecouteurs*, of their own corruption'.[48] She received two life sentences and a sentence of seven years to run concurrently.[49] In 1987 Hindley confessed to the fact that they had murdered two other young people and buried them on the moors outside Manchester. The tabloid press continue to be fascinated by her,[50] so not surprisingly she has spawned more 'True Crime' books than any other female murderer. As Birch points out, the books written of the case have been particularly influential in terms of how Hindley has come to be represented because at the time of the trial the tabloid press was in its infancy.[51] As that press has flourished:

> More and more, she is depicted as the arch-female sadist - even by writers who doubt that she herself killed the pair's victims ... Few male sexual killers - whose pleasure lies not in watching, but in doing - attract the virulent hatred Myra Hindley does (even Brady is not so viciously and constantly reviled). Whatever other crimes she may have committed Myra Hindley has offended against standards of femininity and has been punished accordingly.[52]

To some extent the three main scripts - the wicked woman, dupe and madwoman - are present in most of the five cases, and indeed at the time of Hindley's trial it was probably the Pygmalion story which predominated. For example, Marchbanks contended:

She was patient and kind and the sort of girl any of the mothers in the district would trust implicitly and would encourage to take an interest in their children. They remembered her as a toddler and the loving care she lavished on her dolls, the fondness and gentleness she showed when she played with her grandmother's dog. She was a likeable girl, a shade more responsible than most her age.[53]

Many of the 'True Crime' accounts aim at resolving this contradiction and the obvious solution was to cast her in role of dupe, as Brady unsuccessfully attempted to do at the trial. Under cross-examination he said that his views always prevailed overs hers '[b]ecause she was my typist in the office and this tended to wrap over ... She argued so little - I had to tell her to argue at times. When she did, it had the opposite effect, it was worse'.[54] Other writers also point to the change in Hindley when she and Brady became inseparable in the spring of 1962.[55] This Pygmalion story has also been perpetuated by psychiatrists and her supporters such as Lord Longford and David Astor, and in the 'True Crime' accounts is perhaps the prevalent story:

> He substituted a crazy hotchpotch of evil ideas in place of the workaday attitudes on which Myra had been weaned in Gorton. She committed her crimes (whatever they were) entirely under the influence of Brady.[56]

However in the 30 years since her trial this depiction has been submerged underneath a virulent tabloid campaign, especially in Manchester, to portray Hindley as the dominant partner. A number of factors have contributed to this (re)constitution of Hindley as worse than Brady. It has its roots in essentialist views of women:

> Fear underlies ... anxiety about the case ... it is a fear generated by a failure to comprehend why it happened in the first place. Above all, the incomprehension about Myra Hindley's role: how could a woman offend against her protective maternal instinct that was nurtured into the genes in a process of evolution that spanned a period of two million years?[57]

Overwhelmingly the hatred of the victims' relatives, particularly their mothers, is directed at Hindley rather than Brady, at least in part due to the shock at the time that a woman could be implicated in such crimes. However, even in accounts where Brady is deemed to have been the one who perverted her, Hindley is often implicitly blamed for her susceptibility to corruption.[58]

Since their imprisonment, Brady has receded from view whereas Hindley's visibility has increased. Her campaign for parole, which began only seven years after her conviction[59] has contributed to her demonization. Since breaking off her relationship with Brady, which also contradicted a crucial element of the Pygmalion characterization,[60] she has maintained that her role was secondary to Brady's and failed to display remorse. Brady, by contrast, has accepted that he is destined never to be released and when he was transferred to Park Lane secure hospital for psychiatric treatment in 1985 this official acknowledgment of his mental illness implied that after all she was somehow the stronger of the two. Interestingly, in view of the nature of their crimes, there was little suggestion of madness at the time of the trial, except in Harrison's suggestion that she must have suffered from *folie à deux* - a condition where one individual's mental illness communicates itself to a lover or close relative. As Cameron and Fraser suggest, this adds a clinical gloss to the Pygmalion theory,[61] but was largely due to a desire to explain her complicity.

As the other two stories have increasingly been downplayed, the overwhelming impression of Hindley has become her evil monstrous nature as exemplified in the photograph taken at the time of her arrest, which has 'become detached from its subject ... [and] exceeds the crimes of two individuals at a particular place and time'.[62] A similar image is strikingly conveyed in Johnson's account of her at her trial:

On the whole [Ian Brady] looks ordinary. Myra Hindley does not. Sturdy in build and broad-buttocked ... she could have served a nineteenth-century Academy painter as a model for Clytemnestra; but sometimes she looks more terrible, like one of Fuseli's nightmare women drawn giant-sized, elaborately coiffed ... Her hair is styled into a huge puff-ball, with a fringe across her brows. At the beginning of the trial it was rinsed to a lilac shade, now it is melon-yellow. The stye is far too massive for the wedge-shaped face; in itself, it bears an uneasy suggestion of fetishism. But it is the lines of this porcelained face which are extraordinary. Brows, eyes, mouth are all quite straight, precisely parallel. The fine nose is straight, too, except for a very faint downward turn at the tip, just as the chin turns very faintly upward. She will have a nutcracker face one day ... Now, in the dock, she has a great strangeness, and the kind of authority one might expect to find in a woman guard of a concentration camp.[63]

This was the beginning of the myth making of Myra Hindley as a monster.[64] Given such representations it is not surprising that, against all the evidence, Hindley has been (re)constituted as the dominant partner:

> those who saw Myra in the witness box agree that she was an intelligent, probably tougher character than her lover ... Was Myra in fact the dominant partner: When she heard his views and boasts did she, *woman-like*, say in effect, 'Let's not dream and indulge in these fantasies. Let's do something about them. Let's make them real.'[65]

In her case other sub-themes support the dominant construction. As well as emphasising her monstrous and masculine appearance, her sexual deviance is emphasized. Although she appears to have been a virgin until she met Brady,[66] their sado-masochistic relationship and consumption of both pornographic and Nazi materials are detailed.[67] In Ritchie's biography her lesbian prison affairs are extensively documented.[68]

Ruth Ellis's story is also dominated by the Lady Macbeth model. In contemporary accounts, as well as the biography of her by Robert Hancock, the Pygmalion story is submerged under the Lady Macbeth imagery. For example, in the aftermath of her shooting of her unfaithful lover David Blakely, Hancock emphasises her composure, her lack of emotion - she was 'unbelievably calm and detached',[69] and capable of telling 'sustained, deliberate lies'.[70] This depiction is supported by her ambitious social-climbing: '[t]he pattern was locking together, Ruth was not going to be poor, she had the clothes and she was going to make something of her life. If it entailed, as it did, becoming a prostitute who worked the clubs ... it was unimportant'.[71] Her lack of conformity to appropriate roles is emphasised. She is a failed wife whose marriage, in which we are told she was the stronger character,[72] split up in less than a year,[73] partly due to her 'quite unreasoning jealousy'.[74] Even worse, she is a bad mother, who has had an abortion.[75]

> Ruth went home to see baby Andy when she could, but the all-night parties and the weekends in the country clubs and horse-brass pubs in the Kent and Surrey fringes of London took most of her time.[76]

Similarly even though Myra Hindley has never been a mother she is depicted as antithetical to the ideal:

'Shame', said the women, who stood in groups, protective arms around their children, staring at the windows of the town hall, their eyes burning with resentment. It was Myra Hindley that the women wanted to get their hands on, the woman who had affronted their sex and their sense of motherhood.[77]

As with accounts of Hindley, the spectre of lesbianism shadows Ellis, even though Hancock's evidence for this is ludicrously speculative, dependent on a photograph in which

> Ruth is wearing a faintly lesbian outfit of a severe white jacket whose neck is filled by a silk scarf knotted in that strange square-fronted way then favoured by homosexuals,[78]

and the fact that '[t]o encourage perverts she kept hand-drawn, highly coloured sets of out-of-perspective pornographic pictures printed on white cardboard. Some of these dealt with the relations between the Lesbian headmistress of a girls' school and her pupils'. From this he concludes that '[p]erhaps Ruth was a lesbian, as she knew plenty of them'.[79]

In the cases of both Ellis and Hindley their appearance at the trials worked as a disadvantage in a way that would be inconceivable for a male criminal.

> As the date for her appearance at the Old Bailey approached Ruth was able to ease the tension of waiting by concentrating ... on a vital issue ... her hair was going very dark well above the roots and this, if not treated, would destroy the cool blond image she wanted so much to show when she appeared in court ... She is dressed in a black two-piece with a white blouse; her face is thinner than when she appeared at Hampstead in April but she smiles reassuringly at the blue-uniformed wardress who accompanies her into the box. Nobody will be able to say that Ruth Ellis is not playing her part competently.[80]

Precisely the same theme was to resurface 11 years later at Hindley's trial:

> Her hair had been carefully rinsed a lilac-blue before the trial. The colour would be washed out by the end of the three weeks, but her hair had been recently bleached and there was no sign of dark roots. She listened to the charges against her with blue hair and heard her sentence with bright yellow hair ... She remained impassive and stony-faced almost throughout, only once or twice sharing secret smiles with Brady when something was said that amused them.[81]

Both eschewed the obligatory feminine role of repentance.[82]   Equally a failure to display the requisite repentance seemed to be a factor in many commentators' views of Sara Thornton.[83]   By contrast, much was made of Susan Christie's repentance at her trial, with the inference that it impacted on the outcome of her case.   Christie had killed her lover's wife by luring her to a forest and cutting her throat with a butcher's boning knife - a crime which contrasted starkly with the appearance of its author in court:

> Only an inch over five feet tall and wearing no makeup or lipstick, Christie seemed much younger than her twenty-three years. With her head bowed, her hair covering her forehead, shielding her eyes, she appeared timid and vulnerable, even coy. And she was visibly trembling ... In the dock the jury saw a subdued, insecure, disorientated young woman.[84]

In Christie's case, a strategy of pleading diminished responsibility, coupled with defence emphasis on her role as shy Northern Irish virgin,[85] succeeded in reducing the conviction to manslaughter, for which a five year sentence was initially imposed. However, the power of the Lady Macbeth image, especially when linked to *Fatal Attraction* rhetoric which dominated media reporting of the case, was sufficiently powerful to impact upon the public and feed into the appellate level decision to increase her sentence to nine years.

By contrast, Beverley Allitt's case represents a yet more extreme case of the media's hostility to 'unfeminine' women. Allitt was convicted of the murder of four children, the attempted murder of three others and of causing grievous bodily harm to six more children on the ward where she worked in Grantham and Kesteven hospital and sentenced to life imprisonment. In her case alone there was no trace of the Pygmalion story. She acted alone and perverted her training as a nurse. With much emphasis on her masculine appearance and lesbianism, the Lady Macbeth imagery dominated, and competed with a less dominant script of mental abnormality linked to the possibility that she was suffering from Munchausen's Disease by Proxy.[86] Claims of the existence of the disease did offer an explanation of the inexplicable and a way out of having to accept that a woman had committed these crimes intentionally on her own. As Naylor notes, press coverage of her case also 'reflects anxieties of ... woman as most dangerous when she puts on the soothing appearance of femininity whilst consciously betraying that image'.[87]   The portrayal of the villainous woman as lesbian is a particularly significant discursive tactic.[88]   As Hart has argued, '[l]esbian identity has served many functions, among them as a site where women's aggression has been displaced'[89] - a woman who is perceived as aggressive carries with her the shadow of the lesbian.[90] Again this harks back to the criminology of Lombroso - the idea that the born female offender 'retains the sex of a female but acquires the gender attributes of masculinity'.[91] Although Allitt is the only one of my subjects to clearly identify as a lesbian, as we have seen the strategy of displacing aggression unto lesbians has also operated in the cases of Hindley and Ellis.[92] This, combined with Hollywood's current fascination with violent, transgressive relationships between women may, as Romney argues, reveal more about male fantasies than the female psyche.[93]

The other point worth noting is the manner in which women offenders are infantilised. Glaringly absent from the 'True Crime' stories, as from classical criminology[94] is any conception of the female criminal as politically motivated - only male criminals can be justified in their actions. Legitimately or illegitimately, criminality is constantly a verification of masculinity. As Smart notes, criminological theories 'invoke biological "causes"' in accounting for female criminality 'rather than considering the possibility that criminal action may be cognitively rational action'.[95] In Thornton's case alone is there any trace of a woman who acted rationally given the circumstances in which she found herself. She stabbed her drunken husband to death after he threatened to kill her and her daughter, with a knife she allegedly sharpened to protect herself. In her case a story of how his abuse amounted to cumulative provocation and how the legal requirement that her reaction be immediate discriminated against women permeated the broadsheet newspapers,[96] largely thanks to the efforts of feminist pressure groups like *Women for Justice*. It is also told in a sustained form in Nadel's biography, which is unique amongst the accounts considered in offering a social context for the woman's crime and thus challenging the stock stories.[97] Ironically, in view of the fact that Sara Thornton's case has been perhaps the most high profile of all the 'battered women' cases in Britain,[98] she herself does not fit the particular script which the law is reluctantly beginning to endorse.[99] However her story, which has been taken up in fictionalized accounts, has had tremendous power in changing attitudes to women who kill in these circumstances.[100]

Outside of this one account, however, there is no sense of a challenge to the dominant stories. Yet a different story could be told about all of the other women. For instance, in Ruth Ellis's case, Helena Kennedy has postulated an alternative version:

Her feelings when Blakely finally dumped her, aided and abetted by his circle of friends, were never fully explored ... Every sense of herself as an outsider, beyond the pale of his social class, must have been reinforced, and her head must have been buzzing with visions of Blakely with another woman. None of this reached across the courtroom to the jury. Her irrationality was explained as jealousy, the fury of the woman scorned, rather than as the response of someone who has been systematically abused, exploited and humiliated.[101]

The class factors undercutting the case were clearly crucial, but were never acknowledged.[102] Thus, faced with the prejudices of the men who spoke on her behalf, a very partial account of Ruth Ellis's actions emerged in court.[103] As Kennedy's account demonstrates, there is a much fuller version of Ruth Ellis's story to be told. Had this reached the jury, notwithstanding the law at that time, Ellis would almost certainly have been spared from the gallows. Similarly, Susan Christie's actions in killing her lover's wife with a butcher's knife could be situated in the context of a conservative Northern Irish society and a reactionary army context which left her disempowered *vis-à-vis* her lover and left her isolated with no-one to confide in or counsel her.[104] Beverley Allitt was a nurse who killed four children in her care and harmed nine others. Her story could be rendered differently by focusing on the context of the run-down and demoralised NHS ward in which she worked, where she was inadequately trained and supervised.[105] In Hindley's case, the 'True Crime' writers who do not write her off as inherently evil, depict her as falling under an evil spell, yet as Cameron and Fraser have argued their relationship is not so very different from the acceptable pattern of heterosexual relationships.[106] None of these alternative accounts would serve to fully excuse (much less justify or condone) the women's crimes, and indeed law is unable to take such factors on board, but by providing an alternative reading they might further understanding of it and offer a better informed background for the imposition of punishment.

Punishing women who kill

My argument thus far has been that feminist legal theory, has failed to find a way to discuss, let alone accommodate, the female killer. Yet it is important to address these cases because, with the possible exception of Allitt, all these women have been harshly punished by the legal system. In each case their failure to live up to idealized constructions of femininity at least partly condemned them to that fate. The narratives told in legal cases and 'True Crime' accounts lead logically to the imposition of punishment.[107] Feminist scholars have reached a general impasse in talking not only in relation to female killers but about punishment,[108] although there are now signs that a new feminist theorisation of punishment is beginning to emerge.[109] Whilst there has been some feminist work on deconstructing images of Myra Hindley[110] it has not addressed the issue of how she should be punished.[111] The issue of punishment is exceptionally difficult in these cases where the collective effect of the stereotypes has been silencing. To even try to contest the Lady Macbeth/monster stereotype, or to canvass the issue of parole is to be drawn into a media confrontation with the victims' families. It becomes questionable whether it is even possible to adopt an objective or dispassionate stance in such cases.

The upshot is that law and feminist theory are confronted with two related impasses. Kathryn Abrams has argued that when

> the legal system has reached an impasse, the law has progressed to the limits of what it can accomplish, given an ingrained conception of a particular problem; before it can move again, it is necessary that some reconceptualisation take place.[112]

Given the constraints of the legal process it would seem that the courts are not the best forum for seeking to effect such a reconceptualisation. Feminist legal practitioners have pointed to the problem of experimenting in court when real-life women's lives are at stake.[113] The courts are unlikely to be ready for a new narrative until it gains some currency in the general culture. One example of how such a process has already impacted on law in the United Kingdom is in relation to miscarriages of justice. Such cases were not exposed by effective appeals procedures within the court system, but by journalistic appeals to a wider public, whose support was engaged in trying to reverse the official determination of guilt. Whilst literature may lack the immediate impact of political or newspaper campaigns to bring about legal change, one of the important insights of feminist legal scholarship has been a growing awareness of the transformative value of literary narrative in its relation to legal narrative.[114] Ward has argued that literature can be educative,[115] and it certainly offers new ways of thinking and has the capacity to generate empathy.[116] Thus it is not surprising that feminist narrative scholars have attempted to reconceptualize problems like sexual harassment through the use of narrative. Such a recourse to narrative may be even more necessary in these cases, where it is not only the law, but feminist theory which has reached an impasse. As Heilbrun contends the novel 'gives women the chance to transform narrative and anecdote into jurisprudence'.[117]

The changing shape of the 'True Crime' accounts

One means of using literature to effect change is to utilise the 'True Crime' format, which is already obsessed with violent women and offers a huge audience. And there are signs that feminism is having an impact on the genre. In addition to Nadel's book there is also Artley's moving account of the Thompson sisters who killed their abusive father;[118] a recent collection on the stories of women who killed as a result of domestic violence[119] and some feminist influenced accounts of American 'serial killer' Aileen Wournos.[120] All of these, in common with feminist writing, are contextualized, and present a more complex and nuanced portrait of their subjects than any of the other books in this genre. They are thus challenging to the legal status quo in a way which all the other 'True Crime' accounts are not. They also broaden the framework for debate by calling society, as well as the criminal justice system to account. Whilst there is no guarantee that the narratives which feminist scholars tell of these lives is any more accurate,[121] feminist writers have a different agenda. They aim to contest the accepted narratives and frequently to posit law reform,[122] whereas 'True Crime' accounts traditionally accept the imposition of legal punishment. They thus endorse the legal status quo. However there are indications, in the books cited above, that the genres of 'True Crime' and 'Women's Studies' are beginning to converge.

There are, however, limitations to this format. The 'True Crime' genre is inherently restrictive, as books which seek to contextualize the actions of the offender lose their sensationalist appeal, and also their reassuring conclusion. Moreover because the subject matter is an individual crime, such literature functions best to produce a change where it can be linked to a specific legal or evidential reform - as in the case of Sara Thornton.[123] Although one of the central insights of feminist narrative scholarship is that it is precisely these vivid, particularised accounts which do generate empathy and sympathy so that even 'one woman's story has the potential to force the recognition of a need for ... transformation',[124] such transformations work most effectively when the subject is broadly sympathetic. It is much more difficult to see how a crime like Hindley's or Christie's can be harnessed to explicit law reform proposals - in Birch's words, '[t]here is no easy way to appropriate [Hindley's] actions for the purpose of advancing the cause of women'.[125]   One senses that Nadel's account of Sara Thornton is constrained by being largely factually based - the book has the tone of a vindication of Thornton's actions. Unlike Kennedy's re-telling of Ellis's story, it does not quite render Sara Thornton a victim - she emerges as more of a survivor - but there are traces of the victim story. To some extent 'factional' accounts circumvent this problem, for example Susan Brownmiller's account of the Hedda Nussbaum case - *Waverley Place* - which is written as a fictional account, or Emlyn Williams' account of the Moors murders which is also fictionalized with invented dialogue and scenarios. However such 'factional' accounts cannot depart too far from the known facts of the case. If the 'True Crime' genre is too limited and too reflective of existing law, fiction offers greater possibilities. Not only does it offer an arena for feminist experimentation, but given that historically our images of violent women have been powerfully shaped by the novel, and that the history of legal and fictional representations of violent women are intertwined, it offers a forum for shaping representations of female killers, but this time from a feminist perspective.   Moreover, because it is not, like feminist 'True Crime' accounts linked to law reform, it is better suited to the more diffuse aim of changing the terms of the debate in such a way that will permit justice to be done.

However, in relation to punishment the literary antecedents are not promising. Certainly even though Victorian literature did challenge very restrictive biologically-rooted notions of female crime, it ultimately reinforced law's censure of transgressive women:

> the Victorian novelists were not only members of a society at best unsympathetic and often openly hostile to unconventional women, but they were unable to disguise the threat to stability such women posed. As a result, few violent women are allowed to live after their crimes, and those who do not are restored to social grace.[126]

A good example is Lady Audley in Mary Elizabeth Braddon's *Lady Audley's Secret*. As Hart points out, she is 'a rare example of a Victorian woman who intends to kill with calm, premeditative deliberation and fails to repent with any sincerity'.[127]   However the cost of her perversity, like Lady Macbeth's, is madness, which forms 'both the problem and the solution. It accounts for the woman's aggression *and* recuperates it. Victorian audiences were accustomed to the spectacle of madness to recuperate the evil women'.[128] Thus both literature and law effect a closure which maintains the boundaries of society against dangerous sexualities. The options open to violent fictional women were conformity or madness.

One more promising precedent is the development of feminist lesbian fiction which was instrumental in changing images of lesbians.[129] Clearly the issues are significantly different. In the case of lesbian literature its aim was to shape an identity and bring about a community of lesbian women. However, the voices of both lesbians and women who kill have been silenced in law and there is some commonality in many of the stigmatizing myths perpetrated about lesbians and violent women. Zimmerman argues that lesbian novels were invaluable in revising stereotypes of the lesbian which had been prevalent in literature and other discourses:

> Fiction is a particularly useful medium through which to shape a new lesbian consciousness, for fiction, of all literary forms, makes the most complex and detailed use of historical events and social discourse. By incorporating many interacting voices and points of view, novelists give the appearance of reality to a variety of imaginary worlds ... Lesbian novelists, then, had taken on the project of writing us into our own version of reality. To do this, they have revised the fragmented and distorted plots inherited from the past ...[130]

Literature thus contrasts vividly with law, which is linear, authoritative and dichotomous in form. Catherine MacKinnon and other feminist legal scholars have argued that whilst law purports to be neutral and objective, it is largely masculine in form,[131] a masculinity paralleled in 'True Crime' books. Both reinforce each other in an individualistic theory of liability and methodology. By contrast, novels especially when produced by feminist writers, have been taken to be more subjective, feminine and subversive of patriarchy.[132] Thus, even if one does not fully endorse such essentialism, the novel offers a forum which can incorporate a plurality of women's voices and experiences much more readily than law does, and in novels (and films) the voice of the female killer is beginning to make itself heard.

The new feminist literature

Recent years have spawned for the first time avowedly feminist novels with a
female killer as main protagonist. Phyliss Chessler notes a massive change in
fictional depictions of women: 'Something's up, it's in the air, it's a sea-
change, and suddenly, or so it seems, we are being bombarded by celluloid
images of women killing men'.[133] Film critic Julie Baumgold rejoices in
similar vein that '[w]hat is important is that these warrior women have been
released'.[134] However as Hart argues, what is more important is the
interrogation of how these representations are produced and received. The
most significant factor is the desire to contain even celluloid dangerous
femininities. For example a *Time* cover story sought out feminist scholars to
reassure readers that *Thelma and Louise* was 'not ... a cultural
representation ... but a fairy tale ... not a [literal] description of what's going
on in our society'. As Hart notes the response to these images was an
attempt to restore cultural confidence in *real* women's passivity.[135]

Two recent novels - Andrea Dworkin's *Mercy* [136] and Helen Zahavi's *A
Dirty Weekend* [137] - arouse similar anxieties. Although both novels can be
read as accounts of women who fight back, and are located in a lineage
which stretches back to the Victorian era, what is significant about the
protagonists - Andrea and Bella - is that their target of assault is much
broader. They fight back not against individual men or the constraints of the
home, but seek to elude the public/private dichotomy by making the public
sphere their own. For instance, Bella's defiance of the rules even extends to
wandering the beach at Brighton alone in the early hours of the morning: 'Let
them see her on the shore. Let them try and touch her on the shore. Let them
do it, if they dared'.[138] Andrea and Bella have not simply been victimized by
individual men, but by the legal system and patriarchal society. What unites
the protagonists of both novels with *Thelma and Louise* is that they have
been let down by the conventional forces of law and order.

Ian Ward argues of *Mercy* that '[a]t the heart of this exclusion and this
frustration is the inability of the male-dominated legal order to execute justice
for women'.[139] In similar vein, Chessler describes *Mercy* as reading 'like
something the visionary Cassandra might have written had she escaped life as
Agamemnon's slave-prostitute and become an avenging angel'.[140]

> We surge through the sex dungeon where our kind are kept, the butcher shops
> where our kind are sold; we break them loose; Amnesty International will not
> help us, the United Nations will not help us, the World Court will not help us;

so at night, ghosts, we convene; to spread justice, which stands in for law, which has always been merciless, which is, by its nature, cruel.[141]

In this there are similarities with the Zahavi book, but the style of *A Dirty Weekend* is more conventional. It's anti-heroine Bella, an ex-prostitute, is the 'archetypal victim' who fights back. Once she 'realised she'd had enough' she kills seven men. In both novels society is strongly implicated in the 'crimes' of these women - their source cannot be located in the pathology of the individual woman. It is the failure of law which pushes Andrea and Bella into transgression, although they later willingly embrace it:

> The law-makers have their legal guns. The law-breakers have their shooters. They've built their barricade, and they've shoved her over the other side, and no semantic quibble can stop her now.[142]

They seek equality with a vengeance, and it is their search for equality which marks them as feminist. Furthermore it is stressed that the legal system has not failed just these individuals, but all women 'In the character of Bella, the humiliation and anger of Everywoman has been condensed, compressed and let explode against the oppressive weight of Everyman'.[143] Significantly, they also fight back not solely on their own account, but on behalf of their sisters: 'She hammered her message home the only way she could. She bludgeoned him for all her silent sisters'.[144] And it is the silencing of women which these novels seek to contest. Both books stress the significance of having a story which can be communicated - the very opportunity which real women who kill lack: 'Perhaps it was the thought of having been, and gone, and left no mark. The thought that if she finished it, she would have had no story'.[145] In this it seems to me that they strike a chord with most women readers. As Munt argues, the attraction of *A Dirty Weekend* lies in the fact that

> [t]he plot is wickedly simple, and unimaginable without contemporary feminist discourse. What keeps the reader engaged is the pull of parody, which reveals the seed of truth contained within the absurd. *A Dirty Weekend*, according to my own small straw poll of readers, expresses the desire of many women to pulverize their oppressors. In a way the emotional power of the book is reminiscent of the anger which galvanised early Women's Liberation.[146]

For all its parody it captures the physical and sexual vulnerability of women. It seems to me most women can identify with the book, especially the vulnerability of women in a man's sphere without a weapon - which parallels to the idea of threat of rape being used to control all women:

> She might be a nobody, but the gun makes her somebody. She smiled a smug smile. With the gun in her bag she can go where she likes. With the gun in her bag she can rant and rave. With the gun in her bag she can bide her time. With the gun in her bag ... The smile froze on her face. There's no gun in her bag. The gun's by the bed ... You're in for it, now ... You forgot that you're nothing without your weapons. Less than nothing. Minus nothing.[147]

But significantly this story does not lead to punishment. Andrea and Bella dispatch their own unconventional brand of justice and remain beyond the reach of law and order. They thus elude the punishment meted out to their Victorian counterparts of real-life women who kill. Nor do they go mad. In fact one of the most significant features of their killing is how rational it appears, yet it is a rationality which cannot be accommodated by a criminal justice system predicated on an individual construction of liability. Critics have argued that what made *Thelma and Louise* so transgressive was its ending, when the protagonists embrace death rather than succumb to punishment. As Hart argues

> despite the formal recontainment of these killer women in the iconic final moments of the films, the characters do not succumb to rehabilitation, they do not repent, and the free-frames are hardly the 'tableaux of sympathy' that returned the nineteenth century villainess to the moral order ... As dead women who got away, Thelma and Louise appear to be more dangerous that living women who are locked up.[148]

However both novels go beyond that - Bella and Andrea live on as feminist vigilantes. It is in this regard perhaps that these novels are most transgressive, and why they are beyond the imagination of those who frame the laws: 'Bella in her basement is beyond their imagination. She's beyond belief. She's a video nasty in velvet gloves. Mad-dog Bella has slipped her leash'.[149]

Her actions may be qualitatively different from those who threaten her, but the fact that her killings are premeditated means that the context for her violence - the pervasive threat against all women and the failure of the legal system to offer protection - is too much for law to take on board. Yet it remains possible for feminists to sympathize with her even though her actions are violent and go beyond anything that could be sanctioned by law in self-defence.

Conclusion

Literature thus is valuable in creating extremely violent female killers whose actions can be comprehended, who do not seem to warrant punishment. It is thus the type of work, which as Ward argues, can be extremely useful in serving as a stimulus to discussion in the law school. However it must be questioned what such novels achieve beyond this:

> That women have begun to imagine and befriend women killers - and in print - is very promising. Writers need to create female heroes and anti-heroes, larger than life. Acts of radical compassion are required, acts that embrace other women, not just 'nice' girls, or 'perfect' victims, not when its safe, but precisely when its risky.[150]

Clearly, with both *Mercy* and *A Dirty Weekend* there are hints of a trend in feminist writing to embrace female killers who could not be labelled 'nice'. In this sense they are revolutionary and a break with previous fictional depictions of women who kill. However, in no single instance do either Bella or Andrea instigate that violence - a male aggressor always acts as the trigger. Thus their targets are those who oppress women, and that is how they avoid offending feminist sensibilities. Literature may therefore shed light on women who kill violent men, and broaden our understandings so that women who kill do not have to be victims to engage our sympathies. Thus literary studies (even those in the restrictive 'True Crime' mode) may deepen our understanding of Ruth Ellis or Sara Thornton.

Texts like *Mercy* and *A Dirty Weekend* are valuable additions to Law and Literature courses in affording a perspective on the world which is much broader than that currently accommodated by law. The context and the revolt of the women concerned is much broader. In creating sympathetic heroines who do unspeakable things such novelists may create a different context for speaking about women who kill and rendering their actions more comprehensible. But there are limits to their power to do so. Quite simply, even in our age when stories proliferate there are some stories whose time has not yet come.[151] Stories of women who kill can be revised, which is empowering, as rape and coming out stories have demonstrated.[152] However perhaps the time is not yet right to go beyond deconstructing existing stories when the victims of women who kill are not abusive or sexually predatory men, but others who are disempowered. The question remains, however, whether deconstruction and challenging of existing stories is enough when real issues of justice arise. Furthermore such a conclusion reveals serious limitations to critical legal theories like Law and Literature, given that literary studies are limited in their power to deal with or even imagine the woman who kills another woman or a child like Myra Hindley, Beverley Allitt and Susan Christie. Thus if perhaps the two most progressive forms of critical legal theorising are unable to speak about accommodating the woman who kills unless she is a battered woman who kills an abusive man, how can the legal system be expected to treat her justly? Birch has argued that '[t]he mythology of Myra Hindley reveals, above all, that we do not have a language to represent female killing, and that a case like this disrupts the very terms which hold gender in place'.[153]

Until such a language exists then the power of the law and literature movement will always be limited. One route for exploring whether such a language could be fashioned may be to allow killers themselves to speak. Recently there have been reports that Myra Hindley plans to write her biography, but currently our society deems it necessary to censure such stories.[154] Yet if it were not to be sensationalised, such a first person account might increase our understanding, and it would seem that at the moment all we can do is attempt to understand such killers.[155] If we fail to understand then we are unable to fashion a literature around such killers, much less find a language to express their deeds without resorting to simplistic accounts that they are monsters.

Notes

1. Willbanks (1982).
2. Hart (1994), p. 28. As Worrall has argued, female offenders are constructed within the discourses of domesticity, sexuality and pathology by judicial, medical and welfare personnel; Worrall (1990), p. 74.
3. For example Smart (1976) and Jones (1980).
4. Heinzelman and Wiseman (1994), p. 248.
5. Ward (1994), p. 158.
6. Cameron and Fraser (1987), pp. 145-7.
7. Smart (1976), pp. 28-37.
8. Smart (1976), p. 33.
9. Brown (1990), p. 51.
10. Smart (1976), p. 35.
11. Hart (1994), p. 12.

12. Brown (1990), p. 41.
13. Brown (1990), p. 55.
14. This happened in the cases of both Myra Hindley and Susan Christie discussed below.
15. Frigon (1995) and Worrall (1994), p. 91.
16. Daly (1994), p. 264.
17. Walters (1995), p. 10.
18. Smart (1976), pp. 70-76.
19. Soothill and Walby (1991), p. 90.
20. Worrall (1990).
21. Worrall (1990), p. 84; Kennedy (1992), p. 196.
22. Heidensohn (1985), pp. 88-9, arguing that they serve the dual role of emphasising appropriate gender roles and acting as a warning to other women.
23. Chessler (1993), p. 943.
24. Frigon (1995), p. 27.
25. Morris (1990), p. 3 and Worrall (1990), p. 34.
26. Frigon (1995), p. 28.
27. Showalter (1990), p. 9.
28. Morris (1990), p. 26.
29. Zedner (1991), p. 320; see also Dobash, Dobash and Gutteridge (1986).
30. Morris (1990), p. 27.
31. Hart (1994), p. 39.
32. Hart (1994), p. 44.
33. Morris (1990), p. 27.
34. It has been well documented how Dickens and other Victorian writers took accounts of real-life trials as sources for their fictions. See, for example, Morris (1990), Chp. 3.
35. Victorian crime histories may be seen as precursors to modern 'True Crime' literature.
36. Morris (1990), p. 31.
37. Morris (1990), pp. 24-25.
38. Morris (1990), p. 4.
39. Smart (1976), p. 16.
40. Daly (1994), p. 259.
41. Mahoney (1991).
42. Morris (1990), p. 5.

43. A number of specialist publishing houses devoted solely to the publication of such books exist, whilst they form large sub-divisions of mainstream publishers, such as Harper Collins and Virgin. They are also allocated their own sections in bookstores and in London there is a specialist shop devoted to 'True Crime' and crime fiction.

44. Provost (1991), chp. 1. Symons (1992), chp. 1 points to similar problems in defining crime fiction, which is impossible to clearly delineate from the thriller, spy, novel and mystery novel.

45. In Christie's case it was largely McAllister's version of events which formed the basis for Davies' account of the crime - *A Deadly Kind of Love* (1994).

46. Cameron and Fraser (1987), p. 24.

47. Birch (1993), p. 33.

48. Goodman (1986), p. 10.

49. Hindley's subsequent appeal on the grounds that she should have been tried separately from Brady was dismissed because '[t]he evidence against her was overwhelming' per Parker LCJ in *R v. Hindley*, *The Times*, 18 October 1966.

50. Soothill and Walby (1991), p. 87.

51. Birch (1993), p. 47.

52. Cameron and Fraser (1987), p. 25.

53. Marchbanks (1966), p. 121.

54. Harrison (1986), p. 179-180.

55. Harrison (1986), p. 15 and Johnson (1967), pp. 77-8.

56. Harrison (1987), p. 58.

57. Harrison (1994), p. 17.

58. Sparrow (1974), pp. 85-6. Note how this parallels the prosecution case and tabloid reports of the Rosemary West case. In both cases it is their shared 'depravity' and 'perversion' which is seen as cementing their relationship.

59. Harrison (1994), p. 61.

60. Cameron and Fraser (1987).

61. Cameron and Fraser (1987), p. 145.

62. Birch (1993), p. 33.

63. Johnson (1967), p. 22-3.

64. Naylor (1994), p. 88.

65. Potter (1966), p. 226 (my emphasis).

66. Ritchie (1988), p. 128.

67. Most explicitly in a partly fictionalized account of the case - Williams (1967) pp. 10-11, 138-42, 148-50, 157-60, 168-78 and 245-7.
68. Ritchie (1988), pp. 135-64, 198-200, 217-8.
69. Hancock (1963), pp. 7-8.
70. Hancock (1963), p. 11.
71. Hancock (1963), p. 22.
72. Hancock (1963), p. 28.
73. Hancock (1963), p. 37.
74. Hancock (1963), p. 32.
75. Hancock (1963), p. 39.
76. Hancock (1963), p. 23.
77. Marchbanks (1966), p. 152.
78. Hancock (1963), p. 40.
79. Hancock (1963), p. 41.
80. Hancock (1963), pp. 143 and 145.
81. Ritchie (1988), pp. 108 and 113.
82. Naffine (1987).
83. Upon her release, relatives of her husband Malcolm were critical of her failure to repent.
84. Davies (1994), p. 217.
85. Bell and Fox (1996).
86. As Naylor notes, these allegations were never fully substantiated and doubts surround the diagnosis. The result was that evidence of Munchausens was not made available to the jury at her trial; Naylor (1995), p. 87.
87. Naylor (1995), p. 90.
88. Robson (1995).
89. Hart (1994), p. 9.
90. Hart (1992), p. 89. As Bea Campbell has argued, there has been a trend in recent movies, such as *Butterfly Kiss*, *Fun* and *NBK* to represent lesbians as 'a deadly alchemy'. 'Unruly femininity is increasingly being mobilised to detonate the alarming correlation between crime and masculinity.' Campbell (1995), pp. 34-5.
91. Hart (1994), p. 13.
92. Again this has been an important strand in the construction of the prosecution argument that Rosemary West's crimes were motivated by her sexual deviance.

93. Romney (1995). Romney suggests this in the context of a review of *Fun* and *Butterfly Kiss*, but the most obvious example was in the Hollywood blockbuster *Basic Instinct* which generated much controversy and protests by gay groups. Hart (1994), pp. 124-34.
94. Hart (1994), p. 27.
95. Smart (1995), p. 25.
96. Interestingly Wykes (1995), p. 72, n. 3, notes that this story seems too complex for publication in tabloid newspapers which largely ignored Thornton's case and subsequent appellate level decisions on battered women who killed.
97. Those few accounts which are more reflective, such as Johnson (1967) and Harrison (1987), were written in response to the wider implications of the Moors murders case. They are less concerned with Hindley's aberrations, than with locating the problem in the moral decline of society, such as the rise of pornography and decline of the family.
98. The storm of publicity around the plight of battered women who strike back was largely unleashed by the rejection of Thornton's appeal, and her subsequent high profile campaign which included going on hunger strike.
99. *R v. Ahluwalia* [1992] 4 ALL E.R. 889, *R v. Humphries*, NLJ *Practitioner* 14 July 1995, discussed in Nicholson and Sanghvi (1995).
100. The story which perhaps has had the most impact in Britain has been the storyline in the soap opera *Brookside*. Significantly even in this fictional context of the women who were responsible for killing their abusive father and husband, the daughter was lesbian and the mother became pregnant outside marriage.
101. Kennedy (1992), p. 197.
102. Kennedy (1992), pp. 195-96.
103. The film of her story - *Dance with a Stranger* (1985) offered a more sympathetic account which broadened the frame of reference to portray Blakely as a cad.
104. Bell and Fox (1996).
105. There are traces of this in the Davies (1994) account, but this theme constantly competes with the nightmarish vision of her that emerges from the book. Cf Askill and Sharpe (1993).

106. For example, compare Sparrow (1974), pp. 87 and 96 with Cameron and Fraser (1987), pp. 145-6.
107. See Bennett and Feldman (1981) for an account of the importance of narratives in court.
108. Daly (1994), p. 227.
109. Daly (1994) and Howe (1994).
110. Birch (1993) and Naylor (1995).
111. Even in the case of battered women who kill there has been a reluctance to grapple with the difficult question of how they should be punished; Bell and Fox (1996).
112. Abrams (1994), p. 50.
113. Kennedy (1992).
114. Heinzelman (1995), p. 332.
115. Ward (1994).
116. See further O'Donovan's essay in this volume.
117. Cited in Heinzelman (1995), p. 332.
118. Artley (1993).
119. Kingsley and Tibballs (1994).
120. Kennedy (1994).
121. Robson (1995).
122. For example Artley (1993) and Nadel (1993).
123. However even when such proposals are translated into law they may function in a way different from that intended; Morison (1990). In the case of a battered woman who kills, for example her story may only be heard in court when it is mediated through the voice of experts; Fox (1995).
124. Heinzelman (1994), p. 248. Heinzelman points to Anita Hill's tale of her experience of sexual harassment as an example.
125. Birch (1993), p. 34.
126. Morris (1990), pp. 23-4.
127. Hart (1994), p. 31.
128. Hart (1994), p. 37.
129. Zimmerman (1990).
130. Zimmerman (1990), p. 2.
131. MacKinnon (1983), pp. 644-5.
132. Heizelman (1994).
133. Chessler (1993), pp. 943-4.
134. Cited in Hart (1994), p. 67.

135. Hart (1994), p. 73.
136. Dworkin (1990).
137. Zahavi (1992).
138 Zahavi (1992), p. 171.
139. Ward (1994), p. 151.
140. Chessler (1993), p. 945.
141. Dworkin (1990), p. 331.
142. Zahavi (1992), p.77. It is noteworthy that even when she has transgressed, Bella's aims remain hyper-conventional: 'she would go to London and find a flat, and find a job, and find a man. A gentle kind of man who wouldn't give her pain', Zahavi (1992) p. 141.
143. Review, *The Sunday Tribune* (1991) - as cited on dust jacket.
144. Zahavi (1992), p. 59.
145. Zahavi (1992), p. 2.
146. Munt (1994), p. 203.
147. Zahavi (1992), pp. 129-32.
148. Hart (1994), p. 88.
149. Zahavi (1991).
150. Chessler (1993), p. 945.
151. Plummer (1994).
152. Plummer (1994), p. 114. Very rarely does the late twentieth century tell the tale of a paedophile, a rapist or even a serial murderer from their point of view. See also Birch (1993), p. 61 and Liddle (1995).
153. Birch (1993), p. 61.
154. The response of *The Daily Mail* was to publish an article by Roy Hattersley (former deputy leader of the Labour Party) headlined 'Why we must ban Hindley's pornography', 7 August 1995. In response Hindley sent a letter to *The Independent* denying that she had authorized anyone to write her autobiography, and stating: 'I wholly agree that its publication would be a callous and calculated decision to open wounds of more than thirty years ago'. She added however that if she were to write an autobiography it would not contain details of her crimes nor her claim that she was 'an almost innocent party', *The Independent* 23 September 1995. A similar outcry has arisen over the Official Solicitor's sale of the memoirs of Fred West.
155. Ernst (1993).

References

Abrams, K. (1994), 'The Narrative and the Normative in Legal Scholarship' in Heinzelman, S. and Wiseman, Z. (Eds.), *Representing Women: Law, Literature and Feminism*, pp. 44-56, Duke University Press, Durham.

Artly, A. (1993), *Murder in the Heart*, Penguin, London.

Ashill J. and Sharpe, M. (1993), *Angel of Death: Killer Nurse Beverley Allitt*, Micheal O'Mara Brothers, London.

Bell, C. and Fox, M. (1996), *Telling Stories of Women Who Kill*, in preparation.

Bennett, W. and Feldman, S. (1981), *Reconstructing Reality in the Contrived Justice and Judgement in American Culture*, Rutgers University Press, New Brunswick.

Birch, H. (1993), *Moving Targets: Women, Murder and Representation*, Virago, London.

Brown, B. (1990), 'Reassessing the critique of biologism', in Gelstorpe, L. and Morris, A. (Eds.) *Feminist Perspectives in Criminology*, Open University Press, pp. 41-56, Buckingham.

Brownmiller, S. (1990), *Waverley Place: A True Story of Violence and Neglect*, Mandarin, London.

Cameron, D. and Fraser, E. (1987), *The Lust to Kill*, Polity Press, Cambridge.

Campbell, B. (1995) 'Kiss 'n' Kill', *Diva*, (August/September), pp. 34-5.

Chessler, P. (1993), 'A Woman's Right to Self-Defense: the case of Aileen Carol Wournos', *St John's Law Review*, Vol. 66, p. 933.

Daly, K. (1994), *Gender and Punishment*, Yale University Press, New Haven.

Davies, N. (1993), *Murder on Ward Four*, Chatto and Windus, London.

Davies, N. (1994), *A Deadly Kind of Love*, Blake Publishing, London.

Dobash, R., Dobash, R. and Gutteridge, S. (1986), *The Imprisonment of Women*, Blackwell, Oxford.

Dworkin, A. (1990), *Mercy*, Arrow, London.

Ernst, L. (1993), 'Forum I: Women Who Kill', in Scholder, A. (Ed.), *Critical Condition: Women on the Edge of Violence*, pp. 54-7, City Light Books, San Francisco.

Fox, M. (1995), 'Legal Responses to Battered Women who Kill', in Bridgeman, J. and Millns, S. (Eds.), *Law and Body Politics: Regulating the Female Body*, pp. 171-200, Dartmouth, Aldershot.

Frigon, S. (1995), 'A genealogy of women's madness' in Dobash, R., Dobash, R. and Noakes, L. *Gender and Crime*, pp. 20-48, University of Wales Press, Cardiff.

Goodman, J. (1973, 1986), *The Moors Murders: The Trial of Myra Hindley and Ian Brady*, David and Charles, Newton Abbott.

Hancock, R. (1963, 1993), *Ruth Ellis: The Last Woman to be Hanged*, Orion Books, London.

Harrison, F. (1987), *Brady and Hindley: Genesis of the Moors Murders*, Harper Collins, London.

Hart, L. (1994), *Fatal Women: Lesbian Sexuality and the Mark of Aggression*, Princeton University Press, Princeton, New Jersey.

Heidensohn, F. (1985), *Women and Crime*, New York University Press, New York.

Hinzelman, S. (1994), 'Guilty in Law, Implausible in Fiction: Jurisprudential and Literary Narratives in the Case of Mary Blandy, Parricide, 1752', in Heizelman, S. and Wiseman, Z. (Eds.), *Representing Women: Law, Literature and Feminism*, pp. 309-336, Duke University Press, Durham.

Howe, A. (1994), *Punish and Critique*, Routledge, London.

Kennedy, D. (1994), *On a Killing Day: The Bizarre Story of Convicted Murderer Aileen Lee Wournos*, S.P.I. Books, New York.

Kennedy, H. (1992), *Eve Was Framed: Women and British Justice*, Chatto and Windus, London.

Kingsley, H. and Tibballs, J. (1994), *No Way Out: Battered Women Who Killed*, Headline Book Publishing, London.

Johnson, P.H. (1967), *On Iniquity: Some Personal Reflections Arising Out of the Moors Murders Trial*, Macmillan, London.

Jones, A. (1991), *Women Who Kill*, Victor Gollancz, London.

Lombroso, C. (1895), *The Female Offender*, Appleton and Co., New York.

Liddle, A. M. (1995), 'Child sexual abuse and age of consent laws; a response to some libertarian arguments for "sexual liberty"', in Dobash, R., Dobash, R. and Noakes, L. (Eds.), *Gender and Crime*, pp. 313-339, University of Wales Press, Cardiff.

MacKinnon, C. (1983), 'Feminism, Marxism, Method and the State. Towards a Feminist Jurisprudence', *Signs*, Vol. 8, p. 635.

Mahoney, M. (1991), 'Legal Images of Battered Women: Redefining the Issue of Separation', *Michigan Law Review*, Vol. 90, pp. 1-94.

Marchbanks, D. (1966), *The Moor Murders*, Leslie Frewin, London.

Morison, J. (1990), 'How to Change Things with Rules', in Livingstone, S. and Morison, J. (Eds.), *Law, Society and Change*, pp. 5-32, Dartmouth, Aldershot.

Morris, V. (1990), *Double Jeopardy: Women Who Kill in Victorian Fiction*, University Press of Kentucky, Lexington.

Munt, S. (1994), *Murder by the Book? Feminism and the Crime Novel*, Routledge, London.

Nadel, J. (1993), *Sara Thornton: The Story of a Woman Who Killed*, Victor Gollancz, London.

Naffine, N. (1987), *Female Crime*, Allen and Unwin, Sydney.

Naffine, N. (1990), *Law and the Sexes*, Allen and Unwin, Sydney.

Naylor, B. (1994), 'Fair Trial or Free Press: Legal Responses to Media Reports of Criminal Trials', *Cambridge Law Journal*, vol. 53, pp. 492-501.

Naylor, B. (1995), 'Women's crime and media coverage: making explanations', in Dobash, R., Dobash, R. and Noakes, L. (Eds.), *Gender and Crime*, pp. 77-95, University of Wales Press, Cardiff.

Nicolson, D. and Sanghvi, R. (1995), 'More Justice for Battered Women', *New Law Journal*, Vol. 46, pp. 1122-4.

Plummer, K. (1994), *Telling Sexual Stories*, Routledge, London.

Potter, J. D. (1966), *The Monsters of the Moors*, Elek Press, London.

Provost, G. (1991) *How to Write and Sell 'True Crime'*, Writers' Digest Books, Cincinnatti, Ohio.

Ritchie, J. (1988), *Myra Hindley: Inside the Mind of a Murderess*, Angus and Robertson, London.

Robson, R. (1995), 'Convictions: Theorizing Lesbians and Criminal Justice', in Herman, D. and Stychin, C. (Eds.), *Legal Inversions: Lesbians, Gay Men and the Politics of Law*, pp. 354-81, Temple University Press, Philadelphia.

Romney, J. (1995), 'Well hard women', *The Guardian*, 17 August.

Showalter, E. (1992), *Sexual Anarchy: Gender and Culture at the Fin de Siecle*, Virago, London.

Smart, C. (1976), *Women, Crime and Criminology*, Routledge and Kegan Paul, London.

Smart, C. (1995), *Law, Crime and Sexuality*, Sage, London.

Soothill and Walby (1991), *Sex Crimes in the News*, Routledge, London.

Sparrow, G. (1974), *Women Who Murder*, Tower Books, New York.

Symons, J. (1992), *Bloody Murder - From the Detective Story to the Crime Novel: A History*, Pan Books, London.

Walters, S. (1995), *Material Girls: Making Sense of Feminist Cultural Theory*, University of California Press, Berkeley.

Ward, I. (1994), 'Law and Literature: A Feminist Perspective', *Feminist Legal Studies*, Vol. 2, pp. 133-58.

Willbanks, W. (1982), 'Murdered Women and Women Who Murder: A Critique of the Literature', in Rafter, N. and Stanko, E. (Eds.), *Judge, Lawyer, Victim, Thief: Women, Gender Roles and Criminal Justice*, pp. 151-80, Northeastern University Press, Boston.

Worrall, A. (1990), *Offending Women: Female Lawbreakers and the Criminal Justice System*, Routledge, London.

Wykes, M. (1985), in Dobash, R., Dobash, R. and Noakes, L. (Eds.), *Gender and Crime*, pp. 49-76, University of Wales Press, Cardiff.

Young, A. (1990), *Femininity in Dissent*, Routledge, London.

Zahavi, H. (1992), *Dirty Weekend*, Flamingo, London.

Zedner, L. (1991), *Women, Crime and Custody in Victorian England*, Oxford University Press, Oxford.

7 Newspapers and Crime: Narrative and the Construction of Identity

KIERAN McEVOY

Introduction

Representations of, and discussions about, crime, villainy, rule breaking, anti-social behaviour, whatever one wants to call it, have always been a staple part of human interaction. As David Garland has argued we have always chosen to regulate, account for or represent our behaviour 'whether as myths, cosmologies, theologies, metaphysical systems, or vernacular common sense ...'.[1] We have normally paralleled that discourse with explanations and depictions of rule breaking. A specialist discipline, criminology, has grown exponentially in an attempt to examine and explain this phenomenon.[2] As the factual and fictional portrayal of crime in the media has come to play such a major part in our culture,[3] a sub-discipline within criminology has grown which has looked at the range of cultural representations of crime and the criminal justice process.

In looking at the developments within that sub-discipline, using newspapers as a case-study, I hope to offer some insights to those more traditionally concerned with Law and Literature debates. This chapter is informed by the idea that there are many similarities between developments within the Law and Literature movement and those within criminology and the cultural representation of crime within newspapers. I will suggest that because of the particular significance of the portrayal of crime, as opposed to other 'newsworthy' social phenomenon, discourses upon crime within newspapers and other media outlets are unique cultural artifacts, telling us much about the social, political and moral order of our culture and, as such, playing an important role in the development of an individual's sense of self.

Law and literature as forms of narrative

In the era of television, video, interactive media, information superhighways *et al.*, newspapers are forced to fight ever more vigorously for a dwindling numbers of readers. However as the work of Graber,[4] Ericson *et al*[5] and others has painstakingly demonstrated, much of our knowledge of crime, criminality and its control continues to be derived to some degree from our faith in the written word. While some commentators have argued that newspapers form only a small part of the range of media and cultural outlets which play a role in informing our views,[6] others have gone so far as to suggest that newspapers are an entirely unique cultural form which somehow exercise a greater influence on the individual's thinking.[7] However newspapers are not simply a vehicle for our culturally programmed dialogue, 'hypodermic syringes'[8] injecting information into the social corpus in a one way stream of information. Rather they are active participants and vital contributors in an ongoing dialectic with their readers. They quote themselves as evidence of what 'actually' happened. They are in turn quoted by those who seek to explain or interpret. (Any person who has toiled in a dusty library will recognize the tangible sense of history derived from old yellow stained newspapers, pamphlets and articles.) They are written documents which chart the important events, trends and symbols of a particular culture and in doing so, are in turn themselves cultural artifacts. What they reveal in their content, style or even omissions offers insights into that culture.

As others have pointed out, the Law and Literature debate has been traditionally divided into the two schools of law *in* literature and law *as* literature.[9] Both areas share the premise that there is much to be learnt about the nature of law in the way in which it is represented and interpreted beyond the traditional pursuits of interpreting a series of rules regulating the behaviour between individuals, the state and institutions. Law and Literature studies may be viewed as an attempt to move beyond the traditional positivist philosophy of studying observed, empirical and value free facts to the exclusion of unverifiable statements of values, causes or context.[10] The study of the representation of law within literature[11] or law itself as a form of narrative[12] has attempted to undermine the insularity and autonomy of legal theory.

It will be argued then that the study of the social construction of the media image of crime and the criminal justice process has played an equally useful role in expanding the traditional pursuits of criminology. Criminologists also have sought to examine the portrayal of crime in its various cultural forms including newspapers, television and novels.[13] They too have examined the designation of what constitutes deviant behaviour and the processing of the deviant according to legal procedures as a form of narrative with recognizable characters, value judgments on good and evil, a familiar plot structure and a predictable range of outcomes.[14] This research within criminology is based on the premise that crime, like law (since it is the breach of the latter), is not an empirical 'fact' but rather a socially constructed concept which is represented, understood and reacted to as an integral part of our culture. At the level of narrative, law and news media have similarities.

Both law and news media are concerned with 'policing' in its broadest sense.[15] They 'police' the major institutions of society by setting up a constant public conversation about how the classifications, values and procedures fit with the expectations of various evaluators. For example, in dealing with issues such as corrupt politicians, mentally ill offenders or victims of domestic violence, law and the news media provoke public discourse on the relationship of the particular event to broader structural questions about the moral health of institutions such as the political system, the health system or the family respectively. In this way both law and news media are involved in a discourse involving the construction, articulation, reassurance and ultimately reassertion of a sense of public morality - of what is moral and immoral, right and wrong, good and bad. Based on a claimed neutrality, both news media and law operate by claiming that their policing function is 'in the public interest'. The relationship is symbiotic in the sense that the news media helps to confer legitimacy by presenting law as the natural order of things, by criticising and undermining that which is perceived to be illegitimate or deviant and by ensuring an adaptive capacity to cope with strains or changes in environment.

News media and law share an event orientation, examining conflicts as they arise on a specific, case by case basis. Broader moral principles are grounded, personalized and articulated through an individual conflict rather than summarized and synthesized into abstract concepts. Discourse about the relationship between the individual event and broader social or political concerns are ultimately designed to improve the institutions and reassure the public. This produces 'the appearance (or collective representation) that troubled persons rather than troublesome social structures are at fault'.[16] By individualizing problems, news and law mitigate against systemic and structural accounts which might question the authority of cultural values, the state and the news and legal institutions themselves.

Both news and law place great emphasis on procedure and precedent. Both can be described as social discourses of procedural propriety, referenced and contextualized by past similar occurrences. Journalists and lawyers begin any new story or legal case with a look through the precedents. Any news story or legal case is inevitably portrayed and understood in the context of what has happened before in a similar event. As societies become more diverse and absolute moral or traditional values decline, ensuring procedural propriety becomes ever more important in order to achieve legitimacy.

Despite the fact that both law and news are socially constructed and packaged, they are presented as much as possible as 'natural' or unmediated reality. Press conferences, photo opportunities, backgrounds, interviews etc. are all 'naturalised' as much as possible in the media in order to give the impression to the viewer or listener that they are reading, viewing or listening to a natural event or dialogue unfolding. The scripts, auto-cues, press releases, make-up, cameras - in other words the professional construction of the news story, are all made as discreet and invisible as possible. Elements which are evaluative or even fabricated[17] in a news story are often presented as fact. Similarly law too strives to appear 'natural' in its justification of authority.[18] It is represented as if the relationship between legal 'truth' and the 'facts' are the same thing. In other words, that the proving of a crime beyond reasonable doubt becomes a 'naturalized' account of 'what actually happened'. Law too seeks to underplay the role of rhetoric, bargaining, personal relationships (the behind the scenes equivalent of the auto-cues, cameras etc), presenting the pursuit of truth as unaffected by the impact of human or organizational relations.

Given these similarities, examination of the academic discussion around newspaper representations has insights to offer as to our relationship with 'crime' as a social institution of 'law', not just because of the similarities, but because 'law' also creates 'crime'.

Newspapers and crime

While the portrayal of crime in the media can be traced back at least to eighteenth century provincial and national newspapers,[19] the study of that representation is a relatively recent phenomenon. For most of its history criminology has been mainly concerned with two related endeavours: (i) What are the causes of crime? (ii) How much crime is actually happening? These twin aims had a practical objective; if one could explain the causes of crime and knew how much of it was going on, then it was possible to evolve strategies to deal with it. The history of the search for the causes of crime started in the eighteenth and nineteenth centuries and has continued in various schools and approaches.[20] Criminology's other principal endeavour, the effort to quantify the exact extent of crime, has developed from the straightforward collection of police statistics to crime survey approaches which attempt to plot the 'dark figure' of crime unreported to the police.

In summary criminologists now purport to know so much about the causes of crime and its prevalence, that the discipline might appear at first glance somewhat jaded: all the questions have been asked and the answers that have come up have failed to wholly satisfy. However the attempts to explain and quantify crime have been accompanied by more sophisticated thinking about the way in which particular acts become socially defined as deviant[21] and the way those acts are portrayed in the media.[22] In the same way as the Law and Literature debate opened the way for new ways of viewing law, studies of the cultural representation of crime continue to offer amongst the most interesting possibilities within criminology.

The importance of newspapers has been an axiom within mainstream sociology for at least the last century.[23] The evolving medium of newspapers has, at least since the eighteenth century, contained a healthy ration of crime as part of the daily or weekly diet of either national or provincial newspapers.[24] The radical press also included crime as well as radical politics in their avowedly populist sheets.[25] Following the reduction in the market for revolutionary newspapers in the wake of the Whig government's attempts to eradicate the unstamped press in the 1830s,[26] crime news filled the lacuna of radical politics which had appealed to a mass audience.

In the latter part of the nineteenth century in particular, with the abolition of the advertisement tax in 1853, the stamp duty in 1855 and the paper duty in 1860, there was a proliferation in the number of newspapers being produced. Between 1855 and 1860 the circulation of daily newspapers trebled and then doubled again between 1860 and 1870.[27] With the corresponding increase in the numbers of Sunday newspapers and Quarterlies, aimed by and large at the lower and middle classes, newspapers had taken on their assured place in the regime of the literate classes by the 1870s.[28] Even for those who could not read, there was always the possibility of joining the audience as some literate person held court.[29]

Journalism in the nineteenth and early twentieth century was dominated by an attention to crime, sexual violence and human odditie. Burnham talked of the *Daily Telegraph* as 'thriving on crime'.[30] A review of *Lloyds Weekly News* reveals that 50 per cent of its content dealt with murder, crime and that its advertising featured heavily coverage of fire, robbery and murder.[31]

In summary, the newspaper narrative on crime and its control has a considerable historical pedigree. Studies on more recent newspaper reporting of crime tend to demonstrate that little has changed. Much of the research on the construction of the modern newspaper portrayals of crime can be divided into three main categories. Firstly, those who attempt to demonstrate empirically that the newspaper image of crime and its control is an 'untrue' or 'inaccurate' reflection of reality. Secondly, those who seek to demonstrate how the distorted portrayal supports the dominant capitalist ideology. Thirdly, those who sought to locate the centres of power within the media which lead to that distortion, either focusing internally on individuals (for example owners, editors) or on groups of relationships (journalist to source, journalist to journalist) or externally on other forms of control (technological, bureaucratic or monetary). There is a fourth genre made up of those who seek to measure the 'effects' of media distortion. However I shall deal with this only in so far as it relates to critiques of other genres.

The empirical tradition

The empirical tradition of looking at deviance in newspapers has largely been based on the comparison of column inches devoted to certain types of crime in newspapers, set against their predominance in the official crime statistics. Much of this research has sought to demonstrate a straightforward lack of correlation between the amount of crime coverage news and the number of crimes known to the police.[32] This comparative research has demonstrated that the media clearly overemphasize murder, other forms of serious violence, and offences involving sexual deviance.[33] Newspaper offenders tend to be older and more socially prominent.[34] However, studies of victims in newspaper crimes[35] have tended to dispel the myth that the newspaper victim will be white, old and female, tentatively suggesting that victim depiction in newspapers is broadly in line with their representation in the official statistics.

While much of this research has the straightforward aim of establishing that the newspaper image of deviance is inaccurate when compared to the 'real world' of the official crime statistics,[36] it does have certain obvious methodological and theoretical weaknesses. For example, as noted above, official crime statistics are a notoriously poor guide to 'real' levels of crime. Also, once the 'inaccuracy' is established, putting that inaccuracy into some theoretical context usually involves the 'hypodermic syringe' view of media effects whereby the effect of the distortion on the social corpus can be measured by such indices as an increase in violent or sexual crime or a growth in the fear of crime.[37] Lastly the empirical tradition largely fails to examine in any great detail the social, political and cultural context within which news is produced.

The dominant ideology tradition

Other writers, largely influenced by the radical developments in criminology and sociology during the 1970s, have tried to place the newspaper reporting of deviance in a more ideological and theoretical context.[38] 'Distortion' is taken more or less as axiomatic. Empirically proving such distortion is viewed as neither particularly fruitful nor particularly interesting. Rather this group of sociologists and criminologists attempt to examine the reasons why this distortion might take place.

Robert Cirino, for example, argues that distortion takes place because of the extreme degree of oligopolisation of the mass media in all advanced capitalist societies.[39] Anything that is dangerous to the interest of the status quo such as political conflict in Ireland[40] or industrial strife,[41] is either ignored or deliberately interpreted within pre-ordained parameters. In this way the attention of the reading public is covertly diverted from what concerns them most, poverty, pollution, poor health, by media created myths of delinquent gangs, crazed terrorists, militant miners, from whom the public have much less cause to fear. This process could be viewed either as straightforward censorship or, as Paul Hoch has described, 'the political-economic socialization mechanisms that ensure that the publisher and staff will act "responsibly" without having to be told'.[42] In caricature, this is a straightforward Marxist perspective of the bourgeois press serving the interests of their capitalist overlords.

Others have argued that this distortion arises not so much from explicit or implicit censorship by the ruling elites in the form of newspaper owners, but rather as a result of a more subtle process whereby the newspapers' constant need for a steady source of information leads to the powerful (for example, police, courts or parliament) having disproportionate access to the media and thus becoming the primary definers of society's rules and its infractions.[43]

This idea that the institutional and professional prerogatives of the journalist are influential has been developed. [44] The work of Stuart Hall and others of the Birmingham School have examined how the journalist must respond to both the bureaucratic and cultural exigencies, where s/he must get his/her story and then interpret the story in the light of an accepted paradigm of how things happen and what the world looks like. [45]

Journalists thus may acquiesce with the maintenance of a hegemony either deliberately or unconsciously.[46] This is not a static or one way process, but rather a dialectical process of argument, exchange and speculation by which apparent social consensus emerges.

This approach is open to criticism, particularly for assuming passivity amongst both journalists and consumers.[47] As the detailed work of Graber[48] himself has demonstrated, there are serious pitfalls in assuming that any audience will interpret and act upon media content in a uniform or predictable way. As regards journalists, this work tends to make little use of ethnographic approaches involving actually spending time observing, interviewing and analysing the newspaper from within, or interviewing reporters, editors and news sources. In other words, it ignores those actors who actually produce the product.[49]

The ethnographic tradition

The key element of the ethnographic approach is that the researcher actually spend time with the principal participants, in this case the journalists and editors. This is done so that he/she can best record the aspects of production which are only visible from within. The researcher can allow him/herself a sensitivity to meanings, prerogatives and values as well as an ability to represent and interpret symbols, work practices and forms of cultural production.[50] Steve Chibnall's *Law and Order News*, looking somewhat schematically at the reporting of crime in the British press between 1965-1975, was the most noteworthy of the early attempts at this sort of qualitative analysis. Chibnall looked at the development of crime reporting as a specialist field of journalism which relied heavily on the police as its primary resource. He argues that the ways in which the press distorted reality is not random but rather is systematically governed by a particular set of interests, practices and professional relationships.[51]

Ericson *et al.*, in their important series of three volumes,[52] have outlined in great detail the complex processes by which images of deviance are produced, the importance of the sources of such information and the theoretical and practical consequences of the finished product for social control and social order. They look in detail at the professional culture of journalists[53] and explore empirically the influence of news sources such as the police, courts and legislature to present a picture of the relationships between journalists and their sources as a fluid and complex one. Most recently, Ericson *et al.* have turned to looking at the ways in which the news is really the media image of what constitutes social order.[54] Outlining similarities between law and the media in offering discourse on normalisation and discipline, it is argued that the media is in fact acting as a policing agency, prompting discussion on 'symbolic boundaries, power relations and rules that relate to organising and organised behaviour'.[55] Overall these authors challenge the simplistic view of the media as an instrument of conveying and reinforcing dominant ideology. They argue instead for a much more complex dynamic within the news media institutions and a news product which enables the individual to represent and order his or her life.

Construction of narrative

The ethnographic approach, and to a lesser extent that of the 'dominant ideologists' has demonstrated that the professional, production process of crime news, whereby crime stories are selected and presented in a certain manner, is the result of a complex set of professional and ideological processes. As MacDougall[56] has argued, the billions of events which occur simultaneously throughout the world do not become news until some purveyor of news gives an account of them. Unless we believe that this practice is carried out randomly, then the selection process of what is and what is not news obviously requires some criteria by which the journalist is to judge what is and is not newsworthy. What the journalist chooses to include (and to ignore) informs us not only of his/her professional prerogatives but also of the broader world to which they must ultimately be related.

Whether we view the criteria which guide these decisions as 'news imperatives'[57] which journalists use to recognise and impute significance, or a 'vocabulary of precedents',[58] they are significant because they are chosen and presented in order to represent meaning. Roshier argues that there are four important factors to do with the type of crime news stories which are chosen for coverage; seriousness, ironic and unusual circumstances, dramatic events and high status of actors involved.[59] Ericson *et al* argue that rather than viewing these as the 'news imperatives' of journalism we should see them as elements which journalists use to recognise significance, make choices for which they can account and then take them into consideration in programming the news in conjunction with the elements of social organization which they must consider.[60] In other words this concept of a vocabulary of precedents is a fluid construct by which to articulate the evolution of the journalist's 'on the job' sense of his/her role and responsibilities.

A further criterion which has been suggested is that of simplification, where an event is recognised as significant yet sufficiently uncomplicated to portray a certain meaning.[61] Chibnall has suggested a reduction to binary opposition where certain events are selected and presented in terms of good versus bad, pros versus antis.[62] It is also what is new or what has just happened, geared towards getting the 'latest' on the news stands as quickly as possible. This has been referred to as 'event orientation'[63] where news is centred between the two most recent printing deadlines, supplying just enough information on the background to make the story intelligible, thus encouraging what Barthes has described as 'the miraculous evaporation of history from events'.[64] The selection process also requires dramatization,[65] an emphasis on 'immediacy' or 'impact'[66] and personalization.[67]

Once the journalist has chosen the story, the next key stage is the way that the story is presented. In journalism conventional wisdom has it that the only two sentences people read in a story are the first and last.[68] The idea has been to 'give them blood in the eye on the first one'.[69] This is what Graber referred to as the 'inverted pyramid' style of journalistic writing based on the premise that the most important details must be in the first paragraph because only 18 per cent of news stories are read in full.[70] This idea of the skeleton, or inverted pyramid is certainly very interesting because many of those who have theorised on the consensual nature of the finished story have suggested that these 'key words and phrases' are really the subliminal cultural pointers.[71] Jock Young in his article on the 'consensual paradigm' where the world is divided into 'normal people' and 'deviants' argues that words like 'psychopath', 'mob', 'extremist', 'militant' in time all become cliched labels for those marginalized as 'beyond the pale' in society.[72]

Of course it may not just be the written text within newspapers which may have hidden ideological dimensions. Stuart Hall[73] has suggested that news photographs may be as equally important as a subtle 'agenda setter'. He argues that the newsphoto can repress its ideological dimensions by presenting itself as a literal visual transcription of the 'real world'. If a photograph appears of a policemen being kicked at a demonstration this is shown as a 'truncated reality', the reasons for the demonstration are forgotten or denigrated[74] as the photograph presents this in a 'facts speak for themselves one dimensionality'. It could be argued that, from the multiplicity of photographs that a news photographer takes, the one that is selected for the newspaper and the way in which the corresponding article is presented will be a clear reflection of the slant or angle that the journalist or editor wishes to take.[75]

Theoretically and empirically well informed, the latter genre of research has probably done most within criminology to develop a more complete picture of the production of crime news in the mass media. Crime news as a form of narrative is selected and presented by a fluid set of professional prerogatives and relationships. The only real criticism which I would level at the work of Ericson *et al*, and particularly in their 1991 book, is that they do not look for the same fluidity and variety in their sources for the depiction of law which they see in the production of news. Law and Literature discussions generally do not form part of the common stock of the work of Ericson *et al*. Their view of law tends towards that of black letter positivist law, legal texts acted upon by legal actors engaged largely in a process of textual analysis, rather than as something where the 'reality' of the criminal justice process is itself a narrative or complex set of narratives.

Representations of law and law breaking: narrative and the sense of self

In this final section I will offer some tentative suggestions on the potential significance of the cultural representations of law and law-breaking to the construction of identity. As I noted in the introduction, we have always been fascinated by questions of crime, law and justice. If we view law and law-breaking as the primary cultural device for defining acceptable behaviour, then the journalists who report upon it, the writers who write about it, the directors who make films about it, these are all amongst the more significant of cultural bricklayers constructing the framework of social order. They are all inevitably drawn to deviance and its control because designating deviance is itself so fundamental to the articulation of culture. Our cultural identity, our sense of what we are derives from pointing to what we are not. In being bombarded with stories of misfits and who is authorised to deal with them, the citizen is given his/her sense of place in this administered society.

Anthony Giddens has postulated that the self today is for everyone a reflexive project - a more or less continuous interrogation of past, present and future.[76] In other words our attempts to define ourselves are understood through particular narratives by which we understand our world. In *Modernity and Self Identity*,[77] he argues that the notion of self has become a process where individuals construct a 'revisable narrative' of self identity, based in large part upon the filtering of abstract knowledge systems which the individual may not fully know or understand. As communication systems improve our potential for greater awareness of phenomena of which we have no direct experience (space travel, micro-chips, global warming, etc.) grows exponentially. This may lead to a sense of existential unease or 'ontological insecurity' which makes us more reliant upon abstract systems with which we are familiar and feel we can trust. If we view newspaper stories about crime, as amongst the most familiar form of narrative, then they become amongst the key abstract knowledge systems which we incorporate into our narrative of the self.

News on law and law-breaking must be seen as part of the age old desire to control and command the environment by reference to a common stock of knowledge.[78] The focus on deviancy and its control must be seen as a part of this process designed to reduce environmental equivocality and attain workable levels of certainty. Once the individual is aware of his/her own place and that of other things, this provides an impetus for further organisation since with everything in its place the individual can get on with the quotidian chores in his/her particular sphere of organized life, or 'reality'?

Of course some theorists would strongly dispute this notion of reality at all. For example the French philosopher Jean Baudrillard has offered some interesting and provocative suggestions that in the modern electronic multi-media age, the signs, symbols and images of the media have become autonomous from reality to such a degree that they have usurped and surpassed it to create a realm of 'hyper-reality' which has actually made the term reality both inaccurate and redundant.[79] In *Simulcra and Simulations*[80] Baudrillard postulated that it would be interesting to see whether the repressive apparatus of the state would not react more violently to a simulated hold up than a real one. A real hold up only disturbs the order of things, it only challenges the distribution of the real. Simulation is infinitely more dangerous, since it always suggests, over and above its object, 'that law and order themselves might really be nothing more than simulation'.[81] Therefore he suggests that all hold ups or shootings are no longer in the true sense 'real' since they are inscribed in advance in the decoding rituals of the media, anticipated in their mode of presentation and possible consequences and thus detached from the gravitational pull of the 'real'.[82]

Baudrillard's notion of 'hyper-reality', where the media portrayal of law and law breaking may become completely detached from the 'reality' of the phenomenon being portrayed, is extreme. In deconstructing the cultural representations of deviance in newspapers, and stressing the complex process by which it is produced, it is important not to lose sight of the fact that a phenomena, socially defined as 'crime', does exist.[83] There is nothing so reductionist as the scenario whereby cultural studies become so relativistic that they result in a post modern dog chasing its own metaphysical tail. Real people commit, react to, write about and are the victims of real 'crimes'. Crime and the fear of crime do have real consequences for real people. The error is to try to set up too rigid a division between the 'out there' reality and the cultural representations of that reality.

Nonetheless Baudrillard's work in this context is important because he points the way towards understanding the symbolic importance of what we write, of our discourses on life, politics, crime or whatever. These are not just cultural manifestations, attempts to portray or distort reality, they have an intrinsic validity and reality of their own. Like the picture of Dorian

Gray, the light thrown upon our reality by the 'mirror of representation' offers unique insights, it reflects back and therefore distorts the original reality.

In coming to a view of what we are, there is obviously a dialectic between our 'selves' as individuals, our personalities, our age or sexuality, and the world 'out there'. Law defines our social relations with others with much of that world. But in the melting pot of ideas and influences of the modern era we need certainties, we have little direct experience of many of the phenomena which are relevant to us and therefore we can reduce the equivocality in our world by relying upon a familiar set of narratives. As Giddens has demonstrated our notion of self is itself a narrative project understood by and through other narratives.

There is no narrative more familiar to the individual than that concerning law and law breaking. Like Keith Talent, the anti hero of Martin Amis's *London Fields* (1989), who can only speak of football in pithy tabloid storylines, crime, like law, is understood through its most frequent narratives. Newspaper stories of the senseless mugging, like, for example, the novels of John Grisham or the chicanery of Perry Mason, the portrayal of legality within Kafka, these are some of the ways in which the regulation of our universe is selected, presented and interpreted. By looking more closely at the cultural representations of that narrative, either through the discourses within Law and Literature or in the newspaper representations of crime, we are offered insights into who and what we are which will never be seen in the analysis of black letter law or crime statistics.

Notes

1. Garland (1994), p. 28.
2. See, for example, Bottoms (1987); Rock (1988); Williams and McShane (1994) and Lilly *et al.* (1995).
3. Graber (1980); Sparks (1992).
4. Graber (1980) and (1988).
5. Ericson *et al.* (1987), (1989) and (1991).
6. Altheide (1985).
7. Meyrowitz (1985) argues that newspapers can be distinguished as a form of media because they cannot be read in any state other than isolation. He suggests that those who would normally use television to make their views known to the world such as politicians or pundits,

prefer themselves to use print media as a source for their own knowledge. Similarly Ericson *et al.* (1991) p. 37 argue that while television goes for the widest possible audience or 'lowest common denominator', newspapers may build up their readership by catering for an amalgam of minorities.

8. See generally Guervitz *et al.* (1982) and Collins *et al.* (1986).
9. See further Ward (1993) and (1995).
10. See further Aristodemou (1993).
11. Weisberg (1988).
12. Farber and Sherry (1993).
13. For example Graber (1980); Sparks (1992) and Knight (1980).
14. See for example Hall *et al.* (1978) and Ericson *et al.* (1991).
15. Ericson *et al.* (1991).
16. Pfohl (1985), p. 353.
17. Ericson *et al.* (1987).
18. Goodrich (1986), p. 64.
19. King (1987).
20. For an overview of the history of the development of this type of criminology see Rock (1988); Beirne (1993) and Garland (1994).
21. Becker (1963); Cohen (1972) and Hall *et al.* (1978).
22. Ericson *et al.* (1987), (1989), (1991) and Sparks (1992).
23. Hardt (1979).
24. King (1987).
25. Altick (1972) and Asquith (1978).
26. Weiner (1969).
27. Lee (1978).
28. Berridge (1978).
29. Altick (1970).
30. Burnham (1955).
31. Berridge (1978).
32. Davis (1973); Roshier (1973); Jones (1976); Van Dijk (1979) and Graber (1980).
33. Ditton and Duffy (1982).
34. Graber (1980); Hauge (1965) and Roshier (1973).
35. Cumberbatch and Beardsworth (1976) and Graber (1980).
36. Since Harris (1932) began his examination of newspapers and crime statistics in Minneapolis in 1932, the tradition has continued in America (Jones (1976) - St. Louis; Autunes and Hurley (1977) -

Houston, and Graber (1980) and Sherizen (1978) - Chicago) and spread to Europe with little substantive difference in style or technique. (See generally Marsh (1991); Cumberbatch and Beardsworth (1976); Ditton and Duffy (1983) - United Kingdom; Hauge (1965) - Norway; Van Dijk (1979) - Holland).

37. See for example Howitt and Cumberbatch (1975); Comstock (1976) and Halloran (1978). Mass media accounts were either assumed to have a fairly immediate effect on the individual's propensity for or attitude to socially destructive behaviour (Berkowitz (1990); Tannebaum and Zillman (1975) and Parke *et al* (1977) or, subject to a sustained output, change behaviour over a period of time. Gerbner *et al.* (1979)).

38. Hall *et al.* (1978) and Cohen and Young (1973) and (1981).

39. Cirino (1971).

40. Curtis (1984).

41. Murdock (1973).

42. Hoch (1974) p. 10.

43. Chibnall (1977); Hall *et al.* (1978) and Rock (1973).

44. Chibnall (1977); Galtung and Ruge (1981) and Molotch and Lester (1974).

45. Young (1981). Hall *et al.* (1978) and Hall (1979).

46. In this context hegemony is defined in the Gramscian (1971) sense as the techniques whereby the central and dominant meanings and values of the ruling elite are maintained and diffused throughout society by the ability to incorporate and dilute contradictory or oppositional life styles and opinions.

47. Blumer and Guervitch (1981) and Woollacott (1982).

48. Graber (1980) and (1988).

49. Chibnall (1977), p. 207.

50. Williams (1982).

51. Chibnall (1977), p. 207.

52. Ericson *et al.* (1987).

53. Ericson *et al.* (1989).

54. Ericson *et al.* (1991).

55. Ericson *et al.* (1991), p. 342.

56. MacDougall (1968).

57. Chibnall (1977).

58. Ericson *et al.* (1987).

59. Roshier (1973).
60. Ericson *et al.* (1987), p. 140.
61. Hartley (1982), p. 77.
62. Chibnall (1977).
63. Galtung and Ruge (1981) and Murdock (1973).
64. Barthes (1972).
65. Chibnall (1977) and Ericson *et al.* (1989).
66. Murdoch (1973).
67. Giltin (1980).
68. Ericson *et al.* (1989).
69. Swope (1958).
70. Graber (1988), p. 249. In a letter to the present author a former tabloid journalist described the process in this way: 'obviously one tries initially to arrest the attention of the reader, to make him sit up and take notice. The trick is then to maintain his attention by a gradual reduction in size through two or three stages from the original headline and then to structure the rest of the story on a skeleton. This is done by printing the first paragraph in heavy type and then darkening the type every 30-50 words, on a key phrase or word ... the mechanics of the quality papers ... work along similar principles'.
71. Hall *et al.* (1978).
72. Young (1981).
73. Hall (1981).
74. Murdoch (1973).
75. Using a photograph thus is of course now made all the easier by the advance in computer technology in the storing and developing of news photographs. One notorious example of this was in the case of *R v Taylor* [1993] when the Court of Appeal quashed the convictions of two young sisters for murder on the grounds (inter alia) of prejudicial press coverage involving computer manipulated photographs resulting in 'unremitting, extensive, sensational, inaccurate and misleading' coverage which created a real risk of prejudice. See Naylor (1994), pp. 493-4.
76. See generally Giddens (1991) and (1992).
77. Giddens (1991), p. 5.
78. Ericson *et al.* (1989).
79. See generally Baudrillard (1983) and Gane (1991).

80. (1983).
81. Baudrillard (1988), p. 177.
82. Baudrillard (1988), p. 179
83. Becker (1963).

References

Altick, R.D. (1972), *Victorian Studies in Scarlet*, Dent and Sons, London.
Altheide, D.L. (1985), *Media Power*, Sage Publications, Beverly Hills.
Amis, M. (1989), *London Fields*, Penguin, London.
Aristodemou, M. (1993), 'Studies in Law and Literature: Directions and Concerns', *Anglo American Law Review*, Vol. 22, pp. 157-93.
Autunes, G.E. and Hurley, P.A. (1977), 'The Representation of Criminal Events In Houston's Two Daily Newspapers', *Journalism Quarterly*, Vol. 54, pp. 756-60.
Barthes, R. (1972), *Mythologies*, Jonathon Cape, London.
Baudrillard, J. (1983), *Simulcra and Simulations*, Semiotext, New York.
Baudrillard, J. (1988), *Jean Baudrillard: Selected Writings*, (Ed. Poster, M.), Polity Press, Cambridge.
Becker, H.S. (1963), *Outsiders: Studies In The Sociology Of Deviance*, 111, Free Press, Glencoe.
Beirne, P. (1993), *Inventing Criminology: The Rise of Homo Criminalis*, New York State University of New York Press, Albany New York.
Berkowitz, L. (1990), 'The Contagion of Violence: An SR Mediational Analysis of Some Effects of Observed Aggression' in Arnold, W. and Page, M. (Eds.), *Nebraska Symposium on Motivation*, University of Nebraska Press, Lincoln.
Berridge, V. (1978), 'Popular Sunday Papers and Mid-Victorian Society', in Boyce, G., Curran, J. and Wingate, P. (Eds.), *Newspaper History from the Seventeenth Century to the Present Day*, Constable, London.
Bottoms, A.E. (1987), 'Reflections on the Criminological Enterprise', *Cambridge Law Journal*, Vol. 46(2), pp. 240-63.
Burnham, Lord (1955), *Peterborough Court*, Macmillan, London.
Chibnall, S. (1977), *Law And Order News*, Tavistock, London.
Cirino, R. (1971), *Don't Blame The People*, Diversity Press, Los Angeles.

Cohen, S. (1972), *Folk Devils and Moral Panics*, Paladin, London.

Cohen, S. and Young, J. (1973, 1981), *The Manufacture News: Deviance; Social Problems and Mass Media*, Constable, London.

Comstock, G. (1976,1982), *The Evidence of Television Violence*, Rand, Santa Monica.

Cumberbatch, G. and Beardsworth, A. (1976), 'Criminals, Victims Mass Communications', in Viano, E.C. (Ed.), pp. 72-90, *Victims and Society*, Visage Press, Washington.

Curtis, L. (1984), *Ireland The Propaganda War: The British Media and The Battle for Hearts and Minds*, Pluto Press, London.

Davis, F. (1973), 'Crime News in Colorado Newspapers', in Cohen, S. and Young, J. (Eds.), *The Manufacture of News: Deviance: Social Problems and Mass Media*, pp. 127-35, Constable, London.

Ditton, J. and Duffy, J. (1982), 'Bias In The Newspaper Reporting of Crime News', *British Journal Of Criminology*, Vol. 23, pp. 159-65.

Ericson, R., Baranik, P. and Chan, J. (1987), *Visualising Deviance - A Study of News Organisation*, Open University Press, Milton Keynes.

Ericson, R., Baranek, P. and Chan, J. (1989), *Negotiating Control: A Study of News Sources*, Open University Press, Milton Keynes.

Ericson, R., Baranek, P. and Chan, J. (1991), *Representing Order: Crime, Law and Justice in the News Media*, Open University Press, Milton Keynes.

Farber, D. and Sherry, S. (1993), 'Telling Stories Out of School: An Essay on Legal Narratives', *Stanford Law Review*, Vol. 45, pp. 807-905.

Galtung, J. and Ruge, M. (1981), 'Structuring and Selection News', in Cohen, S and Young, J. (Eds.), *The Manufacture of News: Deviance: Social Problems and Mass Media*, pp. 52-63, Constable, London.

Gane, M. (1991), *Baudrillard, Critical and Fatal Theory*, Routledge, London.

Garland, D. (1994), 'Of Crimes and Criminals; The Development of British Criminology', in Maguire, M., Morgan, R., and Reiner, R. (Eds.), pp. 17-69, *The Oxford Handbook of Criminology*, Clarendon Press, Oxford.

Gerbner, G., Signorielli, N., Morgan, M., and Jackson-Beck, M. (1980), 'The Demonstration of Power: Violence Profile No. 10', *Journal of Communication*, Vol. 29, pp. 176-207.

Giddens, A. (1991), *Modernity and Self Identity; Self and Society in the Late Modern Age*, Polity Press, Cambridge.

Giddens, A. (1992), *The Transformation of Intimacy: Sexuality, Love and Eroticism in Modern Societies*, Polity Press, Cambridge.

Giltin, A. (1991), *The Whole World is Watching*, University of California Press, Berkeley.

Goodrich, P. (1986), *Reading the Law*, Blackwell, Oxford.

Graber, D. (1980), *Crime News and The Public*, Prager, New York.

Graber, D. (1988), *Processing the News: How People Tame the Information Tide* (2nd ed), Longman, New York.

Guervitz, M., Bennet, T., Curran, J., and Woolacott, J. (1982), *Culture, Society and the Media*, Methuen, London.

Hall, S. (1979), 'Culture, The Media and the Idealogical Effect', in Curran, J. *et al.* (Eds.), *Mass Communications and Society*, pp. 314-48, Sage, Beverly Hills.

Hall, S. (1981), 'The Determination of News Photographs', reproduced in Cohen, S. and Young, J. (Eds.), *The Manufacture of News: Deviance; Social Problems and Mass Media*, Constable, London.

Hall, S., Critcher, C., Jefferson, T., Clarke, J. and Roberts, B. (1978), *Policing The Crisis, Mugging, The State and Law and Order*, Macmillan, London.

Halloran, J.D. (1978), 'Studying Violence and The Media; A Sociological Approach', in Winick, C. (Ed.), *Deviance And Mass Media*, Sage, Beverly Hills.

Hardt, H. (1979), *Social Theories of the Press: Early German and American Perspectives*, Sage Publications, Beverly Hills.

Harris, F. (1932), *Presentation Of Crime In Minneapolis Newspapers*, Minneapolis Sociological Press, Minneapolis.

Hartley, J. (1982), *Understanding News*, Methuen, London.

Hauge, R. (1965), 'Crime and the Press', in Christie, N. (Ed.), *Scandinavian Studies in Criminology*, Vol. 1, Tavistock, London.

Hoch, P. (1974), *The Newspaper Game: The Political Sociology of the Press*, Calder and Boyars, London.

Howitt, D. and Cumberbatch, G. (1975), *Mass Media, Violence and Society*, Elek, London.

Jones, E. (1976), 'The Press As Metropolitan Monitor', *Public Opinion Quarterly, Culture, Media, Language*, Vol. 40, pp. 239-44.

King, P. (1987), 'Newspaper Reporting, Prosecution Practice and Perceptions of Urban Crime: the Colchester Crime Wave of 1765', *Continuity and Change*, Vol. 2(3), pp. 423-54.

Knight, S. (1980), *Form and Ideology in Crime and Fiction*, Indiana University Press, Bloomington.

Lee, A. (1978), 'The Structure, Ownership and Control of the British Press 1855-1914', in Boyce, G., Curran, J. and Wingate, P. (Eds.), pp. 117-29, *Newspaper History from the Seventeenth Century to the Present Day*, Constable, London.

Lilly, J.R., Cullen, F.T. and Ball, R.A. (1995), *Criminological Theory: Context and Consequences*, (2nd ed), Sage, London.

MacDougal, C. (1968), *Interpretative Reporting*, Macmillan, New York.

Marsh, H.L. (1991), 'A Comparative Analysis of Crime Coverage in Newspapers in the United States and other Countries from 1960 to 1989: A Review of the Literature', *Journal of Criminal Justice*, Vol. 19, pp. 67-80.

Meyrowitz, J. (1985), *No Sense of Place: The Impact of the Electronic Media on Social Behaviour*, Oxford University Press, New York.

Molotch, H. and Lester, M. (1974), 'News As Purposive Behaviour', *American Sociological Review*, Vol. 39, pp. 101-12.

Murdock, G. (1973), 'Political Deviance: The Presentation of a Militant Mass Demonstration', in Cohen, S. and Young, J. (Eds), pp. 156-75, *The Manufacture of News: Deviance: Social Problems and Mass Media*, (1st ed), Constable, London.

Naylor, B. (1994), 'Fair Trial or Free Press: Legal Responses to Media Reports of Criminal Trials', *Cambridge Law Journal*, Vol. 53(3), pp. 492-501.

Parke, R., Berkowitz, L., Leyens, J.P., West, S. and Sebastian, R. (1977), 'Some Effects of Violent and Non-violent Movies on the Behaviour of Juvenile Delinquents', in Berkowitz, L. (Ed.), *Advances in Experimental Social Psychology*, Vol. 10, Academic Press, New York.

Pfohl, S. (1985), *Images of Deviance and Social Control*, McGraw Hill, New York.

Rock, P. (1973), *Deviant Behaviour*, Hutchinson, London.

Rock, P. (1988), *A History of British Criminology*, Oxford University Press, Oxford.

Roshier, B. (1973), 'The Selection of Crime News By The Press', in Cohen, S. and Young, J. (Eds.), *The Manufacture of News: Deviance: Social Problems and Mass Media*, pp. 28-39, Constable, London.

Sherizen, S. (1978), 'Social Creations Of Crime News: All the News Fitted To Print', in Winick, C. (Ed.), *Deviance and Mass Media*, pp. 205-24, Sage, Beverly Hills.

Sparks, R. (1992), *Television and the Drama of Crime in Public Life*, Open University Press, Buckingham.

Swope, H.B. (1958), 'Statement Recalled In Obituaries After His Death', cited in R. Tripp, (1978), *The International Thesaurus of Quotations*, Penguin, Hammondsworth.

Tannebaum, P. and Zillman, D. (1975), 'Emotional Arousal and the Facilitation of Through Communication', in Berkowitz, L. (Ed.), *Advances in Experimental Social Psychology*, Vol. 8, Academic Press, New York.

Tuchman, G. (1978), *Making News*, Free Press, New York.

Van Dijk, J.J.M. (1979), 'The Extent of Public Information and the Nature of Public Attitudes Towards Crime', in *Public Opinion on Crime and Criminal Justice*, pp. 7-42, France: Council of Europe, Strasbourg.

Ward, I. (1993), 'The Educative Ambition of Law and Literature', *Legal Studies*, Vol. 13, pp. 356-31.

Ward, I. (1995), *Law and Literature: Possibilities and Perspectives*, Cambridge University Press, Cambridge.

Weiner, J.H. (1969), *The War of the Unstamped Press: The Movement to Repeal the British Newspaper Tax 1830-1836*, Cornell University Press, Ithica.

Weisberg, R. (1988), 'The Law-Literature Enterprise', *Yale Journal of Law and the Humanities*, Vol. 1, pp. 1-67.

Williams, F.P. and McShane, M.D. (1994), *Criminological Theory* (2nd ed), Prentice Hall, Englewood Cliffs, New Jersey.

Williams, R. (1982), *The Sociology of Culture*, Schocken, New York.

Young, J. (1981), 'Mass Media, Drugs and Deviance', in Rock, P. and McIntosh, M. (Eds.), *Deviance And Social Control*, pp. 229-59, Tavistock, London.

8 Images of Law in the Fiction of John Grisham

PETER ROBSON

Introduction: The reasons for examining popular fiction

The way people perceive law is crucial for those concerned with the operation of the criminal and civil justice systems. If people see law and lawyers as tools of particular racial, class or gender interests rather than as sources of impartial justice, this has important implications for whether people will adhere to legal rules. Where the legal system and its workings are seen as corrupt there is less likely to be confidence in the integrity of the system in question. Stewart Macaulay has suggested that the role of the televisual media is of great significance in the formulation of people's images of the nature of legal phenomena.[1] He cites the success of such shows as *LA Law*, *Hill Street Blues* and *Perry Mason*. One aspect of popular culture which Macaulay makes only fleeting reference to is fiction. Whilst the legal process and the work of lawyers is generally peripheral in paperback fiction the work of a new group of lawyer writers has thrust the lawyer centrestage and has made a major impact on the bestseller lists replacing spy novels and the sex 'n shopping works of the 1980s. According to Mark Lawson's examination on television of the bestseller in the 1990s, both men and women buy legal thrillers - crime novels not about police procedure but about legal procedure.[2]

This kind of fiction is worthy of examination as part of Macaulay's theme. At the same time an interest has developed in academic law courses in the study of law and literature. This has shifted from being a leisure pursuit[3] to occupying a role in many Law School curricula.[4] One of the central features of this work has been to reveal the socio-political shortcomings of a legal order.

This essay examines the bestselling fictional work of John Grisham in the light of both Stewart Macaulay's comments as well in the context of law in literature. It looks particularly at the way in which lawyers are represented in Grisham's fiction and the extent to which there are consistent themes and typologies in these portrayals. The essay also notes that Grisham's lawyers have a resonance within the legal cultures of Great Britain. The similarities between the United States and British systems of jurisprudence are considerable. The language is superficially the same. Criminal justice practice is based on an adversarial rather than an inquisitorial model. There is a shared basis in a judge-made law and the impact of case law.

There are good reasons for lawyers in Britain and related legal systems to take an interest in the image of law and lawyers provided within the media stemming from the United States. As a result of the common tradition of language and legal approach United States books, films and television works on the legal process are accessible to a British or common law audience. What happens in the courtrooms and lawyers' offices in the United States is recognizable to such viewers and readers. There is evidence, furthermore, that there is an assumption in Britain that the distinctive United States version of legal practice is universal despite major differences.[5]

When taking the oath people in Britain are wont to conclude with the words 'so help me God' - this is not part of the oath they are asked to read but is a feature of American legal portrayals. In the film *In the Name of the Father* concerning the miscarriage of justice involving the Guildford Four we have the example of counsel being asked to approach the bench. In recent years judges in Scotland report that solicitors request that they be permitted to approach the bench. For submissions out of the hearing of the jury there is a standard provision for a request that the jury leave the courtroom. The practice of seeking to 'approach the bench' seems to derive from the popularity of *LA Law* as does the idea of counsel moving about the courtroom for maximum dramatic effect.

Limited examples perhaps and of no major practical consequence except insofar as they show that we in Britain read United States legal material with very limited cultural filters. Part of my thesis is that this indicates why there should be interest in Britain in what kind of images of lawyers are put forward in popular culture. There is also an indication that in other countries the representation of law in the United States model is extensive. Richard North Patterson's most recent work was published simultaneously in nine languages other than English. The work of Friedman and Grisham is also available throughout Europe.[6]

The legal thriller sub genre

Fiction covering the day-to-day work of lawyers was a minor element in crime fiction genre until recently.[7] Since the appearance of Scott Turow's *Presumed Innocent* and John Grisham's *A Time to Kill* in the late 1980s the field has burgeoned so that there are now over one hundred books published after 1988 in which lawyers feature as central protagonists.[8] There are three major strands in this sub genre of crime fiction - courtroom drama; lawyers as private eyes, and works where the central focus is the non-court aspect of lawyers' working lives.

The past decade has seen a new development in crime fiction. This involves books about courtroom lawyers written often by courtroom lawyers like Scott Turow, Philip Friedman and Richard North Patterson. Their influential work concentrates on the locus of the courtroom and the big murder case - *Presumed Innocent*[9] - murder case involving a lawyer as accused; *Reasonable Doubt*[10] - murder case with lawyer defending his daughter-in-law; *Degree of Guilt*[11] - murder case with lawyer as accused defended by her estranged lawyer husband. It is not now difficult to find new writers within this sub-genre with plots frequently centring on whether the lawyer protagonist will secure an acquittal of the client.[12]

The parallel between much of this kind of work and that of the 'Classical Plot' identified by Will Wright in his study of the Western genre[13] appears attractive. The courtroom lawyer as Shane rides into the lives of some oppressed group or individual and by dint of special skills faces down the hired guns of the oppressors. Task accomplished, there is another town to help tame, another river to cross.

Some writers have ostensibly written about lawyers but in fact have written private eye fiction.[14] There are also works which centre on the day-to-day work of lawyers with some coverage of court process. In this strand of work the lawyer is not principally involved as an investigator nor is a big trial the centrepiece of the books. George V. Higgins' work with its lawyer Jerry Kennedy is an example of the 'legal procedural' as well as William J. Coughlin's over-the-hill lawyers Charley Sloan[15] and Jake Martin.[16] More recently, in the wake of the success of John Grisham, William Bernhardt has moved away from the big-time court lawyer to the beginner failing to make his way in the world of corporate law[17] and becoming a poor lone practitioner.[18] His Ben Kincaid series harks back to the days of Henry Cecil with slapstick routines and broad characters[19] in the style of *The Dukes of Hazzard.* In his most recent work the same style and characters are encountered in a tale of murder, racial conflict and neo-Nazis preparing for a race war.[20]

The common factor linking courtroom dramas and the private eye lawyer is the dominance of plot over character. In these works the central feature is whether the hero will secure the verdict sought or discover the perpetrator of the crime in question. Fully rounded personal lives are not crucial for the progression of this kind of fiction. In some circumstances a family context may be provided[21] but we tend to learn little of the broader picture of the legal process or legal practice. The private eye lawyers often have interesting perspectives on the practice of law, but their remarks are essentially those of the outsider and do not carry quite the same weight as the portrayal of law by lawyers. By the very nature of the private eye role, however, there is a lesser opportunity to observe the workings of the legal system. By contrast, courtroom dramas centre on a single aspect of the legal system. They tend to focus on the drama of a trial for a major crime. The action is concerned mainly with courtroom performances. It would be misleading, though, to characterize the lawyers in the courtroom-based lawyer novels as mere ciphers moving the action to its final denouement where against all the odds the client is acquitted. The depth and credibility of these individuals is sometimes a major feature of Grisham's courtroom novels. In Scott Turow's *Presumed Innocent*, District Attorney Rusty Sabich, the accused, finds himself in difficulties precisely because of his private life and his position in the political world of the District Attorney's office. He is painted as a rounded human being with weaknesses rather than some kind of superhero.[22] Similarly the family problems of Christopher Paget in Richard North Patterson's *Degree of Guilt* (1993) are central to the plot and action. While Paget is a less sympathetic character than Sabich, the author is at pains to make clear, however, that his character is a 'cold fish' who has difficulty in social interaction. The point here, though, is not the extent to which the author is convincing at representing lawyers as credible actors in a drama. What is of interest here is the way in which legal practice is presented. How and in what ways do lawyers operate as a category? What different kinds of lawyers do we encounter in these fictional portrayals? In courtroom dramas the lawyers are scarcely abstracted from the courtroom except to plan stratagems and ruses. The trial, even when overlaid with family background, dominates.

Some writers have however loftier ambitions than merely to write thrillers. Philip Friedman summed up his rationale for working within this part of the genre as essentially functional. He found that using the legal system as a base was freer. He was able to deal with virtually every issue in society because virtually every issue in society, in particular in American society, showed up in a courtroom.[23] The big issues from capital punishment and desegregation to abortion and war and peace - these all came before the American courts.[24]

The extent to which the legal thriller as a whole provides consistent images of legal practice and its socio-political significance is a theme I have developed elsewhere and on which I am currently engaged in further work.[25] For present purposes I am concerned with the work of John Grisham and the consistent picture of the legal process being provided there to the huge numbers of buyers of legal thrillers who, according to Macaulay, are gaining their view on law and lawyers from popular culture.

The works of John Grisham

The works of John Grisham are of special interest in their portrayal of what lawyers are about. John Grisham has produced six legal thrillers - *A Time to Kill*,[26] *The Firm*,[27] *The Pelican Brief*,[28] *The Client*,[29] *The Chamber*[30] and *The Rainmaker*.[31] These have all featured in the bestseller lists and some forty million copies of his books are in print in the United States alone.[32] Sixty million copies of his books in the English language have been sold. By 1995 three of his novels have been filmed with such stars as Tom Cruise, Holly Hunter, Gene Hackman,[33] Julia Roberts, Denzel Washington,[34] Tommy Lee Jones and Susan Sarandon.[35] Grisham can justifiably lay claim to the title as the leading figure in modern day crime fiction. He is the fastest selling author in history.[36] His sales figures are staggering. In the United States alone, *The Firm* sold twelve million in paperback, *The Pelican Brief*, eleven million, *A Time to Kill*, nine million. *The Client* sold three million copies in hardback, and the soft-cover has added another six million.[37] Grisham has become something of a shorthand as well as benchmark for the nature and quality of legal thrillers. Book jackets indicate that the novel is the same as, or better than, or at least in the same style as the work of Grisham.

What distinguishes Grisham from most other writers in this field of fiction is the range of his subjects as well as his astonishing sales figures. He has written both within this courtroom format as well as ranging into the day-to-day work of both corporate lawyers, criminal legal practice and, in a small way, legal education.

John Grisham's first novel, *A Time to Kill*, is firmly within the conventional courtroom style. Small town Southern lawyer defends black man accused of murdering the two young rednecks who raped his 10 year old daughter. The novel is extensively concerned with the mechanics of jury selection to ensure a jury can be assembled with some prospect of acquittal.

The Firm concentrates on the problems which emerge when a young rookie lawyer discovers that the apparently respectable firm which he works for is in fact a money laundering front for the Mob in which all the partners are involved. A chase ensues as Mitch McDeere attempts to outwit the Mob.

Grisham again takes up the theme of the implications of a rotten core to respectable institutions in the *Pelican Brief*. Here the corporate forces of evil find it in their interest to assassinate two Supreme Court judges. Only one person, law student Darby Shaw, makes the link. Her thesis unfortunately becomes known to the men in black hats and she dares not trust the authorities. Can she find safety and reveal her discovery to the non-corrupt authorities before evil Capital silences her? A chase occurs.

Returning to the link between lawyers and organized crime John Grisham selects a pre-teenager as the vehicle for the Mob's secret in *The Client*. The scenario involves a *Witness*[38] type storyline after the suicide of a Mob lawyer. The death and its rationale was witnessed by the client. The novel is principally concerned with the lawyer and client trying to work out a strategy to deal with the revenge of the Mob. There is a chase.

The Chamber starts as though there will be a chase. This is, however, a feint. Grisham has adapted the story of Byron de la Beckwith and the murder of 1960s Civil Rights worker Medgar Evers to write on the social issue of capital punishment. The core of the book is about the mental torture engendered by the cruelty of capital punishment when combined with the elaborate and time-consuming appeal procedures which can keep people on death row for many years. The novel's twist is that the Ku Klux Klan murderer's case is taken up by his liberal lawyer grandson who adopts Bob Dylan's view that the murderer is 'only a pawn in their game'.[39]

Finally in *The Rainmaker* we return to the rotten core of institutions. This is a traditional David and Goliath legal tale with a newly qualified lawyer taking up the cause of a family refused assistance under their medical insurance policy. The company acting in bad faith have taken to refusing claims on a routine basis rather than treating them on their merits.[40] To this is added corrupt actions by the most prestigious law firm in Memphis.

The novels can be divided into 'issue' novels and 'chase' novels. The three which have been filmed by 1995 are all in the 'chase' category. They throw light on the legal process but their message is principally about the nature of lawyers rather than social issues. The other books - the serious first novel and the more mature works seem keener to confront social issues - at the expense in all of them of plot development. These are books which are more traditional in the centrality of the court process to the novel.

Grisham's roster

Grisham novels distinguish between several discrete categories of lawyers. Between them they portray the nature and practice of law as highly problematic. The prospect of liberty and justice for all is limited. There is a break between the 'issue' novels and the 'chase' novels. The first work is autobiographical. The story came from an incident which Grisham observed in court. The character of the small town Southern lawyer is Grisham - more or less. As he comments: 'There's a lot of autobiography in this book. I no longer practice law, but for ten years I did so in a manner very similar to Jake Brigance'.[41]

In this book we encounter many more legal characters than in the later novels. Twelve appear in *A Time to Kill*[42] as compared with half a dozen or less in *The Firm,*[43] *The Pelican Brief,*[44] *The Client,*[45] *The Chamber*[46] and *The Rainmaker.*[47]

Looking through this caste of lawyers in the Grisham novels a number of distinct categories recur. Some make such a brief appearance that they make a minimal contribution and have been omitted from this process of categorization. The groupings that emerge from Grisham's texts have resonance outwith the United States and may well transcend cultural boundaries. Grisham's lawyers come in six broad categories. They bear a limited relation to the distinction between 'nice' lawyers and the rest which Weisberg mentions.[48] They do not share the consistent characteristics which he suggests are shared by successful literary lawyers.[49] They occupy different places on a continuum from squeaky clean legality through murky ambivalence towards the goals of the legal system, to simple illegality.

Naive idealists

Whilst women lawyers have a limited role in the work of Grisham when they appear they are always portrayed as idealists. There are the naive idealists Darby Shaw and Ellen Roark. Both are highflying law students seeking to make their way in a male-dominated profession through the application of Stakhanovite principles. To this group one would have to add the perverse and highly principled Rosenberg, the man happy to cause chaos in the pursuit of abstract concepts such as freedom of speech. Mitchell McDeere, the poor boy from the wrong side of the tracks can be placed in this category with his intense ambition to succeed and his overriding desire to assist his imprisoned brother. The lawyer whose death provides the impetus for the capital punishment novel, Marvin Kramer, is right in the thick of the civil rights activism at a dangerous time in a dangerous place in spite of family pressure. Finally Adam Hall is driven to obtain employment with the firm acting for his racist grandfather so that he may have the opportunity to keep him from the gas chamber.

Realist idealists

Those with naive faith in the rule of law and the legal system are few and far between in Grisham's work. Most are realists. There is in his first novel Jake Brigance the small town decent Atticus Finch figure. He is accompanied by a burnt out version of himself in the old style liberal/radical campaigning figure of Lucien Wilbanks.

> He wanted the rapes, the murders, the child abuses, the ugly causes no one else wanted. He wanted to be a civil rights lawyer and litigate civil liberties. But most of all Lucien wanted to be a radical, a flaming radical of a lawyer with unpopular cases and causes, and lots of attention.[50]

The almost burnt-out force of Thomas Callahan from *The Pelican Brief* teeters on the cusp between being the lawyer without illusions and actual disillusion. When he staggers down a New Orleans street to drive his car we may suspect that disillusion has set in after the death of Mr Justice Rosenberg. His auto explosion renders such speculation redundant.

Much of the interest in *The Client* could be said to stem from the fate of Reggie Love. Here we start with a woman recovering from a controlling relationship. She had been trapped in an oppressive and exploitative marriage from which she had fled into a breakdown. From there she had been to Law School and 'found herself'. The burnt out case on the way back to salvation through the healing process of helping through the medium of idealist law practice. This is the same process we see with the representative of the 'slacker' generation growing up in the 1980s Rudy Baylor in *The Rainmaker*. Smart, street wise but not brilliant, he is cynical and opportunistic. These are the initial character traits exhibited by Rudy before he comes to appreciate how harsh and uncaring the jungle of market economics is.

Not surprisingly in a novel like *The Chamber* with a strong polemical thrust about the inhumanity of the practice of the death penalty in the killing belt of the Deep South, Texas, Florida and California there are other realist idealists. The most important, E. Garner Goodman is the conscience of the firm of Kravitz & Bane. He is the driving force behind the *pro bono* work for clients who cannot pay - housing project kids, death row inmates, illegal aliens, drug addicts and the homeless. He has sacrificed his personal life to working round the clock to save society. He is the firm's pet idealist. He is paid large sums of money so that his partners can pat themselves on the back and preach about the social responsibility of lawyers. He knows this but regards himself as the luckiest lawyer in town.

Cynical timeservers

Although they are not a central feature in the works of Grisham there are a number of characters who are not corrupt but who know on which side their bread is buttered. Here we find judges keen to avoid tricky cases for their own peace of mind and prosecutors going though the motions. We meet Percy Bullard the small worrier assigned to hear the preliminary motions in the Carl Lee Hailey case in *A Time to Kill*. Quick and nervous, Bullard has reached his pinnacle as a County Court judge and clearly regards retirement as a boon. Until that time he wants to avoid any trouble. We see the same with the character of Harvey Hale in *The Rainmaker*. He is coasting to retirement preferring to play golf and being quick to dismiss claims to keep his list of cases free of backlog. In the meantime he is happy to cosy up to insurance companies and large corporations and avoid controversy and conflict.

In a slightly different way the Ford County prosecutor Rocky Childers, in *A Time to Kill* has become disillusioned with what the law has provided for him by way of a job. He has a dead-end part-time, full-time job and is 'washed up as a lawyer' and the Carl Lee Hailey case is more than he wants to deal with.[51]

Political careerists

There are also a set of men seeking out the camera to make barnstorming, vote-getting capital out of successfully dealing with criminals. This is something which British audiences have become used to with the Dirty Harry movies. It takes a fresh form where prosecution lawyers are concerned and is one of the central features of the travails of Rusty Sabich in the first major modern legal thriller - Turow's *Presumed Innocent*. The political career founded on successful high profile prosecution features heavily in three of Grisham's novels, *A Time to Kill, The Client* and *The Chamber.*

Roy Foltrigg is ruthless in his pursuit of exposure in the media and loves 'those priceless moments' when the cameras were rolling and waiting for him, when he would 'stroll majestically through the hall or down the courthouse steps'.[52]

Rufus Buckley had his plans too to move from being the youngest District Attorney in Mississippi to another public office on his way to Congress. His problem was that he was not well known outside the Twenty-second District. He needed to be seen, and heard. He needed publicity. 'What Rufus needed more than anything else was a big, nasty, controversial, well-publicized conviction in a murder trial'.[53]

Finally with young district attorney David McAllister, we have a man with a mission to secure a conviction of Sam Cayhall at the third time of asking in order to ensure his own political future. His brilliance, looks and compassion were overlaid by his obnoxious habit of spending all his spare time with the press. The Cayhall trial has a purpose. McAllister has political ambitions on a grand scale.[54] When we next encounter McAllister he is State Governor with the task of deciding whether or not to extend clemency to the man who has spent a decade on death row. His decision-making is solely dependent on the issue of his rating in the polls.[55]

Sleazy/shady wheeler dealers

One of the most controversial characters and the one who most people would surely want to see in his own television series is Gill Teal from *The Rainmaker*. Like Douglas Brackman's half brother in *LA Law* Gill is SLEAZE in capital letters. He is Paul Newman's character from *The Verdict*[56] without the charm. To British readers he is almost unrecognisable. If anything he calls up the world of Gordon F. Newman[57] although in Britain what ambulance chasing exists is carried out through intermediaries - prison warders giving sweeteners to recommend certain lawyers to those in custody.[58] His advertising logo is 'Gill Teal - He's for real', but is he? John Grisham seems to think so given the centrality of ambulance chasing in *The Rainmaker*.

Harry Rex Vonner, a friend of Jake Brigance proves a useful ally with his underhand methods of jury-tampering. There is, however, no question that this 'vile and vicious slob' operates in the shady borders of legality/illegality.

He and Gill would have made a fine partnership.[59] Again in *The Rainmaker* the main protagonist has assistance from another character with only a nodding acquaintance with ethical standards. Deck Skifflet's ethics are what he terms the basics - fight for your client, don't steal and try not to lie. He is the law graduate who cannot pass the Bar Exam and styles himself 'paralawyer': a fully fleshed out relative of Gill Teal. He is an ambulance chaser with no qualms about how he gets clients. He also takes a sanguine view about declining moral standards. If gambling expands in his adopted state this is a good thing. Poor people will gamble. They will lose. Crime will rise. Divorce and bankruptcies will increase and more lawyers will be needed.

These are lawyers who are not sleazy in the sense that Jerry Kennedy's ex-wife described him as sleazy.[60] They do not necessarily have sleazy clients. It is their business methods and ethics which are questionable. Somewhere on the continuum between sleazy and Mob lawyers is Bruiser Stone from *The Rainmaker*. This is man who runs a shady law firm dependant on ambulance chasing. This business is generated through pay-offs to police and other officials. His partners are employed using a version of the sharecropping model. The clients and the lawsuits are genuine enough even if the method of obtaining them and rewarding his employees is all geared to produce income for him. He shades into the more traditional gangster with his protection of gangster clients' business interests. Significant sums of cash are paid to jurors and one suspects threats are made too. He is prepared to rob with a sixgun as well as a fountain pen.

Mob lawyers

Organized crime is central to *The Firm, The Pelican Brief* and *The Client*. This appears in the traditional Italian guise in *The Firm* and *The Client* whilst adopting a slightly different form in *The Pelican Brief*. Mob lawyers include the smooth respectable brand of the Memphis law firm, Bendini, Lambert and Locke in *The Firm* or Leo F. Drummond and his phonetapping firm in *A Time to Kill*. They may be flashy like Bo Marshafsky from *A Time to Kill* or come in the sweaty form of Romy Clifford from *The Client*. These men are hired guns. They are the antithesis of the notion of rule by law although they may disguise this beneath an Ivy League facade. These are men in black hats with no obvious redeeming features.

Jerome Clifford had been defending prominent New Orleans thugs for fifteen years - gangsters, pushers, politicians - and his record was impressive. He was cunning and corrupt, completely willing to buy people who could be bought. He drank with judges and slept with their girlfriends. He bribed the cops and threatened the jurors.[61]

Romy's replacement after his suicide, Willis Upchurch, is straight from the same stable:

a rising star among the gang of boisterous mouthpieces trotting across the country performing for crooks and cameras ... He had become somewhat rich and noted in Chicago for his passionate defense of mob assassins and drug traffickers.[62]

Upchurch, however has rather more ambitions to make it as a personality on his own:

Upchurch was a lawyer who wanted to be seen and heard in magazine articles, news stories, advice columns, quickie books, and gossip shows ... He grinned at himself in the mirror as he tied his ninety-dollar tie and thought of spending the next six months in New Orleans with the press at his beck and call. This was why he went to law school![63]

The same kind of political ambition is shown by the Ku Klux Klan lawyer Clovis Brazelton in *The Chamber*. A secret member of the Klan himself, he wanted to run for governor on a platform of the preservation of the white race. Exactly what happens to these ambitions is not made clear other than that 12 years later he has 'gone onto bigger things'.[64]

Grisham's images of law and legal practice

As indicated, there have been a number of precursors to Grisham's work both in popular fiction as well as in the work of major novelists. The work of William Faulkner provides some interesting resonances with its similarity of lawyer protagonist and location in the South. Grisham also employs the Faulkner device of references to earlier unrelated fictional incidents in later work. Thus we find the protagonists of *The Chamber* visiting Clanton and discussing the Carl Lee Hailey trial from *A Time to Kill*.[65]

Grisham portrays law and its practice as an unattractive pursuit which seems to emphasize the worst traits of those who are involved in its practice. Various explicit views of law are expressed throughout the works. They centre on the plastic nature of law whose content stems solely from the most effective lawyering skills. These skills are deployed ruthlessly. Law is a game for sharks. It involves political manipulation. Practice is portrayed as a home for compulsive personalities, as a cut-throat and competitive enterprise. It has nothing to do with justice but rather is a gravy train to luxury living. It does not conform to the aspirations of Rudy Baylor's tutor Professor Smoot who seeks to enhance the notion of law as public service which is driven out of students by the brutal competition of law school.

The secret of success in the competitive world is how effectively a legal counsel can prevent the truth coming to the surface. In *A Time to Kill*, Carl Lee's army buddy, Cat Bruster, has been involved in drugs, gambling, bribery, guns, racketeering, prostitution. He has been tried but never convicted because he has a smart, mean, crooked lawyer who cheats and plays dirty. Whatever is needed to win the case.[66] Whether it is through the campaigns to defend Carl Lee Hailey or to secure the acquittal or save the life of Sam Cayhall, decision-making in the criminal justice process is portrayed as being driven essentially by short term and narrow political considerations.[67]

The weekly hours worked by the vast majority of the lawyer protagonists in the work of John Grisham are prodigious. Families and any kind of social life are sacrificed to the practice of law. The only major exception to this kind of portrayal is the 'slacker' Rudy Baylor. This is not a recipe for success. The three law firms for which he works collapse over a three month period. Working for himself he adopts a more traditional pattern of work having little time off and minimal social interaction. He becomes a proper legal thriller lawyer following in the footsteps of the majority of Grisham's lawyers.

There is an alternative way out of this lifestyle while still staying in the field of law. One can drop out and become a legal academic. College campus is a home for inadequates unable to function in the real world. It involves books and theories where law is practiced between professional gentlemen, not the real world. It avoids the work habits of contemporaries with 70 hour weeks in pressurized law factories. Thomas Callahan, for instance lasted just 2 years in private practice: 'He was told if he could cram the next 20 years into the next ten, he might just make partner at the weary age of 35'.[68]

Obtaining work for ordinary lawyers is a problem where the profession is portrayed as overcrowded. The methods of procuring that work are often dubious involving crude ambulance chasing. As one of Bruiser Stone's employees points out, however, there is no alternative. There are a lot of rivals eager to pounce and obtain clients. At a collapsed building along with the fire, ambulance and police services we have men with sombre faces trying to sneak close to the families of the victims to hand over their business cards. They would kill for a case, but they only want their third split of the recovered compensation.

Even in the corporate law firms practice is finance driven. Billing is the lifeblood of the firm. Everything revolves around it. Promotions, raises, bonuses, survival, success - everything revolves around how well people are billing. For new employees the quickest route to a reprimand is to neglect the daily billing records.[69]

There is a contrast between the 'ham and egg' struggling street lawyers who are sometimes forced to resort to almost any means to get clients and upmarket colleagues. These are lawyers billing by the hour where speed is not of the essence and work proceeds in leisurely fashion. Seconds mean minutes. Minutes mean hours. Hours mean fees, retainers, bonuses, partnerships.[70] This does not matter. This is the world of the corporation lawyers typified by the ethos at Bendini, Lambert and Locke.

> We only take rich clients - corporations, banks and wealthy people who pay our healthy fees and never complain ... We deal only with people who can pay.[71]

Against this are counterposed the goals of the major protagonists. They seek in a confused way to secure a version of justice. Thus it is that Jake Brigance, Mitch McDeere, Darby Shaw, Reggie Love, Adam Hall and Rudy Baylor are all on the side of the angels. They are individuals with a faith in the ability of the legal process. The illusions of the experienced Jake Brigance and Reggie Love produce a rather more realistic assessment of the way the law operates than the youthful graduates Mitch McDeere, Adam Hall, Rudy Baylor and law student Darby Shaw. Jake and Reggie are street lawyers. Their gloomier message about law and legal practice has the stronger impact. Even ethical Jake Brigance hopes to escape being a 'street lawyer'. He expresses the view that if he gets the Carl Lee Hailey case and wins it then the sky is the limit.

> It's the biggest. I'll practice the rest of my life and never have another reporter from the New York Times stop me in a cafe and ask for an interview. If I win, I'll be top dog in this part of the state.[72]

This dream becomes one not of upward movement but escape when in *The Rainmaker* Deck Shifflet explains what motivates most street lawyers,

> It just takes one, he says over and over. You hear that all the time in this business. One big case, and you can retire. That's the reason lawyers do so many sleazy things, like full-color ads in the yellow pages, and billboards, and placards on city buses, and telephone solicitation. You hold your nose, ignore the stench of what you're doing, ignore the snubs and snobbery of big-firm lawyers, because it only takes one.[73]

In so far as half the protagonists with faith in the system end up out of the system and in hiding at the end of the books it is fair to say that there is a fair degree of pessimism in Grisham as to the value of law as protection for the masses. Over the whole, with his healthy suspicion of the possibility of justice for those without means and the persistence of the theme of rotten core of business and institutions, when he observes that 'the mystery has usually been the province of writers with right-wing viewpoints' Grisham does not conform to the stereotype described by Marvin Lachman.[74]

Grisham and modern culture

Any attempt to derive Grisham's images of law and lawyers from the text alone runs the risk of abstracting Grisham from the development of crime fiction. The rise of the detective novel was seen by Ernest Mandel as mirroring the 'growing, explosive contradiction between individual needs or passions and mechanically imposed patterns of social conformism'.[75] The crime story here is a mirror of the social relations of bourgeois society. The fascination stems, according to Mandel, from the fact that bourgeois society is, when all is said and done, a criminal society. This is something we recognise in the fiction of John Grisham with its corrupt officials, rotten institutions and financially determined justice.

In his examination on television of the world of the legal bestseller Mark Lawson has suggested that the fact that tens of millions of people around the world are suddenly drawn to the same stories must surely tell us something about the way we live now.[76] Success in life is measured in a material way. Lifechances are significantly determined by people's access to resources. In an alienated urban environment some go to the wall. This applies to employment, health care and education. Nowhere is the gap between haves and have-nots made more explicit than in the world of legal rights. Like the

Lottery, however, there is enough publicity for the handful of winners to encourage people to believe that the game is not rigged.

Richard North Patterson is explicit in the political purpose of his writing. His *Degree of Guilt* was written specifically as a critique of the William Kennedy Smith rape trial. Patterson was keen that the issue of past behaviour of the accused be aired. He resorted not to law reform or political campaigning but to writing a legal thriller.[77]

According to Mark Lawson, writers like Grisham, Turow and North Patterson represent a new wave of trained lawyers who have seen the narrative possibilities of the law. This chapter argues that Grisham has seen them a little differently from the other legal thriller writers. Accidentally or not his books are not just readable but eminently filmable too.[78] This translation into film has reinforced the position of John Grisham as the sub genre market leader.[79] He combines the detailed operation of the legal system together with a caste of proper men in black hats. There is in Grisham's 'chase novels' an unreconstructed force of evil seeking to do away with the main character. This is formula writing with an edge. It seems to owe its runaway success to the blending of the fascination of the operation of the legal procedures in court and in the legal office with a good old-fashioned chase. The author's self-proclaimed goals are as an uncomplicated storyteller.[80]

Grisham adopts a simple strategy in these 'chase novels'. From early on in *The Firm* Mitch McDeere is preparing to go on the run.[81] The office is only mentioned as a location for preparation of his scheme of deception. He must flee from the forces of evil who would end his life as he knows that the firm Bendini, Lambert and Locke is a Mafia front. We also have the thrill of the chase in *The Pelican Brief.* From a similar, early stage in the book Darby Shaw is on the run from those who are seeking to kill her. They must silence the knowledge she revealed in her thesis as to the forces behind the murder of the two Supreme Court justices - which forgetfully she has not had copied. Finally in *The Client* Mark Sway commences as a youthful Scarlet Pimpernel and is in hiding of one sort or another for almost the whole of the book. Here the chase is a little different since one of the 'hiding places' is in juvenile custody prior to the final chase episode which occupies the last quarter of the book.

Despite his self-deprecatory aim to be no more than a storyteller, Grisham does provide some intellectual meat in his 'chase novels' - corporate corruption and the notion of professional conduct in *The Firm*; the politics of the Supreme Court in *The Pelican Brief*; client confidentiality and the

treatment of children by the justice system in *The Client*. Points to ponder, however, rather than the central thrust of the work which is the thriller element.[82]

In the 'issues novels' Grisham is much more concerned with the legal issues stemming from social conflict. His first novel *A Time To Kill* was neglected by the world outside Oxford, Mississippi. It was reissued on the strength of the success of *The Firm*. It takes a serious look at the question of jury selection and its significance for affecting the legal process. In this instance the accused is black and living in Mississippi. This is a theme which re-emerges in *The Chamber* and in *The Rainmaker* and is one with which the public is now familiar after the Roderick King and O.J. Simpson trials. The main thrust of *The Chamber* represents a significant shift in style for Grisham. This is a sombre novel on a sombre theme. Perhaps to emphasize the way time passes on death row it is a novel where, in contrast to Grisham's other work, nothing much happens. There is no twist. No unexpected turn of events. By the end of the novel the inhumanity of the various methods of capital punishment have been laid out. The issue occupies a far more central role than any plot or character development.

Finally, *The Rainmaker* explores the problems of poor people trying to use the law against rich corporations. As a refreshing change from bright-eyed enthusiasts the hero reluctantly finds himself reduced to working for poor people when he planned to work for a firm whose sole business was to represent insurance companies in litigation. He gets to see how the poor suffer in the market driven justice system with his exposure to street lawyering. They suffer from their own lawyers as well as those of their opponents. This combined with his discovery as to how ineffective the law can be for women abused by their partners transforms Rudy Baylor's outlook. In line with the enhanced realism in this latest book, Rudy ends up leaving town to become a high school teacher.

There are a number of important dogs that do not bark - gender and sexuality for instance. Following the rather dense coverage of a major issue in *The Chamber* and after Grisham's success in combining social issues and an exciting plot in *The Rainmaker*, it would be surpising if further matters of social conflict are not canvassed in his work. Looking at the corpus of his work it is clear that increasingly John Grisham confronts John Cawelti's hypothesis that formulaic fiction tends to reproduce cultural consensus as opposed to the way elite fiction confronts us with the problematic and contradictory nature of the world as it appears to us.[83] Grisham portrays the world of the criminal and civil justice systems in sufficient detail to have the

appearance of authenticity. His consistent portrayal of law and lawyers is as deeply flawed. We receive few indicators that there is any likelihood of liberty and justice for any but the rich. Given the pervasiveness of Grisham not only in books but in films too the confidence which might have been engendered by *LA Law* is seriously undermined by the corpus of Grisham's work. The rule of law may not be quite dead but is not in good health in this world. The miscarriages of justice uncovered in Britain in the 1980s and the real-life trials involving William Kennedy Smith, Rodney King and O.J. Simpson bear out that this fiction provides a surprisingly accurate representation of a rotten and corrupt system.

Notes

1. Macauley (1987), p. 198.
2. Lawson (1994).
3. Gest (1913).
4. Contrast the study of jurisprudence teaching in British Universities by Barnett (1995) with the earlier study by Barnett and Yach (1985).
5. Robson (1995).
6. There may be subtle shifts of emphasis which this paper does not address such as John Grisham's *The Firm* (1991) becoming *Il Socio* (The Partner) in its Italian version rather than *Lo Studio.*
7. Robson (1995).
8. The author has compiled a data base of such works. Readers who wish for further information will find this on the Internet at the URC: http: //www.strath.ac.uk/Departments/Law/diglib/thrillers.html.
9. Turow (1987).
10. Friedman (1990).
11. North Patterson (1993).
12. The data base (fn. 8 *supra*) yields many examples.
13. Wright (1975), p. 32.
14. These include in Britain M.R.D. Meek's fictional solicitor, Lennox Kemp, Martin Edwards' solicitor Harry Devlin (*All The Lonely People*, (1991); *Suspicious Minds*, (1992); *I Remember You*, (1994)) and Helen West, the public prosecutor featured by Frances Fyfield. In the United States private eye work is also the principal past-time of China Bayles, the lawyer who appears in the work of Susan Wittig Albert (*Thyme of Death*, (1993)), Ed McBain's Florida lawyer

Matthew Hope (*Goldilocks; Rumpelstiltskin; Beauty and the Beast; Jack and the Beanstalk; Snow White and Rose Red; Cinderella; Puss in Boots; The House That Jack Built* and *There was a Little Girl,* 1978 onwards), Boston attorney Brady Coyne (Tapply, *Dead Winter,* (1990)), Albuquerque's Neil Hamel (Van Gieson, *North of the Border,* (1990); *Raptor,* (1990); *The Other Side of Death,* (1990)) and Steve Martini's Sam Bogardus (*The Simeon Chamber,* (1993)).

15. *Shadow of a Doubt* (1991); *Death Penalty* (1993).
16. *In The Presence of Enemies* (1990).
17. *Primary Justice* (1992).
18. *Blind Justice* (1992).
19. *Deadly Justice* (1993).
20. *Perfect Justice* (1995).
21. Brandon, *Loose Among the Lambs* (1994); Irving, *Final Argument* (1993).
22. When portrayed by Harrison Ford these characteristics were somewhat lost by the film star aura of the leading man.
23. Lawson (1994), per Philip Friedman.
24. Lawson (1994), per Scott Turow.
25. Robson (1995).
26. (1992), originally published in 1989.
27. (1991).
28. (1992).
29. (1993).
30. (1994).
31. (1995).
32. Lawson (1994).
33. *The Firm* (1993).
34. *The Pelican Brief* (1993).
35. *The Client* (1994).
36. Lawson (1994).
37. According to *The Guardian* 30 May 1994.
38. Paramount Pictures (1985), CBS.
39. *The Times They are a' Changin,* CBS (1961), 'Only A Pawn in their Game'.
40. A theme which is also found in Shelby Yastrow's *Under Oath* (1994).
41. Author's Note to *A Time to Kill* (1992), p. 11.

42. Jake Brigance; Percy Bullard; Rocky Childers; Omar Noose; Rufus Buckley; Ellen Roark; Lucien Wilbanks; L. Winston Lotterhouse; Harry Rex Vonner; Bo Marshafsky; Norman Reinfeld and the other NAACP lawyers.

43. Mitchell McDeere; Lamar Quin; Oliver Lambert; Royce McKnight; Avery Tolleson.

44. Darby Shaw; Professor Thomas Callahan; Mr Justice Rosenberg; Mr Justice Jensen; Gavin Verheek.

45. Gill Teal; Reggie Love; Jerome Clifford; Roy Foltrigg; Willis Upchurch.

46. Adam Hall; Marvin Kramer; Daniel Rosen; E. Garner Goodman; David McAllister; Clovis Brazelton.

47. Rudy Baylor; Bruiser Stone; Deck Shifflet; Leo F. Drummond; Tyrone Kipler; Jonathan Lake; Harvey Hale.

48. Weisberg (1992).

49. Weisberg (1992), p. 54.

50. *A Time to Kill* (1992), p. 29.

51. *A Time to Kill* (1992), p. 65.

52. *The Client* (1994), p. 73.

53. *A Time to Kill* (1992), p. 101.

54. *The Chamber* (1994), p. 29.

55. *The Chamber* (1994), p. 359.

56. T.C.F., Zanuck-Brown, (1984).

57. *Law and Order,* BBC, (1980).

58. Bankowski and Mungham (1976).

59. The spin-off series would have starred John Candy and Danny de Vito.

60. Higgins (1986), p. 14.

61. *The Client* (1994), p. 25.

62. *The Client* (1994), p. 97.

63. *The Client* (1994), p. 97.

64. Possibly like Imperial Grand Wizard David Duke who was narrowly defeated as Governor in Louisiana in the 1980s when his Klan past was revealed.

65. I am indebted to Ray Geary of Queen's University, Belfast, for this insight.

66. A *Time to Kill* (1992), p. 16.

67. A *Time to Kill* (1992), p. 232.

68. *The Pelican Brief* (1992), p. 62.
69. *The Firm* (1991), p. 51.
70. *A Time to Kill* (1992), p.128.
71. *The Firm* (1991), p. 8.
72. *A Time to Kill* (1992), p. 113.
73. *The Rainmaker* (1995), p. 229.
74. Lachman (1989), p. 15.
75. Mandel (1984), p. 135.
76. Lawson (1994).
77. Lawson (1994).
78. In one interview Grisham indicated that he wrote *The Pelican Brief* with Julia Roberts in mind and *The Chamber* he saw as a vehicle for Paul Newman - *The Guardian* 30 May 1994.
79. Universal Pictures paid $3.5 million for the film rights to *The Chamber* before a word had been written.
80. *The Guardian* 30 May 1994.
81. At page 182 of a 421 page book.
82. Jerry Palmer (1984) identifies three elements which seem to be present in Grisham's 'chase novels' - everything from the point of view of the hero: the hero is distinguished from the other characters by his professionalism and his success and the hero undertakes to solve a henious, mysterious crime which is a major threat to the social order.
83. Cawelti (1976), chp. 1, pp. 5-36.

References

Bankowski, Z. and Mungham, G. (1976), *Images of Law*, RKP, London.
Barnett, H. (1995), 'The Province of Jurisprudence Determined - Again!', *Legal Studies*, Vol. 15(1), pp. 80-127.
Barnett, H. and Yach, D. (1985) 'The Teaching of Jurisprudence in British Universities and Polytechnics', *Legal Studies*, Vol. 5(2), pp. 151.
Cawelti, J. (1976), *Adventure, Mystery and Romance*, University of Chicago, Chicago and London.
Friedman, P. (1990), *Reasonable Doubt*, Headline, London.
Gest, J.M. (1913), *The Lawyer in Literature*, Sweet and Maxwell, London.
Grisham, J. (1991), *The Firm*, Arrow, London.

Grisham, J. (1992/i), *A Time to Kill*, Arrow, London.
Grisham, J. (1992/ii), *The Pelican Brief*, Arrow, London.
Grisham, J. (1993), *The Client*, Arrow, London.
Grisham, J. (1994), *The Chamber*, Century, London.
Grisham, J. (1995), *The Rainmaker*, Century, London.
Higgins, G.V. (1986), *Kennedy for the Defense*, Sphere, London.
Lachman, M. (1989), 'Ed Lacy: Paperback Writer of the Left', in Breen, Jon L. and Greenberg, Martin Harry, (Eds.), *Murder off the Rack: Critical Studies of Ten Paperback Masters*, pp. 15-34, Scarecrow, Metuchen NJ and London.
Lawson, M., *The Bestseller Brief*, BBC 2, 2 February 1994.
Macaulay, L. (1987), 'Images of Law in Everyday Life', *Law and Society Review*, Vol. 21(2), pp. 185-218.
Mandel, E. (1984), *Delightful Murder - A Social History of the Crime Story*, Pluto, London.
Newman, G.F. (1980), *Law and Order*, Sphere, London.
North Patterson, R. (1993), *Degree of Guilt*, Arrow, London.
Palmer, J. (1984), 'Thrillers', in Pawling, C. (Ed.), *Popular Fiction and Social Change*, Macmillan, London.
Robson, P. (1995), *Watching the Detectives*, University of Strathclyde.
Turow, S. (1987), *Presumed Innocent*, Penguin, London.
Weisberg, R. (1992), *Poethics and Other Strategies of Law and Literature*, Columbia University Press, New York.
Wright, W. (1975), *Sixguns and Society*, University of California Press, Berkeley.

9 Victorian Values: Law and Justice in the Novels of Trollope

PETER INGRAM

Introduction: legal themes in Trollope's novels

'He speaks from beyond the grave in sturdy vindication of his aged', wrote Michael Sadleir of Anthony Trollope in his classic biography first published in 1927.[1] In similar vein Lord David Cecil noted that Trollope 'was brought up, an English gentleman with an English gentleman's standards, and his experience of the world only served to confirm him in the view that they were the right ones'. Like other mid-Victorian gentlemen 'he accepted unquestioningly the existing state of society'.[2] These opinions, voiced as Trollope emerged from a period of relative, though by no means complete, neglect following his death in 1882 seem to have stood the test of time as permanent judgments about his work. They are readily confirmed by the comfortable setting of his English novels, each having as a typical background one or another of the principal social institutions of Victorian England: the Church, politics, law, land, commerce, class.

Trollope has by no means the range of social observation that came so naturally to a writer like Dickens. For the most part he remained close to an actuality with which he felt familiar, even when this was based more on imagination than on a genuine everyday acquaintance with the particular variety of social life which he chose to portray (as was largely the case, for example, with his ecclesiastical characters and their lives). His expression of the mid-Victorian spirit takes place within the limits and limitations of the social class and background which he found congenial. Although he extends his settings into the upper class on the one hand and the lower reaches of the middle class on the other, in his English novels at least 'he is the chronicler, the observer and the interpreter of the well-to-do, comfortable England of London and the English shires'.[3] He writes supportively of (to borrow a phrase from one of his own novels) 'the English order of things'.[4] The success of his familiarity with the facts and incidents of comfortable upper-middle-class life in nineteenth-century England is sufficiently evident in the sales of his works, which Trollope himself took care to record.

The limited reach of the social setting of much of his writing emphasizes that, although he was a staunch Liberal in name, Trollope was very much a conservative by nature. The world he created was not one which seemed to itself to require radical reform. On the contrary, it was a world which sought if not to isolate itself from the forces of change at least to hold them back. Individual arguments for change are often heard in the mouths of Trollope's characters, but the forces of reform rarely intrude significantly on the English novels in an organized way; the episodes involving John Bold and the Jupiter in *The Warden*, which was Trollope's first work to achieve popular success, have few parallels in subsequent novels. As for the targets of reform that do occur in the novels, these belong in any case within the experiences of the middle and upper classes. Whatever the faults of ecclesiastical charities or the law of entail, seemingly Trollope's own *bête noire*, they hardly presented objects of urgent reform for the masses. Of the widespread social problems of poverty, disease and exploitation we hear little. The Irish novels are notably different; *The Landleaguers*, which was unfinished at Trollope's death, as well as the much earlier novels set in Ireland, confront the reader with social problems, attitudes, and members of a class whose English analogues, where they exist, are seldom encountered in Trollope's other works. In any event, the general movement for reform which explains the action of *The Warden* is hardly vindicated by the novel's outcome.

Unattractive though reform may seem, Trollope is not unaware of the failings of the social institutions he portrays; he does not conceal or disguise them. In fact, his criticism is expressed on many occasions in both the mouths of his characters and his own authorial comments. In *The Warden*, after all, the reformers' case against the Warden of Hiram's Hospital (as the holder of the office) is a good one. But the abstract principle meets the concrete case; the abstraction of the office is one thing, the real person of the office-holder, Septimus Harding, quite another. Reform does not seem to be an unmitigated good, or even a good at all, when its effects are felt by individual people. To capture the problem as that of 'situation ethics', as one commentator has done,[5] makes a good point, although in the end not a convincing one, since Trollope does not tell us unequivocally what the agent ought to do in relation to either the rule or the situation. Criticism there is, but it is a criticism that seeks no particular outcome; giving effect to the reform appears an unhappy course of action in the circumstances, but the old unreformed rule is not to be justified either. Trollope has the ability to look continually at institutional weaknesses - to state the fault, to portray the problem, and yet to come down in the end on neither side, only implying, gently, that acceptance is preferable to change. If he adopts this stance it is not because of any inherent merits the pre-existing situation may have or because the faults can be excused; he is only saying, in effect, 'Leave well enough alone'.

Nowhere else does Trollope's conservative outlook on society show itself more directly than in his especial interest in questions of land, property and inheritance. From such questions, of course, law is inseparable. It was a bequest and its legal consequences which laid the foundation for the plot of *The Warden* (Trollope's first popular success, published in 1855). Trollope's interest in other aspects of law is shown through his notable depiction in the same novel of Sir Abraham Haphazard and other aspects of the legal process. However, the concerns underlying this preoccupation - at least in relation to law - are not so evident in this book and the other Barsetshire novels, or in the Palliser novels (where law and lawyers often figure), as in other works from the author's later period falling outside these groupings. In particular there are the three major novels: *Orley Farm* (1862), *Lady Anna* (1874), and *Mr Scarborough's Family* (published posthumously in 1883). These are not the only novels concerned with inheritance. Between 1868 and 1873, preceding the publication of *Lady Anna*, Trollope seemed almost obsessed with the subject, which figures centrally in three other novels from these years: *Sir Harry Hotspur of Humblethwaite* (1871), *An Eye for an Eye* (1879, but completed in 1870) and *Ralph the Heir* (1871). They are, however, the novels in which the legal aspects of inheritance are most clearly to the fore.

The action of *Orley Farm* arises from the forging of a codicil to her husband's will by the novel's chief character, Lady Mason. By this codicil the small estate of Orley Farm is supposedly bequeathed to her son Lucius, whereas her husband in fact bequeathed all his property to Joseph, the child of his first marriage. Although disputed, the codicil was affirmed after a trial, and Lady Mason and Lucius remained in possession. Twenty years after her husband's death, the codicil is contested for a second time by Joseph after the chance discovery that the will and the codicil were apparently signed and witnessed by the same persons on the same day, although these witnesses are sure that they attested only one document. The novel focuses on the character of Lady Mason. Her guilt is fully revealed by Trollope before the halfway point of the novel but it has become obvious to the reader long before this. Nevertheless, within the novel she is a person whose guilt seems most unlikely to all those who are close to her and give her their support. Much of the interest of the book therefore is to be found in the way Trollope handles the story, and particularly in his treatment of the legal aspects of the affair, namely Lady Mason's trial and acquittal, thanks to the forensic skill of her barrister, Mr Chaffanbrass. A special skill of Trollope's is revealed in the ending of the novel which leaves Lady Mason in irredeemable and justified disgrace but still likely to retain most readers' sympathy.

Lady Anna begins with the marriage of Josephine Murray, an ambitious woman, to Earl Lovel. He soon claims that the marriage is not valid, on the ground that his wife by a previous marriage was still alive at the time of the wedding. However no evidence is adduced to support this claim. The Countess is nonetheless constrained to quit the Earl's residence of Lovel Grange, taking her daughter, Anna, to live with a tailor who comes to take up her cause. As Anna grows up she forms a deep attachment to the tailor's son, Daniel. The Countess institutes a prosecution for bigamy, something of a neat trick since either the Earl will be found guilty or, with no substantiation of the first marriage to hand, the prosecution will be sure to fail (which in fact it does), with the Countess's claim to her proper title and status becoming publicly recognized. After a lengthy period away the Earl returns to Lovel Grange with an Italian woman but dies not long after. It is his will that sets in train the main action of the book. The document renews the Earl's claim that Josephine Murray was never his lawful wife, asserts that Anna Murray is his illegitimate daughter, makes no mention of the true heir to the title, his cousin, and leaves everything to his last companion. His cousin, the new Earl, destined to inherit only the title and the small estate at Lovel Grange, is prepared to contest the will on the ground of the old Earl's insanity, but the chances of success are not promising. Attempts are made by the Countess in concert with the lawyers to make a love match between the new Earl and Lady Anna, both to bypass all the litigation in prospect and to produce a solution that is somehow fitting. However, these efforts fail and Anna retains her affection for Daniel. They are married and emigrate to a new life in Australia. It seems that Trollope had it in mind to write a sequel to this novel, although he never returned to take up the story of these two characters.

The plot of *Mr Scarborough's Family* turns on Mr Scarborough's intention of protecting his estate against the law of entail. At the beginning of the book Mr Scarborough is close to death. His elder son, Mountjoy, has run up huge gambling debts secured against his future inheritance. Seeing the ruin of the estate in prospect, the father claims that at the time of

Mountjoy's birth, he had not been married to the boy's mother, and that therefore Augustus, his younger son, is in fact the true heir. Eventually convinced of this, Mountjoy's creditors are in the end content to abandon their extortionate securities and settle for a straight repayment of what they had lent. Augustus has meanwhile revealed himself to be a selfish and cold-blooded individual who repels his father, while Mountjoy attempts to free himself from his addiction to gambling. Mr Scarborough then reveals to his lawyer that he had duplicitously gone through two ceremonies of marriage - 'with the intent of enabling him at some future time to upset the law altogether, if it should seem good to him to do so'[6] – and that Mountjoy is indeed the legitimate son and the true heir. Nevertheless, the novel ends with Mountjoy succumbing once again to the vice of gambling with little hope of redemption for him (or his property) in the future.

Although these three books are relatively little read at the present time, they have always had their admirers. *Orley Farm* received high praise from friends. Although Trollope, in his *Autobiography*, expressed the belief that, notwithstanding their opinions, this was not the best novel he had written, he was nevertheless sure that its plot was the best he had ever made.[7] (The accolade of best novel he accorded to *The Last Chronicle of Barset*, despite his assertion that he was 'never quite satisfied with the development of the plot' of that book.[8]) *Orley Farm* was quickly criticized - fairly enough - for its legal inaccuracies and prejudices, but Trollope was still proud of it and believed that there was not a dull page in the book.[9] *Lady Anna* is arguably the most accomplished of Trollope's legal novels, containing his greatest lawyer, the Solicitor-General, Sir William Patterson. He has been considered 'a lawyer's lawyer, one to whom most other lawyers, past middle age, with ambition, ideas and common sense, would point as representing what they themselves would like to be'.[10] As for *Mr Scarborough's Family,* this book is described in the Introduction to a recent edition as 'essentially a dark comedy which, as well as being one of the most intelligent of English legal novels, also offers a penetrating study of Victorian attitudes in the grip of change'.[11]

A legal theme in a novel is hardly unusual; most prominently Charles Dicken's *Bleak House* (1852-53), had converted an example of apparently sterile chancery law into a fruitful source of storytelling and social comment. Still, it is surprising to find that a popular writer like Trollope returns so often to focus on the legal ins and outs of inheritance, which is after all a fairly technical and abstruse area of law, and that he does so for the most part successfully (in a literary if not a legal perspective). He is repeatedly drawn back to the same theme because for him, uniquely, the legal fiction becomes the reality, and ultimately, 'real' property (in the legal sense) comes to matter above all else. The culmination of the process which values property for its own sake occurs in *Mr Scarborough's Family* where it is clear that, even as he lies dying, Mr Scarborough is concerned not that his property may ruin Mountjoy, but that it should not be ruined by him.

With the concern for property comes a concern for propriety, centring on the proper disposition of bequests and inheritance, and a desire for punctilious correctness in the laws and customs associated with property. Trollope was a strict positivist in these matters. 'Even a wretch such as Joseph Mason must have that which was clearly his own' are the thoughts of Sir Peregrine Orme in *Orley Farm*,[12] but they are an accurate echo of Trollope's own thoughts. Trollope possessed the faith of a true conservative in the need to keep estates intact, because he believed them to be part of the foundation of that social order of England which he loved and wished to preserve. It is therefore natural enough that themes of property and inheritance should provide the occasion for numerous principal and secondary plots. Further, law and property are in turn in a relationship with society; law, and in particular the law relating to property, is there to serve the social order. Consequently, in *Lady Anna*, although Anna has claim to all the old Earl's property by law, it is right that the development of the plot should ensure that Anna's cousin, the new Earl, should come to possess the real property that is his due by reason of his social station. Trollope's formalist approach to the relationship between law, property and society - an approach which places principles above individual circumstances - sits at odds in some ways with his dislike of the reformers' disregard of circumstances in their commitment to their own abstract principles. Of course, in both cases there is a tension between general principle and particular situation, but Trollope usually keeps faith with his own ideals. The tension between the abstract principle and the concrete situation is most to the fore in *Lady Anna*, but even here, although the almost working-class Daniel and the not wholly upper-class Anna can be married, it is possible in the end only because both are in their individual ways *déclassé*.

Trollope's almost obsessive interest in the legal side of property - the legal nature of 'real' property comes close to excluding the reality of the physical property - appears to be a source of one major weakness of his writing.[13] With reference to Mr Scarborough's house in *Mr Scarborough's Family,* Sadlier has remarked:

> The house and grounds are left almost unpictured, for the very practical reason that their importance to the tale is as a mere mass of property, a conglomerate wealth to be left in a will, something to be inherited, to serve as security for a debt, to set a family against itself. It does not matter how they looked, it only matters that they are property.[14]

The same holds true in *Lady Anna* and *Orley Farm*, where the reader is given only brief descriptions of Lovel Grange and Orley Farm respectively, and sketchy suggestions as to the character of the remaining properties or the origin or present nature of the wealth at issue. It has been noted how generally the reader is not invited to become aware of the architectural or aesthetic qualities of the houses of Trollope's great families (and the same observation holds for the presumed glories of Barchester Cathedral and its close). And just as one aspect of great houses is their architecture, another is their history and that of their families. Yet again, the history behind his characters and stories rarely comes to life in Trollope's novels. *Orley Farm*, it is true, has a brief but unspirited historical introduction, but *Lady Anna* tells us virtually nothing of the Earldom and its history, despite its seeming illustrious enough for Lady Anna to sacrifice much of her inheritance for its sake. In *Mr Scarborough's Family* the wealth involved is vaguely attributed to successful brick-making. Hiram's Hospital in *The Warden* is the prototype: history, like property, is reduced to being no more than a cause of nineteenth-century dispute. Even people can become mere props. We remain ignorant about the person of Mr Scarborough's wife (even to call her Mrs Scarborough seems unduly intimate). We know only that, according to Mr Scarborough, she was 'the purest and the best of women'. She is mentioned incidentally in the novel, but at any significant length only once, and even then late on and only as a character necessary for the plot.[15] In fact, as a character in the story she is necessary for the plot of the book to be possible, since Mr Scarborough must have had a wife and his sons a mother, but beyond that the author does not and the reader need not have any curiosity about her. Ironically, Trollope's own work suffered a similar fate. In his *Autobiography* his concern with income and property reduced even his novels to items on a balance sheet; his pride in his work was not insignificantly attributable in part to the material success it had brought him.

Trollope's characters: law vs. justice

If it is true that 'Trollope was particularly fascinated by the conflict between legal and moral principles, law and justice',[16] *Orley Farm, Lady Anna* and *Mr Scarborough's Family* successfully capture the deep problem here just because they do not satisfactorily resolve that conflict. The reason that it is not resolved is simple: what polarizes on the surface as a straightforward opposition of interests in the offices of solicitors and the adversarial proceedings of the courts is a state of affairs constituting a moral muddle. In *Orley Farm* Lady Mason herself arouses the reader's sympathy, as well as the author's, but not unequivocally. Her acquittal is on a charge of perjury not forgery (for which she is never tried), and perhaps for Trollope it was forgery - the perversion of the proper course of inheritance - which was the greater crime; of that Lady Mason could not have been acquitted. The rectification of the latter offence has to bypass the courts and be brought about extra-legally. Whatever the justice of her original claim - to modern sensibilities it seems unfair (however legally correct) that Lucius should not have received something from his own father - the property must be restored to its rightful owner and Lady Mason cannot be saved from utter disgrace. But even the working out of a plot which allows Lady Mason to be found not guilty, perhaps because the victory the law seeks and wins is too often the reverse of what is morally right, and then has her give over the estate to its legitimate owner (keeping the morality of the tale straight and maintaining the rightful order of society) can hardly be found satisfying by many modern readers. And at the same time as the story follows this morally tortuous path, the verdict of not guilty and the process of the trial which leads to that verdict clearly mock the law, and do so in law's own terms. Finally, Trollope is prepared to undercut the harshness of society's judgment both by confessing that he 'has learned to forgive her' and by suggesting, in a passage that may seem mawkish to modern tastes, that Lady Mason will once again know happiness.[17]

Confusion in *Lady Anna* – more evident to the Victorian than the late twentieth-century mind unconcerned about a person's station in life - is found in the opposition of inclination and duty, both personal and social. Anna loves Daniel and has also placed herself under an obligation to him, while, given Victorian social values and Trollope's own commitment to a class-structured society, she ought to marry the young Earl, to whom, for much of the novel, she feels a certain attraction. If Lady Anna comes close to being a sweet Victorian heroine, we are nevertheless made aware that she is headstrong, if not obstinate, and - despite what she says and the manner in which her position is characterized - self-centred. Perhaps her mother suggests the presence of a worm in the bud when she declares in her anger that Anna has her mother's brow but her father's heart.[18] The novel ends with Daniel and Anna bound for Australia and its classless society. Yet a return to England to fulfil Daniel's ambitions is already presaged. With this must come a return to the conflict-riven existence which is produced not only by character - neither Daniel nor Anna is a simple person - but by society itself acting on character. (It need hardly be recalled how common a theme in Trollope's work is the social definition of character.)

In *Mr Scarborough's Family* the desire to secure justice in spite of the law will not seem reprehensible to many late-twentieth-century readers. Yet Mr Scarborough is hardly a likeable character and his motives are mixed. His intentions go beyond securing personal justice; he 'delighted to get the better of the law', for law was hardly less absurd to him than religion. It consisted of a perplexed entanglement of rules got together so that the few might live in comfort at the expense of the many.[19] (As is the case elsewhere in Trollope's novels, this shockingly radical opinion about both law and religion is neither refuted nor followed through.) Mr Grey, Mr Scarborough's solicitor, is also conscious that his client's whole life 'had been passed in arranging tricks for the defeat of the law'.[20] Nevertheless, to an extent Mr Scarborough has respect for the law, even though it is no more than a pragmatic respect for its formal requirements. He is precisely aware of what the law of entail requires and permits. In the spirit of the archetypal 'bad man' he appears only to regret that there is no time for that kind of finished revenge, which, while respecting the law, could produce a 'scorched earth' of the estate at Tretton, leaving only 'bare acres' to the legitimate heir while bequeathing all the substance of his wealth to the other son.[21] Mr Scarborough's assault on the law is carried out scrupulously according to law; to defeat the law is not possible, but (since law is made for man and not man for the law) he avails himself of the opportunity of controlling the law in his own interests in preference to the law controlling him in the service of its own impersonal logic. In the end Mr Scarborough has still to rely on the law to sanction his wishes, but by skilful manipulation of the law to his own ends he can get the better of it. He beats the system by working with it.

As in *Orley Farm*, albeit in a different way, the law is mocked by being neatly turned against itself. Did Trollope identify with his character's mockery of the law? Of Mr Scarborough he wrote:

> For the conventionalities of the law he entertained a supreme contempt, but he did wish so to arrange matters with which he was himself concerned as to do what justice demanded. Whether he succeeded in the last year of his life the reader may judge.[22]

In its development the story of *Mr Scarborough's Family* challenges some of the conventional assumptions of Victorian England in such a way as to leave the reader uncomfortable and uncertain as to whether this or some other outcome is or could be morally the best. Any doubts about Trollope's detachment are surely dispelled as he, seemingly washing his hands of the business, leaves judgment to his reader. Are we to consider Mr Scarborough's success in practical terms alone, or is Trollope inviting us to probe more deeply into the moral basis of social arrangements and the requirements of true justice? Or in this novel, as in the others, are we merely offered from time to time an invitation to harmless armchair philosophizing? The moral elements in Trollope's stories are frequently incongruous if not discordant. Most parties have their virtues and their faults; when they do not they all too easily become caricatures (which happens rarely with the principal characters of Trollope's novels). There are divergent and conflicting points of view and, for the most part, none has some privileged status. Subversive possibilities repeatedly emerge in the novels, but disappear again to leave no permanent effect. Trollope's addition of law to the moral mix increases this confusion of values. The author himself did not dwell on complexities too long. As we know, he could be finished with one book, quite ready to start another the next morning.

Trollope's legal institutions and lawyers

To side clearly with established ways, giving them unquestioning support, would obviously leave no stories to be told but, more seriously, would imply that the system was perfect, with no failings evident and no reforms needed. On the other hand, to provide a single acceptable outcome for each novel, unarguably right and just above all possible outcomes, would point too clearly to the reforms that were necessary and would impart to the novels a didactic, moralizing character quite alien to the successful Trollope.

Why is Trollope so lacking in reforming zeal when he appears so aware of the failings of the system? His ability to portray characters sympathetically with all their failings as well as their good qualities in a tolerant and humane way is well known. Unlike many other Victorian novelists Trollope did not use his characters to make moral points, nor did he sit in judgment on them. Their goodness or badness seldom becomes a caricature. Can such an attitude be acceptably extended from people to institutions? His detachment can make him almost a social anthropologist reporting on the mores of middle-class Victorian England, interested and amused, but unconcerned about taking sides. Law is one more element in this total picture, an institution which acknowledges certain principles and proceeds according to certain rules but also a practice which in effect ignores the substance of its principles and acknowledges only the letter not the spirit of its rules.

If this is a correct interpretation of Trollope's depiction of law, we seem through his authorial manner to be constantly reminded that this depiction is reportage not condemnation. Why does Trollope not create for the reader a clear moral path through his stories in the manner of other Victorian writers (including Thackeray, whom Trollope admired so much)? The frequent involvement of the law in his stories could have given Trollope a special opportunity to praise or damn the law for what it did and could do for people's lives and, through the words and deeds of his characters rather than his own comments, to hint (at least) at constructive reform. But for Trollope it seems that institutions, like people, are what they are. Trollope sought a realistic portrayal of people which would be entertaining in itself, and this in turn required a realism in describing those conditions of society which made them what they were - but no more than that. Reporting the discrepancies between principle and practice is therefore unavoidable, but there is no ulterior motive. 'The book was read, and I was satisfied'[23] would not be an unfitting epitaph for Trollope the novelist. The lack of accord between principle and practice only contributes to the complexity of good and bad features in both institutions and people which provide the novelist with fertile sources of entertainment for the reader.

Trollope is not sparing in his comments on law and lawyers; the faults of the system are not played down. The most obvious fault is the cost of law, and the point made in *Orley Farm* is a familiar one for many litigants. When Joseph Mason first thought of contesting the codicil to the will,

> [h]e was minded to press the case on to a Court of Appeal, up even to the House of Lords; but he was advised that in doing so he would spend more money than Orley Farm was worth, and that he would, almost to a certainty, spend it in vain. Under this advice he cursed the laws of his country, and withdrew to Groby Park.[24]

The pecuniary interests of lawyers are similarly apparent. Trollope's comments on this subject and others can approach the cynical (and perhaps the trite), 'Legal gentlemen are, I believe, quite as often bought off as bought up'.[25] With reference to Mr Furnival in *Orley Farm*, we are told: '[a]ny cause was sound to him when once he had been fed for its support, and he carried in his countenance his assurance of this soundness'.[26] As to the character of law itself, 'with us the law is the same for an Italian harlot and an English widow; and it may well be that in its niceties it shall be found kinder to the former than to the latter'.[27]

From superficial sneers Trollope can move to more troubling observations. In what is hardly more than a passing quip Trollope can convey a wealth of meaning, as when Mr Chaffanbrass is referred to as 'this great guardian of the innocence - or rather not-guiltiness of the public'.[28] More considered opinions are offered by Trollope in relation to the character of Mr Chaffanbrass

> To him it was a matter of course that Lady Mason should be guilty. Had she not been guilty, he, Mr Chaffanbrass, would not have been required. Mr Chaffanbrass well understood that the defence of injured innocence was no part of his mission.[29]

> As to Mr Chaffanbrass and Mr Solomon Aram - to them the escape of a criminal under their auspices would of course be a matter of triumph. To such work for many years had they applied their sharp intellects and legal knowledge.[30]

In these passages we are reminded that the paramount commitment of lawyers is to success. Septimus Harding, of all Trollope's main characters the paradigm of a legal *ingénu*, represents the antithesis of the professional legal mind: 'He was not so anxious to prove himself right, as to be so'.[31] The adversarial process puts winning and success − appearing to prove oneself right - above all else, including the truth. As he describes the interview between Mr Furuvial and Lady Mason in *Orley Farm* the author himself muses:

> If I, having committed a crime, were to confess my criminality to the gentleman engaged to defend me, might he not be called on to say: 'Then, O my friend, confess it also to the judge; and so let justice be done. *Ruat coelum*, and the rest of it?' But who would pay a lawyer for counsel such as that?[32]

Downright lying is against the rules, but anything else is allowed and indeed required: 'no amount of eloquence will make an English lawyer think that loyalty to truth should come before loyalty to his client'.[33] Therefore it is common and accepted practice either to conceal the truth or to make truth look like falsehood. Mr Flick in *Lady Anna* is 'in his way, an honest man' but 'if the real truth were adverse to his side, why search for it?'[34] The consequence of the adversarial nature of proceedings is clear enough for Mr Flick - and for any lawyer: 'It was not up to him to get up evidence for the other side'.[35] Deception and disregard for truth are not against the rules:

> As for himself, Mr Chaffanbrass knew well enough that she [Bridget Bolster] had spoken nothing but the truth. But had he so managed that the truth might be made to look like falsehood, - or at any rate to have a doubtful air? If he had done that, he had succeeded in the occupation of his life, and was indifferent to his own triumph.[36]

This way of proceeding is not something to be ashamed of but correctly professional and worthy of pride:

> That those witnesses had spoken truth he also knew, and yet he had been able to hold them up to the execration of all around them as though they had committed the worst of crimes from the foulest of motives! And more than this, stranger than this, worse than this, - when the legal world knew - as the legal world soon did know - that all this had been so, the legal world found no fault with Mr. Furnival, conceiving that he had done his duty by his client in a manner becoming an English barrister and an English gentleman.[37]

Kenneby, one of the witnesses in the Orley Farm case, gives stark expression to the astute layman's attitude. He knows that he will have to tell his story

> in two different ways. There'll be one fellow'll make you tell it his way first, and another fellow'll make you tell it again his way afterwards; and its [sic] odds but what the first'll be at you again after that, till you won't know whether you stand on your heels or your head.[38]

Yet, whenever we are confident that Trollope is pointing his finger at a clear abuse, it is always possible to find him throwing in an equivocating aside:

> There are gentlemen at the bar ... who have confined their talents to the browbeating of witnesses, - greatly to their own profit, and no doubt to the advantage of society.[39]

If the last few words are intended ironically, is there also truth in the irony?

The very basis of the common law system in adversarial proceedings is placed in question in *Orley Farm* by Felix Graham (we may inquire here if he is speaking for Trollope himself):

> We ask him [the accused] whether or not he confesses his guilt in a foolish way, tending to induce him to deny it; but that is not much. Guilt seldom will confess as long as a chance remains. But we teach him to lie, or rather we lie for him during the whole ceremony of his trial. We think it merciful to give him chances of escape, and hunt him as we do a fox, in obedience to certain laws framed for his protection.[40]

But if we are persuaded for the moment that Trollope had reform in mind, the discordance between the pronouncements of Felix Graham and the facts of the Orley Farm case should disabuse us. Felix Graham's grand ideas about improving the law are rendered worthless by the target of his good intentions, Lady Mason herself, who is in fact (though never found so in law) guilty of forgery. Wholly deluded, he declares:

> It is one of those cases ... in which the sufferer should be protected by the very fact of her own innocence. No lawyer should consent to take up the cudgels against her.[41]

Unwittingly, in arguing for the protection of Lady Mason, Felix Graham stands condemned in the light of his own somewhat pretentious utterance a few pages previously, to the effect that all should do their best to protect the innocent, but as to the guilty man, 'for the concealing of his guilt let no astute or good man work at all'.[42] Felix Graham, it is surmised, could not defend a case where he was not convinced of his client's innocence. Ironically, just when he is most charitable in wishing to protect the innocent from the distress of a trial he is most wrong. But however exemplary his intentions, he is in any case deceived as to a proper understanding of law in practice.

> He had ideas of his own that men should pursue their labours without special conventional regulations, but should be guided in their work by the general great rules of the world, such for instance as those given in the commandments:- Thou shalt not bear false witness; Thou shalt not steal; and others. His notions no doubt were great, and perhaps were good; but hitherto they had not led him to much pecuniary success in his profession. A sort of a name he had obtained, but it was not a name sweet in the ears of practising attorneys.[43]

The consequence is summed up in Lady Staveley's musing about Felix Graham that 'he belonged to a profession which he would not follow in the only way by which it was possible to earn an income by it'.[44] This neatly complements the earlier opinion of Mr Chaffanbrass: 'He does not understand the nature of the duty which a professional man owes to his client.'[45] Mr Grey in *Mr Scarborough's Family*, on the other hand, knows his duty very well. Despite his intense personal dislike of Mr Scarborough and his two sons, despite the deception and dishonesty that has placed him in a morally awkward situation, aware that Mr Scarborough has been thoroughly dishonest, and believing him to be the wickedest man who has ever lived, he is not prepared to abandon an old client and has no qualms about carrying on so long as he is assured of the legal correctness of what he is doing.[46] And Trollope presents Mr Grey as a sympathetic figure.

Felix Graham may wish zealously to reform the law, but in the end law *is* a game played according to certain rules, where the factual truth of the matter is of no account. The point is stated clearly in a few lines in *Mr Scarborough's Family*. Should a murderer be defended? Dolly, Mr Grey's daughter, thinks not, but her father points out that he might not have been a murderer after all 'or not legally so, which, as far as the law goes, is the same thing'.[47]

Trollope is realistic about the legal process. To be a lawyer of any kind is to seek the success of being seen as right rather than to be right. *Orley Farm* centres its plot on a criminal action, while *Mr Scarborough's Family* and *Lady Anna* remain confined to civil actions. In *Orley Farm* Trollope has the lawyer, Mr Furnival, taking part in an international legal congress in Birmingham, where 'the wisest Rustums of the law from all the civilized countries of Europe' are inquiring whether any and what changes might be made in the modes of answering that great question, 'Guilty or not guilty?' and that other equally great question, 'Is it *meum* or is it *tuum*?' To answer which question justly should be the end and object of every lawyer's work.[48]

The tone of the whole description from which this quotation is extracted leaves us in no doubt about Trollope's attitude to self-professed legal reformers but also, more seriously, seems to preclude us taking everything that the author says at this point with anything less than heavy irony. We must conclude, with respect to both questions, that the underlying message from Trollope is the same - and it is a message repeatedly emphasized throughout *Orley Farm, Lady Anna* and *Mr Scarborough's Family*, as well as elsewhere in Trollope's fiction. The law is not about justice, at least in a substantive sense. It is in the contrast between Sir William Patterson, the Solicitor-General in *Lady Anna,* and the barrister, Mr Hardy, that we are to understand what the practice of law is really about. Sir William, though portrayed as an essentially humane man, thinks little about justice. Concerned about the Lovel property, he is anxious only 'that the vast property at stake should not get into improper hands'. To which Mr Hardy adds, '[a]nd that justice should be done'. To this Sir William assents almost as an afterthought.[49] But Mr Hardy, the reader has already been told, 'hated compromise and desired justice, - and was a great rather than successful lawyer'.[50]

But does Trollope not believe that law ought to be about justice? Trollope's concern with property and inheritance focuses on areas where the law can seem to be (from the point of view of justice) at its most arbitrary. Rules of inheritance are not about what is required by justice - this concept may require quite different outcomes from what the law dictates - but about what the social order requires. Trollope is repeatedly intent on preserving rules of inheritance and the social order they underpin. This intent of his is clear, because he is prepared to move beyond the law in support of the social order. Lady Mason has to restore Orley Farm to its rightful owner without any legal compulsion to do so. Mr Scarborough eventually fails of his own volition to defeat the law of entail. At the end of the book Mountjoy surely receives all his inheritance because this is his formal entitlement - what other outcome would be right? - even though it is doomed to be lost through his gambling. Lady Anna is prepared to give up a sizable portion of her inheritance for no convincing reason of her own - legal, moral, or emotional - just because the new Earl Lovel must have sufficient property to keep himself in the manner to which society believes earls should be accustomed. Even the humanity of Sir William Patterson works towards a solution that is pragmatically workable, one which compromises legalism but which at the same time does not seek moral justice of a black-and-white clarity. Sir William believes that the marriage of Lady Anna with Daniel Thwaite 'would be a grievous injury to the social world of his country', and in that regard 'it behoved him to look to his client's interests, rather than his client's instructions'.[51] Really, Sir William surely has society's interests at heart.

Trollope's fatalism: social order before justice

The mature Trollope was no more than passively critical. The tendency to preach, to moralize, or to express indignation, a tendency present in his earliest novels (up to and including *The Warden*) disappears. Trollope has 'no itch to set the world to rights'.[52] He was critical of the law of his time. Many of his comments in *Orley Farm*, *Lady Anna* and *Mr Scarborough's Family* are overtly critical and many more passages imply criticism. However, although the criticism is usually to the point, it is often dampened by a quality of wry humor or sardonic comment which allows us to infer a relaxed detachment on the author's part. Trollope has no personal or social axe to grind. His commitment, if there is anything so strong in his work, is to the way things are. In consequence, he enjoys a rare freedom to contemplate with a significant degree of disinterest certain aspects of life in his own time, observing and recounting the tensions of his society. Yet the combination of this detached attitude with the setting of moral complexity in his characters and situations implies at least one message, that social conflicts cannot be brought to an end in terms of a neat and tidy morality. If we are to leave things as they are, this is a conclusion resulting not from complacency but from profound understanding. Realistically, his novels often have endings that can seem curiously (for their time) unresolved and unsatisfying, with their characters destined for neither certain happiness nor tragic completeness.

Sadleir remarked that Trollope's novels 'are almost without exception novels of a conflict between individual decencies and social disingenuities'.[53] Yet the individual decencies are often flawed and it is the social disingenuities which triumph - in law and politics (both parliamentary and ecclesiastical) especially - and it is these disingenuities which support the social order. For much of the time Trollope is detached from his own criticism, but finally he is prepared to accord social order the paramount place in his scheme of things. If each must get his own, this is not because of any personal moral claims that may be made, but because his station in life demands it. The maintenance or restoration of the order of things forms a major theme in many of his novels even when it is not the basis of the principal plot. He asserts an inherent social order and fitness which is dependent as much or more on outward form than on inner substance. The very artificiality of the particular part of the social order - the importance of 'real' property and the law of entail - that the legal system sustains in the three novels considered here emphasizes just this point.

Like the social order it supports, the legal system is artificial too. This is emphasized in the extreme absurdity of that aspect of legal procedure which determines that Mr Chaffenbrass, who is leading Mr Furnivall in the Orley Farm case, cannot cross-examine both of two key witnesses even if it means losing the case.

> The success or safety of a client is a very great thing; - in a professional point of view a very great thing indeed. But there is a matter which in legal eyes is greater even than that. Professional etiquette required that the cross-examination of these two most important witnesses should not be left in the hands of the same barrister.[54]

Law maintains the social order, and it is better to accept all the faults of law, which Trollope fully recognizes, than threaten this order. Order comes before justice, and perhaps justice comes nowhere at all, for the outcomes of Trollope's stories are neither just nor unjust. The faults of law and society are to be lived with, but is this so great a sacrifice in a world which is not morally black and white? 'Who can say what is the justice or the injustice of anything after twenty years of possession?' the solicitor Crabwitz replies to Dockwrath, who has (in *Orley Farm*) made appeal to both public policy and justice.[55] Indeed, who can decide all the rights and wrongs of any issue after so many years of law and custom and dispute?

Trollope's novels end with a mixture of happiness and unhappiness, success and failure, certainty and uncertainty, satisfaction and dissatisfaction. Other outcomes to his stories there could be, but none would finally square the moral account. About *Lady Anna* he wrote that everybody found fault with me for marrying her to the tailor. What would they have said if I had allowed her to jilt the tailor and marry the good-looking young lord? How much louder, then, would have been the censure![56]

Such outspokenness is unusual however. Most of the time, Trollope could so accept the inherent imperfections of people *and* institutions, as well as the complexities and constraints of social life, that in his comments on them he found no need to tell his readers that there is no right answer. On one level Trollope, like a detached anthropologist, records social customs and practices and does no more than describe what the law is and does, how it works and what society expects of it. Nevertheless, on another level the society that Trollope describes is his own society. If the detached part of his self records the typical failings of law in a dispassionate manner, the other part still identifies that law as his own and rests content with it - not least as to the law of property.

Notes

1. Sadleir (1945), p. 14.
2. Cecil (1948), pp. 186-7.
3. Sadleir (1945), p. 15.
4. *Ralph the Heir*, Vol. I, p. 337.
5. ApRoberts (1981), p. 150.
6. *Mr Scarborough's Family* (1935), p. 522.
7. *Autobiography*, p. 143.
8. *Autobiography*, p. 236.
9. It is worth noting, since illustrations were an almost essential element of the published Victorian novel with a significance that is often forgotten or ignored today, that he was equally proud of Millais illustrations; these were, he wrote, 'the best I have seen in any novel in any language'. In the previous year he had not been so pleased with the same artist's illustrations to *Framley Parsonage*. (*Autobiography*, p. 144).
10. Drinker (1950), p. 40.
11. *Mr Scarborough's Family* (1935), Introduction, p. xxi.
12. *Orley Farm* (1935), Vol. II, p. 46. The selfsame idea occurs in *Ralph the Heir*.

13. Notable exceptions occur in *The Belton Estate* (1866), and *Sir Harry Hotspur of Humblethwaite* (1871).
14. Sadleir (1945), p. 192.
15. Ironically, Trollope's own work suffered a similar fate; in his *Autobiography* his concern with income and property reduced even his novels to items on a balance sheet; his pride in his work was not insignificantly attributable in part to the material success it had brought him. See his *Autobiography*, p. 298.
16. *Mr Scarborough's Family* (1935), Introduction, p. viii.
17. *Orley Farm* (1935), Vol. II, pp. 404-5.
18. *Lady Anna* (1936), p. 450.
19. *Mr Scarborough's Family* (1935), p. 194.
20. *Mr Scarborough's Family* (1935), p. 526.
21. *Mr Scarborough's Family* (1935), p. 298.
22. *Mr Scarborough's Family* (1935), p. 567.
23. *Autobiography* (1953), p. 298. (The reference is to *Lady Anna*.)
24. *Orley Farm* (1935), Vol. I, p. 16.
25. *Orley Farm* (1935), Vol. I, p. 95.
26. *Orley Farm* (1935), Vol. I, p. 98.
27. *Lady Anna* (1936), p. 20.
28. *Orley Farm* (1935), Vol. I, p. 342.
29. *Orley Farm* (1935), Vol. II, p. 282.
30. *Orley Farm* (1935), Vol. II, p. 165.
31. *The Warden* (1918), p. 35.
32. *Orley Farm* (1935), Vol. I, p. 118.
33. *Orley Farm* (1935), Vol. II, p. 169.
34. *Lady Anna* (1936), p. 42.
35. *Lady Anna* (1936), p. 43.
36. *Orley Farm* (1935), Vol. II, p. 323.
37. *Orley Farm* (1935), Vol. II, p. 331.
38. *Orley Farm* (1935), Vol. II, p. 213.
39. *Orley Farm* (1935), Vol. I, p. 97.
40. *Orley Farm* (1935), Vol. I, p. 178.
41. *Orley Farm* (1935), Vol. I, p. 189.
42. *Orley Farm* (1935), Vol. I, p. 179.
43. *Orley Farm* (1935), Vol. I, p. 175.
44. *Orley Farm* (1935), Vol. II, p. 116.
45. *Orley Farm* (1935), Vol. I, p. 345.

46. See *Mr Scarborough's Family* (1935), pp. 151-7.
47. *Mr Scarborough's Family* (1935), p. 155.
48. See *Orley Farm* (1935), Vol. I, p. 115.
49. *Lady Anna* (1936), p. 67.
50 *Lady Anna* (1936), p. 46.
51. *Lady Anna* (1936), p. 204.
52. Sadleir (1945), p. 155.
53. Sadleir (1945), p. 153.
54. *Orley Farm* (1935), Vol. II, p. 22.
55. *Orley Farm* (1935), Vol. I, p. 319.
56. *Autobiography* (1953), p. 298.

References

ApRoberts, R. (1981), 'The Shaping Principle', in Hall, N.J. (Ed.), *The Trollope Critics*, pp. 138-52, Macmillan, London.

Cecil, D. (1948), *Early Victorian Novelists: Essays in Revaluation*, Penguin Books, Harmondsworth.

Drinker, H.S. (1950), *The Lawyers of Anthony Trollope*, The Grolier Club, New York.

Sadleir, M. (1945), *Trollope: A Commentary*, Constable, London.

Trollope, A. (1953), *Autobiography*, Oxford University Press, London (first published 1893).

Trollope, A. (1936), *Lady Anna*, Oxford University Press, London (first published 1874).

Trollope, A. (1989), *Mr Scarborough's Family*, Oxford University Press, London (first published 1883).

Trollope, A. (1935), *Orley Farm*, Oxford University Press, London (first published 1862).

Trollope, A. (1993), *Ralph the Heir*, Penguin Books, Harmondsworth (first published 1871).

Trollope, A. (1918), *The Warden*, Oxford University Press, London (first published 1885).

10 The Law *of* Literature: Folklore and Law

NORMA DAWSON

The other contributors to this collection may have assumed a ready supply
of literature around which to weave their themes but the reader may care to
pause to consider the factors which guarantee, regulate and shape that
supply. Besides the creative urge, the organization and profitability of the
publishing industry and legal regulation of literature are dominant factors.[1]
Law has an impact on literature at various points: through obscenity law,
the laws of defamation and of confidentiality, and most fundamentally of
all, copyright law, that part of our law which allows authors to own literary
property. It is instructive to examine the impact of copyright law on a
particular genre or literary form or style, whether it be the novel, sequels,
drama, poetry, satire, biography, the writing of history, and so on. In this
way, students of law or of literature can gain a real sense of the purpose and
extent of copyright protection, the values which underpin it, its political
bias and its impact on published literary work. In addition, they can learn
how literary theory has helped to shape the content of copyright law. As
Gaines states, 'the two discourses [copyright law and literature] inform
each other because they share the same cultural root buried deep in the
seventeenth century.'[2]

The focus of this essay is on expressions of a particular literary form -
folklore - which are considered to be beyond the margins of copyright
protection, at least in the developed world. As a distinct form, folklore
predates all copyright laws and yet little or no accommodation has been
made for it as copyright has developed. Folklore presents unique
challenges to the copyright systems of the world and to the distinction
between private forms of intellectual property, such as copyright, and
public forms, such as the public domain. We shall see that the legal
treatment of folklore either as a form of literary property or as part of the
public domain has reflected the value placed by different societies on their
own folklore as a form of literary or cultural expression: the creation of
legal value, in the form of property, has followed the attachment of cultural
value at a national level. But the imbalance and inequity caused by national
copyright laws in a global system of cultural exchange are thorny issues in
a debate engendered by Western exploitation of the folklore of indigenous
peoples and distinct ethnic groups within developing nations. The story of

law and folklore continues to unfold; as we read this story and imagine the ending, our understanding of copyright will be uniquely illuminated.

Copyright: literary property

Copyright is a somewhat paradoxical device designed to make literary works and other cultural forms available to the public by restricting their availability.   Copyright, an exclusive right in the author to control exploitation of his or her work, is generally exercised by the grant to a publisher of a licence to publish the work.   Provided that the author can offer a licence on terms which are attractive to the publisher, such as an exclusive licence to publish in paperback within a particular territory or territories, publication of the work becomes a commercially viable venture. Similarly, exploitation of the work for television or film will require the involvement of other entrepreneurs.   In each case, a licence or assignment of copyright from the author forms the basis upon which the various media become involved.[3]   Published literary and other works, therefore, come to us courtesy of copyright law which has effectively replaced patronage as a means of securing financial backing for publication.

Copyright is in effect a right to engage in literary enclosure.   Having created a work, the author is entitled to ring fence it and erect a 'keep out' sign, meaning 'read, but do not take or use without consent'.   To some extent, the enclosure of a literary work can be justified on the ground that without the author's creative act, that area of literary territory would not exist at all; thus, copyright is a reward for creativity and a recognition of the author's natural right of property in his or her creation.[4]   While this was historically the original justification for copyright in continental European countries, in Anglo-American legal theory, rewarding the author has been a secondary consideration.[5]   The preamble to the first Copyright Act in Great Britain, the Statute of Anne 1710, declared the purpose of the legislation to be

> for the encouragement of learning, by vesting the copies of printed books in the authors, or purchasers, [i.e. publishers] of such copies during the times therein mentioned.[6]

The 'times therein mentioned' were two consecutive periods of 14 years.[7] Not content with the duration of the copyright term under the statute, publishers mounted a campaign in the 1760s and 1770s to establish that copyright in published works also existed at common law, based on the author's natural right to his or her intellectual creation, and that this was a perpetual right of property.[8] In Blackstone's words:

> every author hath in himself the sole exlusive right of multiplying the copies of his literary productions ... independent of [statute] ... Universal law has established a permanent perpetual property in bodily acquisitions: and reason requires that the property in mental acquisitions should be equally permanent.[9]

Ultimately, in the leading case of *Donaldson v. Beckett*,[10] the House of Lords ruled that the time-limited copyright under the Statute of Anne 1710 had replaced any common law copyright in published literary works, thus excluding notions of perpetual natural rights.

United States copyright law reveals the influence of the Statute of Anne. The 'copyright patent' clause of the Constitution provides that:

> The Congress shall have power ... To promote the progress of science and useful arts, by securing for limited times to authors and inventors the exclusive right to their respective writings and discoveries.[11]

The first federal copyright legislation of 1790 begins in the following way:

> [a]n Act for the encouragement of learning, by securing the copies of maps, charts and books to the authors and proprietors of such copies, during the times therein mentioned.[12]

Yet while the principal motivation is to encourage learning by creating a market in literary and other works, the means by which this is achieved is to give authors exclusive rights in their works. Authors are practically, if not philosophically, central to Anglo-American copyright law. As expressed in one United States Supreme Court opinion:

> the immediate effect of our copyright law is to secure a fair return for an 'author's' creative labor.[13]

Thus, the practical operation of Anglo-American copyright law and that of other common law systems is not fundamentally different from that of civil law systems founded on the natural rights of authors. This is important because the market in literary and other cultural works extends throughout the globe, making international cooperation on copyright a practical necessity. Global harmonization of copyright laws has come about largely as a result of the growth in membership of two international copyright unions, established by the Berne Convention 1886, administered by the World Intellectual Property Organisation (WIPO),[14] and, to a lesser extent, the Universal Copyright Convention 1952, administered by UNESCO.[15] The third, relatively recent, development in international copyright law is the TRIPS Agreement 1993,[16] concluded in the GATT Uruguay Round and administered by the World Trade Organisation, the net effect of which will be to accelerate the pace at which countries adhere to the minimum copyright standards established under the Berne Convention.

Within the Berne Union, copyright systems based on common and civil law approaches co-exist in relative harmony. Thus in the opening words of the Berne Convention:

> the countries of the Union, being equally animated by the desire to protect, in as effective and uniform a manner as possible, the rights of authors in their literary and artistic works ... have agreed as follows:
> The countries to which this Convention applies constitute a Union for the protection of the rights of authors in their literary and artistic works.

This is an acurate view of the position for all of the member states whether they view the protection of authors' rights as an end in itself or as a means to some greater end. The effect of copyright law throughout the two international copyright Unions is to reward authors for their creativity by giving value in the form of literary property in their work.

But literary works are not created in a vacuum. While a new work may pass the minimum threshold of 'originality' set by copyright law, namely that the work was not copied, the work will be the result not only of the author's creativity but also of the many influences which have consciously or unconsciously shaped the work, including the literary works of others.[17] This provides one reason for us to be suspicious of the author's claim to have an exclusive right to control his or her work. A second reservation is that the stated purpose of our copyright law, namely the encouragement of learning, can be achieved without giving authors unlimited rights over their literary property. Indeed, it can be more fully achieved by giving authors limited property rights. The extent of permissible literary enclosure is in fact limited by a number of legal principles, all of which have relevance to a study of the legal regulation of literature.

First, some unauthorized copying of copyright works is allowed by virtue of the fact that copyright does not protect ideas underlying a work, but only the form of expression of those ideas.[18] This is linked to a requirement in many Berne Union member states, including the United States and the United Kingdom, that a work must be 'fixed' or recorded in some material form for copyright to subsist in it.[19] Ideas unexpressed in the author's mind cannot be protected under copyright law. While the purpose of the idea/expression dichotomy is to control the monopoly created by copyright,[20] the dividing line between unprotected idea and protectable expression is difficult to draw in practice and indeed is differently applied to different genres of literary work.[21] Secondly, some use of copyright works is permitted as 'fair dealing', for example, the use of quotations from a work for the purpose of criticism or review.[22] This is important for biographers and literary critics, but affords no defence for imitation artists and others who help themselves to others' works, albeit in the name of art or culture. Thirdly, copyright is not a perpetual right of property. The standard copyright term for original literary works throughout the Berne Union is currently the author's life and 50 years, or, for anonymous works, simply 50 years, at the end of which the work passes into the public domain and can be copied and used at will by anyone. This period will shortly be extended to life and 70 years throughout the European Union,[23] and a similar extension is being considered in the United States.

Each of these limits on copyright go some way towards ensuring that copyright increases but does not impede 'the harvest of knowledge.'[24] However, the authors of copyright works also enjoy 'moral rights' which remain with them even when copyright is assigned. These rights permit authors to prevent derogatory treatment of their work,[25] and in some countries, not including the UK, to withdraw a licence to publish, where the author has had a change of heart and decides to suppress a work. In *Anatole France v. Lemerre*,[26] the defendant publishers had bought the manuscript of the plaintiff's history of France written in 1882, but took no steps to publish it until 1907. The plaintiff, believing that publication after such a lengthy interval with no opportunity to revise the work, would damage his reputation, successfully sued for the return of his work. Moral rights protect the author's integrity and reputation. Clearly, their exercise could have a significant impact on published literature, although for their own purposes publishers will try to minimize the impact of moral rights by controlling the terms of publishing contracts and by exploiting uncertainty surrounding moral rights legislation. Moral rights as established in the UK are not wide enough to prevent every derogatory treatment of a work. For example, one area of doubt relates to book covers. If a publisher designs a book cover which the author finds insulting or offensive, it is a moot point whether the use of the cover can be enjoined under the moral rights provisions of the Copyright, Designs and Patents Act 1988.[27]

Law and Folklore

At first glance, the organizing concepts of copyright law - originality, fixation, and the need for an author or authors to exploit and enforce the copyright - would seem to exclude expressions of folklore. And yet, folklore is as susceptible as other literary forms to unauthorized exploitation and derogatory treatment. 'Folklore', a term coined in 1846 by William Thoms[28] but which lacks a generally accepted definition even among folklore scholars,[29] is wide enough to include literary works - folktales, myths, legends, drama, poetry; artistic works including artefacts; and musical works, the three main categories of author's works under copyright law, as well as folk customs, festivals, rituals, sayings and beliefs.[30] Our interest here is in literary expressions of folklore. The essence of folklore is 'oral tradition channeled across the centuries through human mouths'.[31] This oral tradition involves repetition and continuity with some inevitable variation.[32] The important 'events' in folklore are the repeated transmissions of folktales from one generation to another, not the fixation of the work in printed form, as in the case of other forms of literature. In this sense, folklore is more in the nature of a performance than a work in material form.[33]

Since the nineteenth century when folklore scholarship began to flourish, folklorists have been collecting folktales and other literary expressions of folklore from many parts of the world. Means have been devised of cataloguing and classifying these according to type and motif. In the collection of folktales, folklore scholars rely upon the Aarne-Thompson Index known as *The Types of the Folk Tale*,[34] which catalogues 299 types of animal tale, over 400 types of magic or supernatural tales, or 'Marchen',[35] over 100 types of tales of lying, tall tales such as those told by Baron von Munchausen, and so on.

Often, an interest in folklore has accompanied a tide of nationalism as in Ireland, Finland, Nasser's Egypt (he established a Pan-Arab folklore centre), and more ominously, in Hitler's Germany. The work done by folklore collectors employed by the Irish Folklore Commission since its establishment in 1935 has formed the basis of a vast archive and led to the creation of an index to some of the archival material, *The Types of the Irish Folktale*.[36]

In some cultures, folktales and other forms of folklore are essentially dead, mere relics of a bygone age, but in other societies, sometimes preliterate, folklore in all its forms is a living tradition of major cultural or even spiritual significance. A further distinction must be drawn between folklore which is not 'owned' in any sense by one particular group or people, as in the case of folktales which have travelled vast distances and of which variants can be found across the globe,[37] and folklore which is unique to a particular culture and highly valued as a form of self expression within that society. Where folklore is a living tradition created and sustained within the identifiable bounds of a particular ethnic group, then it 'reflects reality and integral wish rather than cultural lag in a way which it cannot in our "alienated" modern societies'.[38] It is in this context that folklore assumes the appearance of intellectual property created and owned collectively by the members of the group and of special cultural importance and value to them.

Folklore can be used and exploited in various ways. It is often a source of inspiration for individual authors creating their own 'original' literary works. Shakespeare, for example, used fairytales in the writing of *A Midsummer Night's Dream*; folktales inspired Chaucer's *Canterbury Tales*; Henry Longfellow drew inspiration for his *Song of Hiawatha* from tales of the Ojibwa Indians, tales which had been collected by the folklorist Henry Rowe Schoolcraft, and more recently, a local legend, 'the Beauty of Buttermere',[39] was the source of inspiration for Melvyn Bragg's novel *The Maid of Buttermere*. Then there is the work of folklorists whose collections of folktales and legends, as gathered in the field, are deposited in archives or published under their own names. Other folklorists may dip into existing archives to create compilations or anthologies, again published under their own names. Further along the spectrum are the popularisers of folktales and other folklore, those who publish their own stylized versions of folklore. Examples include the *Uncle Remus* tales (Brer Rabbit, Brer Fox and so on) of Joel Chandler Harris, who popularised the folktales from the black community of the southern states of the United States;[40] the poet Sir Thomas Malory's *Morte D'Arthur*,[41] a distillation of Malory's extensive researches into Arthurian legend; and the fairytales of the brothers Jacob and Wilhelm Grimm.[42] With this example,

> Jacob, the scholar, wanted to print the stories as he found them, whereas Wilhelm, the literary man, displeased with the imperfect style of the collected versions, touched up the texts to make them worthy of the natural poets who created them: the Folk.[43]

A fourth kind of folklore exploitation is the modification and adulteration of folklore solely with a view to gain. The opportunities to peddle 'fakelore'[44] have greatly increased in recent years with a growing demand for folk or 'ethnic' cultural products.

How does copyright regulate the relationship between the 'creators' of folklore and the exploiters of folklore? It is often said that the creators of folklore are in principle beyond the scope of copyright protection on three interrelated grounds. First, their works are not or may not be 'fixed' or recorded in a material form; secondly, their works are not original; and thirdly, the creators are not identifiable: they are not merely anonymous but also span the generations. The first of these problems is probably the real obstacle to the use of copyright law to protect literary expressions of folklore, even though many folktales and legends are eventually recorded, by folklorists or others. Where a work becomes 'fixed' in some form, on tape or in print, the act of recording can create a copyright in the work recorded; any copyright which arises in the work recorded will belong to the person who spoke the literary work, and the recordist will obtain a separate copyright in the recording.[45] Where folktales are not 'fixed', copyright cannot be relied upon to prevent their exploitation. It is a sad irony that folklore in the oral tradition should be found not to meet the copyright requirement of fixation when it can be the most enduring form of literary work. As Niedzielska puts it,

> folklore suffers from an inherent contradiction: while its actual existence is solely for the duration of each performance, it does exist and last - despite its ephemeral character - in the collective consciousness and memory of a people, ethnic community or tribe.[46]

And in fact the legal requirement of fixation could be waived. Under article 2(2) of the Berne Convention, the requirement for fixation is a matter to be decided by national legislatures and need not be applied to all categories of work.[47] Most industrialized states, however, continue to make fixation a requirement for copyright works, partly for evidential reasons, since if a work has not been recorded, it is difficult to establish originality and authorship. For the owners of living folklore, their difficulty is not merely that folktales in their current form are not fixed or recorded, but that the tales have never been recorded, making it impossible to show that the changes which have occurred in the tales' evolution are sufficient to meet the originality requirement. Thus, it is assumed that folklore is not original in the copyright sense of 'not copied'. Even if the legal requirement of fixation were removed, the absence of fixation would in practice continue to create great difficulties in establishing originality. Repetition or copying is the essence of the transmission of folklore, with changes, often imperceptible, being made on each transmission. Each narrator or performer of folklore is 'author' only to the extent of his or her contribution to the tale's evolution. Where folklore is part of the culture of a definite group, one could say that all the members of the group and their forebears are collectively the creators and owners. While anonymous authorship and collective ownership are recognised and facilitated by law, the requirement of originality will usually be sufficient to defeat a claim to copyright in folklore.

> This [is] so because whereas an expression of folklore is the result of an impersonal, continuous and slow process of creative activity exercised in a given community by consecutive imitation, works protected by copyright must, traditionally, bear a decisive mark of individual originality.[48]

But the absence of originality is assumed from the absence of evidence inherent in the oral tradition.

These principles have been tested in a number of Australian cases in which some Aboriginal bark painters were able to prevent unauthorised exploitations of their work, artistic expressions of folklore.[49] In each case, the plaintiff sued individually to enforce the copyright in his original artistic work, asserting that his work was sufficiently different from that of his ancestors to meet the requirement of originality, a fact which, as already noted, is easier to establish in the field of visual art than in relation to literary folklore. In addition, a cultural difficulty may arise in finding members of the creator group willing to act as individuals pursuing legal rights on their own account.

Where the creators of folklore take steps to record their own work, they will obtain copyright in the recording, even though they do not enjoy copyright in the underlying expression of folklore (which lacks originality).[50] This is, however, in most cases, a theoretical means only of securing copyright, since the creators are unlikely to be acquainted with the intricacies of copyright law.

In sum, the creators of expressions of folklore will only obtain copyright protection in exceptional cases. Not only does copyright law fail to accommodate works of folklore, it actually rewards those who, without consent, exploit folklore. Thus, as noted above, folklorists who record folktales[51] and who publish collections and anthologies obtain copyrights in the recording and in any compilation of such tales. Some commentators suggest that the work of folklorists is sufficiently useful to justify the award of copyright,[52] but contrary views are sometimes forcefully expressed.

> Of course, no one wants to prevent, or would try to prevent the folk from singing their own songs privately ... But heaven help anybody that tries to sing a printed song ... for money. The money to be made out of folklore (and we are learning to our surprise just how much money there seems to be) belongs to the owners of the folklore. And the owners of the folklore - God bless us all - now turn out to be the folklorists who collect and print it, generally on government and university money; but who did not create it, who are as a matter of fact, forbidden by the rules of the game even to try to create it, and who - one ventures to say - bloody well cannot create it.[53]

For popularisers of folklore, writers inspired by folklore and peddlars of 'fakelore', as described earlier, what they add to the folklore base of their work will generally be sufficient to secure a copyright in their own 'original literary work'.

Thus, copyright which regulates the global system of cultural exchange denies the developing nations and ethnic groups within them any return from or control over the exploitation of expressions of folklore, because the manner of their creation does not conform to the pattern of creativity in the developed world. In addition, the cultural mores of the developing nations and particular groups within them are not such that writers and artists emphasize their 'decisive mark of originality'.[54] The apparent reluctance to accommodate folklore within the international copyright regime reveals a cultural bias which has very damaging consequences for the developing nations.

> The accelerating development of technology, especially in the fields of sound and audiovisual recording, broadcasting, cable television and cinematography may lead to improper exploitation of the cultural heritage of the nation. Expressions of folklore are being commercialised by such means on a world-wide scale without due respect for the cultural or economic interests of the communities in which they originate and without conceding any share in

the returns ... to the peoples who are the authors of their folklore. In connection with their commercialisation, expressions of folklore are often distorted in order to correspond to what is believed to be better for marketing them.[55]

For 30 years, a debate has been fostered on the legal protection of expressions of folklore by WIPO and UNESCO, the guardians of the international copyright conventions.[56] Those involved in that debate are broadly agreed that the failure to protect expressions of folklore is unfair and unacceptable, but little progress has been made on mechanisms for change. Essentially two options have been suggested: the adaptation of copyright law to accommodate folklore, or the creation of a *sui generis* intellectual property right in folklore.

Since copyright as it has developed will only exceptionally protect works of folklore, some radical changes to copyright laws would be necessary to bring folklore within its reach. The legal requirement of fixation could easily be waived, as already permitted under the Berne Convention.[57] But a separate category of protected copyright work - expressions of folklore - would have to be added, exempt from the requirement of originality. Copyright would be enforceable by some competent authority on behalf of the generations of anonymous 'authors' who collectively created the works. To reflect the nature and cultural significance of folklore, copyright would be perpetual, not time-limited. Copyright in folklore would be accompanied by moral rights, such as a right to object to derogatory treatment, which could be used to prevent the publication of 'fakelore' or representations of folklore which cause offence to the creator group.

Some national laws currently protect expressions of folklore in terms such as those just outlined: in Tunisia, Bolivia, Chile, Iran, Morocco, Algeria, Senegal, Kenya, Mali, Burundi, Ivory Coast, Sri Lanka, Guinea, Barbados, Cameroon, Madagascar, Rwanda, Benin, Burkina Faso, Central African Republic, Ghana, Zaire, and Indonesia.[58] In some states, folklore works have become assimilated to such an extent within copyright law that the acts of infringement are the same as for other copyright works, but in other states, the range of infringing acts is more restricted for works of folklore than for traditional copyright works. Where folklore has been accommodated within national copyright laws, the changes to standard provisions embodying the fundamental concepts of copyright protection have been so substantial that the rights created in folklore are copyrights in name only, at least in the eyes of developed nations. This view is summed up by Sherman:

> while copyright law is cognitively open to new forms of subject matter, it is normatively closed in the manner in which it deals with and treats that subject matter.[59]

A variation on the use of copyright in this context has been a suggestion that the concept of 'paying public domain' could be used to protect works of folklore. The underlying assumption here is that these works either never attracted copyright at all and have therefore always been in the public domain, or that they theoretically attract copyright when originated by an unknown author, but that the copyright term has expired long ago and they are now in the public domain. The doctrine of 'paying public domain' is that when copyright expires and the work passes into the public domain, then, although the author can no longer control the exploitation of the work, anyone who exploits it must nevertheless pay a royalty not to the author but to the State or to some 'competent authority' such as an Arts Council. It is a tax on cultural products to raise revenue to encourage fresh cultural endeavours.[60] In 1987, Ricketson reported that 19 Berne Union members had legislation establishing a paying public domain,[61] although the Berne Convention itself makes no reference to the concept.[62]

Difficulties, practical, moral and theoretical, arise with the use of the doctrine. Paying public domain would give the creators of folklore no right to control or prevent the use of their works, merely a right to receive royalties. It has become clear that the developing nations are arguing for a fully-fledged property right with power to exclude others from their works, as well as a right to receive a fair return for their works. In other words, the owners of folklore should be treated in the same way as the owners of copyright works. Further, the use of paying public domain in the context of folklore is misconceived. It is a fallacy to say that because works are not literary property under copyright, they are necessarily in the public domain. The public domain is what remains after the law has accommodated such property rights as are considered necessary. Many current forms of property have at earlier stages in our legal history not been capable of appropriation but have become so in response to social, economic and political pressures. New forms of intellectual property may yet emerge, such as the relatively new 'performers' rights', the right of performers in their live performances, granted under the Copyright, Designs and Patents Act 1988, following intensive lobbying from sections of the entertainment business concerned about activities such as 'bootlegging', the unauthorised recording of live performances.[63]   Indeed, the protection of live performances, considered too ephemeral for ordinary copyright protection, provides an interesting parallel with oral transmissions of folklore, and it may be that performers' rights could fortuitously be used to protect folklore in some states. But, like copyright, performers' rights cannot be used on any systematic basis to protect expressions of folklore.

The early efforts of WIPO and UNESCO to encourage the legal protection of folklore were conducted under the copyright rubric. In the 1960s, India raised the question of making provision for expressions of folklore in the Berne Convention, but other member states were concerned that folklore failed to meet the fundamental criteria for copyright protection and was in the public domain. By way of a compromise, article 15(4) was added to the Berne Convention in 1967.[64] Article 15(4) provides that in relation to the unpublished works of unknown authors who are presumed to be nationals of a member state of the Berne Union, that state may designate a competent authority to protect and enforce copyright on behalf of the unknown authors in other member states. Thus, works of folklore are treated as a category of anonymous works, but in other respects must meet the basic criteria for copyright protection. It seems that only India has notified WIPO that it has designated a competent authority to act under article 15(4) of the Convention.[65] Very reluctantly, the UK has enacted legislation enabling competent authorities designated in other Berne Union states to act in the UK under article 15(4).[66] The adoption of article 15(4) has done nothing to enhance the position of works of folklore, and significantly does not even refer to folklore. Restricted as it is to *unpublished* works of unknown authors, it could only be of limited value even if implemented by Berne members, since much folklore is published in the copyright sense. The use of copyright to protect folklore was, however, pursued further by WIPO and UNESCO. The Tunis Model Law on Copyright for developing countries produced by WIPO and UNESCO in 1976 formed the basis for some of the national laws referred to earlier. Since the early 1980s, however, the international copyright organizations have abandoned the idea of adapting copyright to protect expressions of folklore and made efforts to develop a *sui generis* intellectual property right in folklore, with no requirements of originality, authorship (in the copyright sense), or fixation, and no time limit on protection. WIPO and UNESCO have produced *Model Provisions for National Laws on the Protection of Expressions of Folklore against Illicit Exploitation and other Prejudicial*

Actions.[67] These would create a new property right in expressions of folklore ('characteristic elements of the traditional artistic heritage developed and maintained by a community'), enforceable in perpetuity by a competent authority to be designated in national legislation.

The rejection of copyright in favour of a *sui generis* intellectual property right to some extent clarifies the theoretical issues but the remaining practical problems are legion. The evidential difficulties of establishing protectable folklore will be very considerable and will require the use of expert witnesses such as folklorists and anthropologists.[68] The difficulties surrounding regional folklore created by an identifiable ethnic group which straddles national boundaries may be impossible to resolve under national laws and may require regional arrangements. The choice of competent authority and the mechanisms for ensuring that royalties reach the peoples who created the folklore will be contentious.[69] Building checks and balances into the system to allow 'fair use' of folklore, for example, educational or archival use, or merely as inspiration for authored works, will be necessary.

More important than all of these is the absence of widespread consensus among the nations that the current treatment of expressions of folklore under copyright law is inequitable and requires new thinking on intellectual property to redress the cultural and economic balance. Only 33 states were represented in the group which adopted the UNESCO/WIPO *Model Provisions*. Ultimately, all of the legal problems, theoretical or practical, surrounding folklore protection can be resolved with a little imagination. What has been lacking to date is the political will to accord property status to expressions of folklore. The unwillingness of the developed nations to encroach upon the public domain in this way is in marked contrast to the extension of the copyright term from life and 50 years, to life and 70 years, creating a considerable bonanza for copyright owners.

But the times they are a-changin'?

The copyright concepts of authorship and originality reflect the Romantic view of authors and authorship of the eighteenth and nineteenth centuries. Revered for possessing and exercising the power to create, the author was rewarded by a right of literary enclosure or the power to colonise the literary imagination which at times borders on censorship. The extent of copyright as revealed in the caselaw of the United States, for example, reveals an awesome power to control other creative artists.[70] Yet the standard of originality which the author has to achieve is merely that the work was not copied but originated with him or her; beyond this, no particular creative skills need be displayed. Does the 'author' of an 'original literary work' do anything very different from those engaged in the oral transmission of folklore? In each case, the 'work' may rely heavily on previous 'works', but what the owners of folklore lack is the ability to demonstrate that a folktale as told today is sufficiently different from the version handed on yesterday. And of course there will be cases where the evolution of folklore is very gradual indeed and proof of originality and authorship at any stage in the folktale's life is impossible. The exclusion of expressions of folklore from copyright protection has caused the international copyright organizations to consider the creation of a new intellectual property right. But simultaneously, copyright is itself under attack, provoked in part by recent legislative extensions of copyright and consequent encroachments on the public domain, in part by judicial interpretations of copyright law which show undue regard for copyright ownership and fail to protect the vital resources of the public domain, but also in part by new perspectives in literary theory, challenging the traditional views of authorship which underpin copyright law.[71] Interest in the public domain has never been greater than it is today. This bodes ill for any lobby seeking the creation of a new *sui generis* intellectual property right. But this does not mean that a property-based solution is entirely inappropriate; merely that fresh approaches to the concept of property in intangibles are necessary.

Current legal and literary discourse begins to restore the public domain to a position of preeminence. If we see this as the principal asset to be protected, a doctrine of *cultural* property can develop from this base. Within this doctrine, concerns of national heritage or cultural patrimony will compete more effectively with individual rights of property than at present under the narrower rubric of intellectual property law. As cultural property, folklore could be protected without the creation of a new property right but as a result of more refined analysis of the public domain, possibly as 'protected public domain' rather than the more limited 'paying public domain' described earlier. As a recent gathering of interested persons declared,

> [w]e call on the international community to expand the public domain through expansive application of concepts of 'fair use', compulsory licensing, and narrower initial coverage of property rights in the first place. But since

existing author-focused regimes are blind to the interests of non-authorial producers as well as to the importance of the commons, the main exception to this expansion of the public domain should be in favor of those who have been excluded by the authorial biases of current law.[72]

Can lawyers and literary scholars, with others, 'reimagine the "author function" in ways that will be useful for the next century'[73] and at the same time reimagine property law to achieve changing cultural ends? Can the law *of* literature be revitalized, like the folktale, as we hand it on to the next generation?

Notes

1. Posner (1988), chp. 7.
2. Gaines (1992), p. 23.
3. While broadcasting and film production companies rely upon the author's copyright, they will at the end of the process enjoy their own copyrights in the broadcast or film: see Copyright, Designs and Patents Act 1988, ss. 5-7.
4. Copyright is a somewhat blunt instrument in that the words 'literary work' have been loosely interpreted to apply to any written or printed matter regardless of content or quality: *per* Peterson J. in *University of London Press v. University Tutorial Press* [1916] 2, Ch. 601, 608.
5. *US v. Paramount Pictures Inc.* [1948] 334 U.S. 131, 158.
6. 8 Anne c. 19.
7. The second 14 year term only arose if the author was still alive at the end of the first.
8. The story of the 'battle of the booksellers' is told in Patterson (1968), chp. 8. See also Rose (1994) and Sherman (1994), p. 115, for a discussion of the 18th century litigation in England.
9. Blackstone was counsel for the plaintiff in *Tonson v. Collins*, 1 Black. W. 322, 96 Eng. Rep. 180.
10. [1774] 4 Burr. 2408, 98 Eng. Rep. 257. A perpetual copyright in *unpublished* works continued at common law and from 1911 under statute until the enactment of the Copyright, Designs and Patents Act 1988, Sched. 1, para. 4.
11. U.S. Const., art. I (8), cl. 8.
12. 1 Stat. 124 (1790). Patterson (1968) explains that several state copyright laws passed before 1790 and effectively superseded by the

federal legislation were expressly based on the natural rights of authors (pp. 186-7). See also Abrams (1991).

13. *Twentieth Century Music Corp. v. Aiken* [1975] 422 U.S. 151,156.

14. There are now some 111 members of the Berne Union. The 1886 text has been revised several times. For an exhaustive account and for the latest text, see Ricketson (1987).

15. See Cornish (1989), paras. 9-011 *et seq.*

16. The text of the TRIPS Agreement can be found in (1994) 25 IIC 209.

17. Hermeren (1975) explores various types of causality in art and literature, analysing the necessary conditions for influence and methods for measuring its extent.

18. For example, *Ravenscroft v. Herbert* [1980] R.P.C. 193, and *Harman Pictures NV v. Osborne* [1967] 2 All E.R. 324.

19. Copyright, Designs and Patents Act 1988, s. 3(2).

20. A huge literature has developed around the idea/expression dichotomy. A useful starting point is Kurtz (1993).

21. Cornish (1989), para. 11-010 and Copinger and Skone James (1991), paras. 8-30 - 8-50.

22. Copyright, Designs and Patents Act 1988, ss. 29-30.

23. Council Directive 93/98/EEC, OJ L290/9, 29 October 1993.

24. *Harper and Row Publishers Inc v. Nation Enterprises* [1985] 471 U.S. 539, 545, *per* Justice O'Connor.

25. Copyright, Designs and Patents Act 1988, chp. IV, and see Dworkin (1995) and Dietz (1995).

26. Cited in Roeder (1940), p. 560.

27. In *Ravenscroft v. Herbert* [1980] R.P.C. 193, the plaintiff had written an historical account of the Hofburg Spear, reputed to have been used to pierce the side of Christ and removed by Hitler, who believed in its mystical powers, from Vienna to Nuremberg. The book was published in paperback under a cover showing 'a diminutive Hitler wearing a sort of red Roman toga and holding the spear and a swastika shield, depicted against a lurid background of Hitler's face in electric blue' (p. 197). This was done without the plaintiff's consent while he was abroad. It is very doubtful if the 1988 Act would provide a remedy in such a case.

28. Thoms (1846).

29. Leach (1949) provides 21 definitions of 'folklore'; these are analyzed in Utley (1965).

30. See Dundes (1965), p. 3, and Utley (1965), pp. 8-9.
31. Dorson (1959), p. 2.
32. Variation is encouraged or tolerated in some cultures but frowned upon in others: Dundes (1965), pp. 269-70.
33. Abrahams (1972).
34. First devised by the Finn Antti Aarne and revised by a leading American folklorist Stith Thompson in 1928, with a later edition in 1961. Thompson devised a motif index also: Thompson (1955-8).
35. From the German *mar* meaning a short story.
36. O'Sullivan and Christiansen (1965).
37. See Dorson (1983), p. 21, and (1972), p. 9.
38. Utley (1965), p. 21.
39. Bailey (1981), p. 67.
40. Harris (1880) and (1883).
41. Printed by Caxton in 1485. Malory died in 1471.
42. Grimm (1812-4).
43. Degh (1972), p. 54.
44. The term was coined by the American folklore scholar, Richard Dorson, in 1949: Dorson (1959), p. 4.
45. Copyright, Designs and Patents Act 1988, ss. 3(2) and (3).
46. Niedzielska (1980), p. 344.
47. See Ricketson (1987), paras. 6.13-6.
48. UNESCO/WIPO, 1985.
49. See Golvan, (1989), Puri (1993) and Sherman (1994).
50. See generally Ficsor (1993/ii). Some reliance on performers' rights may also be possible: Copyright, Designs and Patents Act 1988, Pt II. See also Arnold (1990).
51. There is some authority to the effect that the mere reporting of another's words may give rise to a 'reporter's copyright' if skill and judgment is used in the composition of the report: *Express Newspapers plc v. News (UK) plc* [1991] F.S.R. 36.
52. Niedzielska (1980), p. 343, Uchtenhagen (1993), p. 1.
53. Legman (1962), quoted in Klarman (1964), pp. 703-4. And for a United Kingdom example, see *Roberton v. Lewis* [1976] R.P.C. 169.
54. UNESCO/WIPO, 1985.
55. UNESCO/WIPO (1985), para. 2.
56. See generally Niedzielska (1980); Gavrilov (1984); *Report of the Committee of Governmental Experts on the Intellectual Property*

Aspects of the Protection of Expressions of Folklore, UNESCO/WIPO/FOLK/CGE/1/6; *Commentary on the Model Provisions for National Laws for the Protection of Expressions of Folklore* (1985), UNESCO/WIPO; *Report of the Group of Experts on the International Protection of Expressions of Folklore by Intellectual Property* (1984), UNESCO/WIPO/FOLK/GEI.1/4; and Ficsor (1993/i).

57. See above.
58. See Ficsor (1993/i), para. 3. In the overwhelming majority of the countries listed, copyright in works of folklore has perpetual duration.
59. Sherman (1994), p. 115.
60. A novel suggestion was made by the famous folk singer Pete Seeger that recording companies which exploited folk music could pay a royalty to a public domain fund which could be used to sue those who unjustly claimed copyright over folksongs; for Seeger, folk music was *ex hypothesi* in the public domain. See Klarman (1964), p. 711.
61. Ricketson (1987), para. 7.41.
62. It was incorporated in the Tunis Model Law on Copyright for Developing Countries 1976, published by UNESCO and WIPO.
63. See Arnold (1990). No copyright exists in a live performance which is too ephemeral and has no material form, until recorded, like folklore?
64. The Stockholm text of the Convention: Ricketson (1987), paras. 6.82-4.
65. Art. 15(4)(*b*) of the Convention and Ricketson (1987), p. 959.
66. *Report of the Whitford Committee on Copyright Law*, (1977), Cmnd. 6732, para. 50(iv), and Copyright, Designs and Patents Act 1988, s. 169.
67. Adopted by a Committee of Governmental Experts in 1982 and published with a commentary by WIPO and UNESCO in 1985.
68. A registration system has been suggested: *Report of the Group of Experts on the International Protection of Expressions of Folklore by Intellectual Property*, UNESCO/WIPO/FOLK/GEI.1/4, para. 30.
69. See Weiner (1987), p. 87.
70. See Gaines (1992), p. 210 *et seq*, and Helfand (1992).
71. See Sherman and Strowel (1994), *passim*, esp. pp. 7-22, by Chartier.

72.   The Bellagio Declaration, a statement by the participants in an international conference of lawyers, literary scholars, political scientists, anthropologists and others, March 1993. See O'Keefe (1995), p. 391.
73.   O'Keefe (1995), p. 388.

References

Abrahams, R. (1972), 'Folklore and Literature as Performance', *Journal of Folklore Institute*, Vol. IX, pp. 75-94.

Abrahams, H. (1991), *The Law of Copyright*, 2 Vol., Clark Boardman Callaghan, New York.

Aide, C. (1990), 'A More Comprehensive Soul: Romantic Conceptions of Authorship and the Copyright Doctrine of Moral Right', *University of Toronto Faculty Law Review*, Vol. 48, pp. 211-28.

Arnold, R. (1990), *Performers' Rights and Recording Rights*, ESC Publishing, Oxford.

Bailey, B.J. (1981), *Lakeland Walks and Legends*, Granada, London.

Bogsch, A. (1986), 'The First Hundred Years of the Berne Convention for the Protection of Literary and Artistic Works', *Copyright*, special issue, WIPO, Geneva.

Cornish, W.R. (1989), *Intellectual Property*, (2nd edition) Sweet and Maxwell, London.

Cornish, W.R. (1995), 'Authors in Law', *Modern Law Review*, Vol. 58, pp. 1-16.

Degh, L. (1972), 'Folk Narrative' in Dorson, R. (Ed.), *Folklore and Folklife*, pp. 53-84, University of Chicago Press, Chicago.

Dietz, A. (1995), 'The Moral Rights of the Author: Moral Rights and the Civil Law Countries', *Columbia VLA Journal of Law and the Arts*, Vol. 19, pp. 199-227.

Dorson, R. (1959), *American Folklore*, University of Chicago Press, Chicago.

Dorson, R. (1972), *Folklore and Folklife*, University of Chicago Press, Chicago.

Dorson, R. (1983), *Handbook of American Folklore*, Indiana University Press, Bloomington.

Dundes, A. (1965), *The Study of Folklore*, Prentice Hall, New Jersey.

Dworkin, G. (1995), 'The Moral Rights of Authors: Moral Rights and the Common Law Countries', *Columbia VLA Journal of Law and the Arts*, Vol. 19, pp. 229-67.

Ficsor, M. (1993/i), 'Attempts to Establish International Protection for Folklore through Intellectual Property Rights', *WIPO/FOLK/BEI/93/1*.

Ficsor, M. (1993/ii), 'Indirect Means for the Protection of Folklore', *WIPO/FOLK/BEI/93/6.Rev.*

Gaines, J. (1992), *Contested Culture*, British Film Institute, London.

Gavrilov, E.P. (1984), 'The Legal Protection of Works of Folklore', *Copyright*, February 1984, pp. 76-80.

Ginsburg, J. (1994), 'A Tale of Two Copyrights', in Sherman, B. and Strowel, A. (Eds.), *Of Authors and Origins: Essays on Copyright Law*, pp. 131-58, Clarendon Press, Oxford.

Golvan, C. (1989), 'Aboriginal Art and Copyright: the Case for Johnny Bulun-Bulun', *European Intellectual Property Review*, Vol. 11, pp. 346-55.

Helfand, M.T. (1992), 'When Mickey Mouse is as Strong as Superman: the Convergence of Intellectual Property Laws to Protect Fictional Literary and Pictorial Characters', *Stanford Law Review*, Vol. 44, pp. 623-74.

Hermeren, G. (1975), *Influence in Art and Literature*, Princeton University Press, New Jersey.

Jaszi, P. (1994), 'On the Author Effect: Contemporary Copyright and Collective Creativity', in Woodmansee, M. and Jaszi, P. (Eds.), *The Construction of Authorship: Textual Appropriation in Law and Literature*, Duke University Press, Durham and London.

Klarman, B. (1964), 'Copyright and Folk Music - a Perplexing Problem', *Wayne Law Review*, Vol. 10, pp. 702-15.

Kurtz, L.A. (1993), 'Speaking to the Ghost: Idea and Expression in Copyright', *University of Miami Law Review*, Vol. 47, pp. 1221-61.

Leach, M. (1949), *Standard Dictionary of Folklore, Mythology and Legend*, 2 Vols., New York.

Legman, (1962), 'Who owns Folklore?' *Western Folklore*, Vol. 21, pp. 1-12.

Niedzielska, M. (1980), 'The Intellectual Property Aspects of Folklore Protection', *Copyright*, November 1980, pp. 339-46.

O'Keefe, P.J. (1995), 'Cultural Agency/Cultural Authority: Politics and Poetics of Intellectual Property in the Post Colonial Era', *International Journal of Cultural Property*, Vol. 4, pp. 388-96.

O'Sullivan, S. (1974), *The Folklore of Ireland*, Batsford, London.

Patterson, L.R. (1968), *Copyright in Historical Perspective*, Vanderbilt University Press, Nashville.

Posner, R.A. (1988), *Law and Literature: A Misunderstood Relation*, Harvard University Press, Cambridge, Mass.

Puri, K. (1993), 'Protection of Expressions of Folklore - the Australian Experience', *WIPO/FOLK/BEI/93/8*.

Ricketson, S. (1987), *The Berne Convention for the Protection of Literary and Artistic Works: 1886-1986*, Queen Mary College and Kluwer, London.

Roeder, M.A. (1940), 'The Doctrine of Moral Right', *Harvard Law Review*, Vol. 53, pp. 554-78.

Rose, M. (1994), 'The Author as Proprietor: *Donaldson v. Becket* and the Genealogy of Modern Authorship', in Sherman, B. and Strowel, A. (Eds.), *Of Authors and Origins: Essays on Copyright Law*, pp. 23-55, Clarendon Press, Oxford.

Sherman, B. (1994), 'From the non-original to the Ab-original: a History', in Sherman, B., and Strowel, A. (Eds.), *Of Authors and Origins: Essays on Copyright Law*, Clarendon Press, Oxford.

Sherman, B. and Strowel, A. (1994), *Of Authors and Origins: Essays on Copyright Law*, Clarendon Press, Oxford.

Thompson, S. (1946), *The Folktale*, Holt Rinehart and Winston, New York and London.

Thoms, W. (1846), Letter to *The Athenaeum,* 22 August 1846, reprinted in Dundes, A. (1965), *The Study of Folklore*, Prentice Hall, New Jersey.

Uchtenhagen, U. (1993), 'Protection of Adaptations and Collections of Expressions of Folklore', *WIPO/FOLK/BEI/93/5*.

UNESCO/WIPO (1985), *Commentary in the Model Provisions for National Laws for the Protection of Expressions of Folklore*.

Utley, F.L. (1965), 'Folk Literature: an Operational Definition', in Dundes, A. (Ed.), *The Study of Folklore*, Prentice Hall, New Jersey.

Weiner, J. (1987), 'Protection of Folklore: a Political and Legal Challenge', *IIC*, Vol. 18, pp. 56-92.

11 Law as Art: An Introduction

GARY BAGNALL

Introduction

This chapter will introduce a new conceptualization of 'law', what I call the *Law as Art Hypothesis* (LAH). 'Law' conceived as a form of art work, differentiated as art by the *Law as Compound Artistic Type Hypothesis* (LCATH). Both hypotheses take 'art' and 'law' seriously and, in my judgment, may be demonstrated to provide the best explanation for 'law'.

Present ambitions are limited to articulating the key features of the LAH and LCATH, locating them within contemporary scholarship. Since scepticism has generated a pernicious anti-aestheticism, any putative theory of 'law *as* art' must be developed within a framework of epistemology, art and artistic value. This framework can be found in Part I of my forthcoming book, similarly titled *Law as Art*,[1] which also provides (in Part II) a development of both hypotheses. For now, I will introduce philosophical assumptions without attempting to defend them further, therefore my ambition for the present essay reduces from 'best explanation' to a 'plausible explanation'.

My method is unorthodox, especially with regard to theoretical progress. There is no 'one true theory of law'. Instead, working hypotheses are tested for explanatory 'fit' with experience of 'facts' (not in the sense of foundational truths, but a firm class of belief from which truth is logically derived), seeking the 'best explanation' available. Findings are testable and fallible, all theorizing being within an ongoing tradition of inquiry. The degree of 'fit' the LAH and LCATH offer is ultimately a collective judgment.

The general idea of law: semantics and basic facts

My epistemology considers semantics knowledge 'driven', not prior to knowledge of reality. Developing knowledge requires expression through developing semantics. Following Allott's typography,[2] both LAW and ART are abstractions from experience of laws and art works, but how is inquiry into LAW to proceed?

267

The situation therefore is that, as with physical science, one starts with a *working hypothesis*, usually based on sufficient evidence or analysis (or it would not need to be a hypothesis). One is willing to amend this hypothesis, or even abandon it, if the facts do not fit. There is two-way feedback between the particular and the general.

Allott illustrates this method by reference to western jurists' engagement of African customary *Legal* systems.

Equipped with their knowledge of western *Laws* at different points in time, they had constructed an abstract LAW, which to them expressed the essence of LAW. They came across customary legal systems, found they did not match with western *Laws* in various ways, and concluded that therefore they were not LAW, or that these societies did not have or recognise LAW. The original western hypothesis was applied to and worked in regard to the small area from which it drew its data; was then applied to a larger area, and found not to work ... The response of some western jurists was ... to elaborate a new and broader construct of LAW. They had revised their hypothesis. It was not a question of LAW changing its nature, but of the users of the term admitting new referents or new characteristics in *Laws* upon which their use of LAW was based.

The main function of a working hypothesis is to work. The work that such a hypothesis does is *heuristic*, i.e. it assists in the discovery of new facts, new systems, new perceptions of connection, new perceptions of the functioning of those systems. A juristic hypothesis with low heuristic value needs discarding - it is not effective. LAW as a term is thus effective only in this sense.[3]

In dismissing imperative analysis, Allott notes that one cannot construct a 'pure' theory of LAW, if one means a theory devoid of experiential input, providing facts reality, against which any theory is tested for heuristic 'fit'.[4] LAW accounts for a distinct aspect of experienced reality, experience inherently 'theory saturated'. The LAH is a working hypothesis (heuristic) used to gain epistemic access to *Law* and laws, abstracted as LAW.

It is important to detail the basic facts about LAW which I use to connect the LCATH with *Law*/law.

Any metaphor's attractiveness is gauged by degree of explanatory 'fit', needs no *a priori* justification, but must have *some* connection with the reality to be explained. How? Working hypotheses are used to explain selected basic facts. This provides knowledge of degree of 'fit' of the new framework with those facts, as well as knowledge about the framework itself. A minimalist position is preferable when selecting basic facts, since the fewer facts that are used in the construction *of the theory* (e.g., in the fixing of parameters) the more facts will count as potential confirmation for the theory when its ... consequences are tested.[5]

Minimalism is of facts used in constructing the 'theory', which is tested for explanatory weight against the *complete* reality experienced. The following basic facts underpin the LAH and ground the adoption of my preferred model for the LCATH:

1. LAW is a complex reality, known abstractly and conceptually (LAW), socially and functionally (a system of *Law*) and semantically (as 'LAW', '*Law*', 'law').
2. LAW embraces LAW, *Law*, and law experienced as a unified, elementally heterogenous homoeostatic entity.
3. LAW is elementally compound, dominantly 'text' (written or oral) and therefore representational, but not reducible to text.
4. LAW is anthropocentric but not ethnocentric.
5. LAW is about the expression of power through textual representation.

Facts 1-5 are contentious, and I would be surprised if the reader did not question one or more of them. That is not the point. They are five basic beliefs derived from *my* experience of *Law* and laws, given my theoretical preconceptions about LAW. This is sufficient to justify their use as basic distinguishing criteria of LAW, in order to apply the LAH and LCATH. It is my argument that, given facts 1-5, the model I shall detail later has general explanatory 'fit', sufficient to support the transfer metaphorically of my preferred model to LAW.

LAW and ART as action type

The LAH is radical: LAW *is* a kind of ART work. It is a complex working hypothesis, not least because it presumes a philosophy of ART and ARTISTIC value (discussed in Part I of *Law as Art*[6]). My philosophy of ART derives its ontology (the *Action Type Hypothesis* - ATH) from the work of Currie[7] and its theory of value (which differentiates ART as class of action type) partly from the work Budd[8] and partly from my epistemology: the *Sophisticated Realist Hypothesis* - the SRH (again, explained in *Law as Art*[9]).

The primary elements in the LAH can be expressed in the formula:

LAW is an artistically valuable (*i.e.*, intrinsic, sentiment-dependent, inter-subjective, anthropocentric, incommensurable, contextual, contingent, non-ethnocentric, objective) action type (*i.e.*, performance achieved by the artist, possessed of structure and heuristic, capable of multiple instantiation).

Consider any LEGAL art work L. To claim L is ART is an ontological claim about the kind of entity L is, as well as a judgment as to its value as a work of kind K. L, as work, is the sum of its elements: activity, structure, heuristic, and ARTISTIC value, and this is what I experience. As action type, L is a performance, an activity achieved by the artist(s). Four elements: (1) artist(s), (2) structure, (3) particular time of composition, and (4) the way of arriving at (2), the heuristic. To know (2) and (4), and to experience L as possessing ARTISTIC value, is to know and correctly judge L ART.

Aside from structure, (the primary differentiating aspect) the ontological criteria of the LAH have important implications. First, L as action type, an activity, cannot be reduced to any single structural element, such as text (whether written or oral). It is a homoeostatic cluster property, of compound, highly developed, yet fully integrated elements. It is an event type achieving or discovering structure S by heuristic path H, experience of which may possess a degree of value. Furthermore, heuristic H is constitutive of, and not instrumental to, the kind of entity L is. The LAH emphasises the constitutive elements of work L, individual characteristics of the originators being *un*constitutive, yet the artist is *not* irrelevant to the experience, understanding, and response to L. Indeed, the opposite is the case. Similarly, the temporal aspect (time of composition) is also not constitutive of L. To take the analogy further, the creator(s) of L instantiate event type *discovering L via a certain heuristic*, whereas system officials (draughtsmen, enforcement officers, adjudicating officials) are analogous to singers and musicians in a musical work, enacting event type *performing structure L*. Given what Currie calls the *Instance Multiplicity Hypothesis* (IMH),[10] there can by any possible number of instances of action type L, which are all L, and not tokens of L.

Together, these criteria conceive LAW as ART, going beyond the structure of L, to emphasise both the heuristic path by which L was discovered *and* its ARTISTIC value. Importantly, the LAH embraces (through the Action Type Hypothesis) both a legal realist concern with what officials do and a formalist concern with structure and pedigree of origination. LAW is not the activity of *Legal* officials, as an activity type, it is an enactment of structure possessed of distinctive generative heuristic. LAW is not the activity of *Legal* practice: LAW is a work, an action type, an enactment of structure, possessed of distinctive heuristic.

But the LAH demands more, since *L*, to be LAW, must have ARTISTIC value to be ART at all. Extending the criteria for valid LAW beyond the activity of enacting structure and heuristic, to its value is an important development in re-conceptualizing LAW. The value of *L* is a property intrinsic to *L*, experienced by engaging *L* in the correct manner. This affirms legal realist concern with the experience of *Legal* activity, but, although the intrinsic ARTISTIC value of *L* is deeply personal, sentiment-dependent, and incommensurable, it is not the experience itself but the type of experience which matters. The sense of satisfaction (or reward) with *L*, is incommensurable, but not the correctness of the judgment that *L* possesses ARTISTIC value, that is, produces a feeling of satisfaction of a given type. Since it is the possession of value which differentiates *L as* ART, then all the validating criteria (enacting activity, structure, heuristic, and value) are commensurable, communal, inter-subjective and non-ethnocentric. Furthermore, since a sense of attraction to *L* is possible because there are facts about *L* to know, and my theory of value accepts the possibility of both moral and ARTISTIC facts, it is possible that experience of moral facts about *L* may contribute to convincing that *L* is rewarding. A sentimental response, drawn from experience of *L*, which may form the basis for the judgment that the type of experience *L* produces is intrinsically attractive, and therefore *L* possesses value. There are facts about *L*. These facts may, depending upon the engaging conceptual framework (within moral theory - relating to what is considered 'good' or worthwhile: within theory of ART - relating to the attractiveness of *L* as a work of kind *K*) may be semantically labelled 'moral' or 'ARTISTIC facts'. Given my epistemology, fact *F* about *L* may have moral and ARTISTIC significance simultaneously. Moral and artistic truths require justification (*i.e.*, coherence with a prior belief system) and remain fallible, but the deep sense of reward which the experience generates, is incommensurable (*i.e.*, sentiment-dependent and prior to the logico-epistemic process) yet remain significant, as input into the truth-generating process.

It is also significant through offering the possibility of transcending the antinomy between positivistic formalism, (grounded upon an unverifiable, *a priori* verification principle), and classical moral realism of natural LAW theory, (employing diverse fixed, universal, moral frameworks as determining criteria of validity). It explains how moral belief can be constitutive of judgments of LEGAL validity by showing that moral beliefs (as 'fact' and 'truth', in my epistemology) can input the process of ascribing value. Claims to moral 'truth' require justification, but moral 'facts' are what we know, in the sense of being a firm class of belief, and as inputs into the truth-generating, epistemic process are incommensurable, products of a 'theory-saturated' experience of reality. Just as the judgment that L possesses value may be correct or incorrect, so too judgment that (part) of what I find valuable is its moral value. Correlatively, both moral and ARTISTIC worth experienced, to the extent that it is what I know as distinct from justify, is epistemologically valid, but incommensurable, data. LAW, as ART, is the activity of enacting structure and heuristic that possesses *some* degree of value, and value is dependent upon the worth of L, and that experience of worth, as type, *may* include moral worth. In this way the positive/natural LAW antinomy is transcended through the value requirement of the LAH, because there can be both formal *and* moral criteria for a valid LAW. Such moral criteria can have no predetermined substance, and may or may not be coherent (and thus true) and LEGAL validity/invalidity does not guarantee the veracity of moral judgments made during the validating process. The ARTISTIC value of L depends upon how rewarding the type of experience of L is, as kind K, but the sense of reward may turn on the moral worth of moral (dis)value expressed, therefore the moral worth of L may, as type, determine value and thereby validity.

To conclude: the LAH, in its account of LAW affirms the 'common-sense' view of LAW, as something encountered within experience of *Legal* practice (the law/work), yet irreducible to official action nor to abstract frameworks of rules, principles or other purely rational constructs. The LAH holds validity determined by engaging the *work* as action type; it is partly sentiment-dependent, but not sentimental or relativistic. Validity is *not* determined either by pre-experiential application of purely formal criteria nor by acceptance of a universal *a priori* moral system. LAW, as ART work, may (and often will) be multiply enacted and experience of each enactment is engagement with the same work. Legal realists were correct to connect LAW with judicial action, but wrong to have limited their conceptualization to it. For the LAH, LAW is the activity of enacting a distinctive structure and heuristic, a structure judged correctly as possessing *some* degree of ARTISTIC value. Judgments of validity are commensurable, fallible, and contingent, and simply impossible without engaging the work.

LAW as ART and the Operatic Music Drama metaphor

The question is: Assuming LAW is ART, what kind of ART? The model (metaphor) I consider most analogous to LAW is the structurally compound

Operatic Music Drama (OMD). Metaphor (as artistic heuristic) is a distinctive mode of constructing hypotheses which input into the epistemic process. To say a metaphor is 'true', is to say that any proposition(s) which it generates are 'true'. Metaphor assists in cohering experiences of the world: it functions to assist in the truth-generating process, its verification does *not* lie prior to it. To gain insight into the claim that this model possesses general epistemic 'fit' with the five basic facts about LAW, I need to describe the principal distinguishing characteristics of OMD. An account of the derivation of OMD can be found in *Law as Art* (forthcoming), for present purposes they can be summarized schematically, which I call OMD_1

> OMD_1 is a distinct kind of compound operatic art work; as opera, it is within the Italian tradition of musico-dramatic art; it is a dynamic and inchoate artistic activity; each performance or instantiation being a unique art work of variable cohativity; text and dramatic action are of far greater importance than in other opera, and are united with music and theatrical arts generally into a single art work, through the imaginative receptivity of the audience; performance environment is of greater importance to the overall experience of the work than in opera generally.

Employing 'morphological criteria'[11] it is possible to further differentiate OMD_1 as ART. This morphological differentiation is also fully detailed in *Law as Art* (Part I)[12], but the findings generate a revised schema OMD_2.

> OMD_2 is a distinct kind of compound operatic art work (predominantly audiovisual and bisensory; structurally significant; elementally highly developed, complex and integrated); as opera, it is within the Italian tradition of musico-dramatic art; a dramatic enactment (as compositional framework type it is basically representational, but unlike opera generally its thematic and expository accessory types are more highly developed, additionally it has a significant utilitarian accessory in the shape of its performance architecture; as compositional type it employs pictorial and sculptural representation in both static and mobile types; visual dramatic representation in mobile type; both musical and non-musical auditory mimetic/descriptive representation; linguistic-symbolic/literary representation including writing, narration and dramatic text/libretto); as action it is a dynamic and inchoate artistic activity; each performance or instantiation being a unique art work of variable cohativity; text and dramatic action are of far greater importance than in other opera, and are united with music and theatrical arts generally into a single art work (musical motivic structure and unending aria vocal score enhance integration with text/libretto and sound effects; developed costuming, scenery, architecturally and acoustically sympathetic performance environment,

rejection or developing of dramatically disruptive operatic forms *e.g.* recitative; spoken dialogue; chorus, and the imaginative receptivity of the audience further enhance integration); performance environment is of greater importance to the overall experience of the work than in opera generally; possessed of style, understood historically as a set of common structural and heuristic traits of disparate works sharing a common provenance (interpreted widely including individual, group, society, race, geography, chronology).

That LAW is a compound type of ART, analogous in kind to OMD_2, I call the *Law as Compound Artistic Type Hypothesis* ($LCATH_1$). It is not that LAW *is* OMD_2, but that OMD_2 is the closest analogous kind of ART. A further revision of OMD_2 is achievable by using it explain the reality of *Legal*/legal experience: laws as ART works, *conceived as compound artistically valuable action type*. A revised OMD_2/$LCATH_1$ can be distinguished as $LCATH_2$, which will express both analogous qualities between the two models, as well as distinctive qualities of LAW. $LCATH_2$ is *not* the 'one true theory of LAW', but offers the best explanation, and remains subject to ongoing revision.

Progression from $LCATH_1$ to a revised $LCATH_2$ is very important to the conceptual framework of the LAH, but a detailed account is beyond the scope of this chapter. Revisions can be signposted. First, it is not in ontological type, but as differentiated type, particularly as regards compositional structure, that LAW is distinguished from its metaphor OMD_2. LAW shares with OMD_2 compound structure, within which different ARTs are each highly developed and integrated into a single, complex, cohesive kind. Whereas OMD_2 is predominantly bisensory, LAW will be multisensory, with more developed and complex integral elements. Both are dramatic enactments, but of quite distinct compositional type. For example, whereas OMD_2 is predominantly representational, with developed thematic, expository and utilitarian/performance accessories, LAW is dominated by the utilitarian/performance and representational framework types with expository and thematic accessories. As performance type, LAW is dominated by linguistic/literary representation, but will still include other forms, albeit to a different degree than OMD_2, although there is an interesting analogy between the non-representational aspect of the musical element in OMD_2 and the power element in LAW. Both, as action types, are dynamic and of variable cohativity. Costuming and scenery will, in proportion to degree of dramatic enactment, be of varying significance, but of far greater importance than presently acknowledged. The same is true of architectural performance environment, an aspect of LAW that has not been seriously considered.

Related to performance is the important cohesing function of the 'audience' to both, where the function may be the same but of variable importance, not least regarding the kind and size of audience to which each kind of ART is directed. The effect of LEGAL art work upon its audience appears to offer important insights for explaining compliance, which has also never been satisfactorily accounted for by existing theoretical frameworks. With style, comes an idea that first emerged within early classical American realism, but here becomes an important aspect of the chronological development of the *work* within and between traditions. In both OMD_2 and LAW, style is important but always subservient to the *work,* an over-preoccupation detracting from the work, and ultimately appreciation, response to, and judgment of it as ART.

Much needs to be said about the derivation of $LCATH_2$, (I have said little or nothing so far about 'judge', 'rights', 'duty', 'obligation', 'justice', and so forth). In what remains of this chapter, I will seek to demonstrate that the LAH and $LCATH_2$, and the use of metaphor, have support within contemporary scholarship.

LAW and ART in contemporary scholarship

A neotraditionalist movement is identifiable in contemporary LEGAL theory, which countenances a pre-modern idea of LAW *as* art work. In Posner's words, for some neotraditionalists, 'law is an art - the art of social governance by rules'.[13] I doubt Posner had in mind anything quite like that proposed, yet the LAH and $LCATH_2$ do share *some* similarities with neotraditionalism.

Western European LEGAL theory, as a specialist field of enquiry, 'scarcely existed before the end of the Middle Ages',[14] although inquiry into LAW and ART both have a rich tradition of scholarship, much remaining vital and relevant. As regards the *Arts*:

> Nowadays we may take it for granted that there is a group of activities, 'the arts', which come naturally together as activities of the same general kind; and on this basis we proceed to ask what it is that they all have in common, which makes them different from other activities. The truth is ... that 'The Modern System of the Arts', as P.O. Kristeller has called it, only emerged, after a good deal of argument, in the eighteenth century.[15]

Since the eighteenth century, theory of ART and LAW has increased in specialization, bringing increasing intellectualization, conceptual differentiation (and a tendency to conceptual autonomy and incommensurability) and, until this century, the predominance of both reason over experience and emotion, and of the 'scientific method'. As LEGAL inquiry has become increasingly 'scientific', so the gulf between LAW and ART has widened - the cry of 'ART for ART's sake' rendering the ARTS impotent through rigorous differentiation, or subjective and incommensurable, through labelling them 'emotional'. ART reduced to taste, an artistic 'experience', denigrating reality and diminishing the significance of the entity experienced - the art work.

This *cri de coeur* is not inapplicable to LAW. 'LAW for LAW's sake' could be a fitting slogan for western societies, who have exponentially generated laws seeking to regulate more effectively. The idea of autonomous LAW premises this fetishism, and is central to orthodox political liberalism, which has dominated twentieth century scholarship. Orthodox LEGAL theory remains dominated by the basic ideas of the eighteenth century 'cult of reason': 'rule', 'principle', 'right', 'system', 'technique', 'form'. Just as 'ART for ART's sake' diminishes the reality of the work in favour of the experience, so the conceptualization of LAW within rational, formal, validating criteria, distances understanding of LAW from real works (laws). Often, scepticism of 'fact' and 'rule' deconstructs both rational construct *and* work, dismissing LEGAL theory entirely. LAW reduced to a 'matter of taste' or the relative indeterminacy of the interpretive act.

The legacy of the second half of this century may be the abandonment of the 'cult of reason' in favour of the 'cult of *un*reason', unless a satisfactory *via media* can be established between rationalism and scepticism. The SRH is one such path, differentiating a unified reality as a 'tool' to inquiry, and the labels 'art', 'science', 'law', 'morality', 'politics' etc., viewed as contingent, epistemologically driven, and forming a constantly reviewable attempt to express the reality experienced. My epistemology raises no *prima facie* impediment to the LAH, *if* that is the best explanation of LAW. If LAW *is* ART, then LEGAL inquiry is methodologically an ARTISTIC enterprise.

Recently, a movement within LEGAL philosophy has emerged, focused upon the connection between LAW and one established ART form: the literary work. As this comes closest to linking LAW and ART it also merits examination.

The law and literature movement and neotraditionalism

As Ward observes in a recent review of the achievements of the movement,[16] it is now 16 years since Allen Smith predicted the 'coming renaissance in law and literature'.[17] Ward traces the first stirrings to J. Boyd White's *The Legal Imagination*[18] and there is now a rich literature on the subject.

Ward opens by identifying what is an important distinction, between those who conceive the relationship as one of insight drawn from how LAW is represented *in* literary works, and those who argue that LAW (or law) ought to be methodologically engaged, if not conceptualized *as*, literature.[19] This differentiation *is* important, since I am explaining LAW, therefore, the second claim, that LAW/law ought to be engaged *as* ART (literary art work) is more interesting. I do not claim that scholarship regarding the representation of LAW *in* literary works has made, or can make, no valuable contribution. It does, especially regarding the use of metaphor and narrative in LEGAL inquiry, which Ward traces from Aristotle, Aquinas, Hobbes, and Locke, to Bacon's celebrated Creation 'story'.[20] The LAH shares Ricoeur's judgment of the legacy of the Enlightenment as one of unwarranted elevation of 'scienticism',[21] and embraces both metaphor and narrative. Posner[22] denies the jurisprudential significance of narrative to LAW, but 'appears prepared to accept the validity of metaphor as a means of enhancing judicial style',[23] whereas Ricoeur[24] and Rorty[25] are prepared to embrace both. Fish[26] and White[27] both give weight to narrative in their work.

Of present concern is not how LAW/law is represented *in* literary works of ART, but whether LAW/law ought to be engaged *as*, or is best explained *as*, a kind of literary ART? Ward opens his account of 'LAW/law *as* literature' scholarship by noting that it seeks to do two things which appear paradoxical.

> In one sense it wishes to impress the necessity of our existence in language as a living force. The keynote here is perhaps Heidegger's much-used trope: 'Language is the house of being.' Language need not be reified, although it can be. Language is something which we all use, and as such it is language which we can all design. Language is the construction of the community, and not some sort of transcendental force ... Among contemporary philosophers, perhaps the most revered exponent of this position is Richard Rorty ... [28]

But at the same time

while it may wish to stress the 'ordinariness' of language, law *as* literature also wants to intellectualise legal study. It wishes to both widen and to deepen. In other words, law *as* literature suggest that both teachers and students must be aware of all the various 'isms' of literary theory, structuralism, post-structuralism, deconstructionism and so on, which can be then be used so that as lawyers we can better understand what a text means, both functionally and interpretively. As a complement to law and literature scholarship, law journals have increasingly presented articles about revered figures in the philosophy of language such as Derrida, Foucault, Heidegger and Wittgenstein. Law and literature scholars, on the other hand, have tended to concentrate instead on resurrecting the art of rhetoric ... Perhaps the accommodation of this essential paradox in law and literature lies in the resurrection of rhetoric as a primary concern in law teaching ... The essence of 'law *as* literature', then, is the suggestion that the techniques and methods of literary theory and analysis are appropriate to legal scholarship.[29]

Saying such techniques are 'appropriate' to legal scholarship is claiming that law, as text, is to be engaged *as* one would a literary text, but this is not to claim that LAW *is* such a text. The influence of philosophers of language has been, (most perniciously in the work of Fish), to reduce knowledge to language, relativise language to an interpretative activity, and finally, to relativize interpretation to open-ended creative possibility. The deconstructionist, linguistic nihilism of Fish exposes Ward's paradox most acutely: the reifying, 'intellectualising' of language has undermined the 'ordinariness' of language, especially the common-sense quality of providing knowledge of the reality.[30] The claim to linguistic 'ordinariness' is weakened by denying that language provides epistemic access. The effect is trivializing. Both law and the literary text are not a 'work' to be interpreted, but an endless interpretive 'process', a purposeless game we are destined to play until death. It is because such manifestations of the 'LAW/law *as* literature' movement reduce the literary work to a creative, subjective, indeterminate, interpretive dynamic that they find little point in addressing whether LAW is or is not a kind of literary ART work, since what is important is their textuality and interpretive possibilities.

It is this understanding of 'LAW/law *as* literature' that Posner criticizes,[31] for, as Ward puts it,

just as literary texts are unusable as legal texts, so the methods of literary theory are inappropriate for the interpretation of legal texts ... this inappropriateness is rendered by the very different roles and ambitions of fictional and legal writing ... Despite the relative virtues of pragmatic or utilitarian concerns, 'in legal interpretation the subordination of the interpreter to the 'speaker' is a condition of legitimacy. In other words, if in any doubt, original intent enjoys an 'authority' over creative interpretation. The concession ... Posner is prepared to make to the 'law *as* literature' position, and it is an important one, is that although lawyers have little to learn from the various techniques of literary theory they have much to gain from the study of rhetoric ... Thus, although he is keen to maintain the distinction between literature and politics, Posner is prepared to admit that 'there is still the possibility that immersion in literature might make a person a better judge by enlarging his knowledge of the human condition'. Even the most sceptical of detractors is prepared to concede some virtue in the accommodation of literature in legal theory.[32]

To paraphrase Dworkin, Posner wants to 'take LAW seriously', stressing the structural distinction: LAW is not literature and literature is not LAW. Posner argues from a pragmatism which conceives ART generally, and literary ART in particular, as instructive, pleasing, but ultimately a recreational, lesser experience, whereas LAW is much more socially important. Posner judges the movement's claim to solve the perennial problems of jurisprudence to be overstated,[33] whereas Ward, acknowledging the movement's many contestable claims, offers a more optimistic prognosis, stressing its ambition, 'user friendly' and educative qualities.[34] I share Posner's sceptical view about the movement generally, but for different reasons. With ambition to enlighten and educate, and bearing in mind the paradox of at the same time seeking to deepen and widen legal theory, Ward's analogy with the early socio-political Critical Legal Studies provides a reminder of how early promise can dissipate, especially if politically subverted. To flirt with political dogmas, Ward writes,[35] is up to a point necessary, but to 'illustrate politics is one thing ... using it to replace one political dogma with another' is to undermine ones critical credibility and effectiveness. I would add to Ward's critique another epistemological problem shared by both: extreme relativism/scepticism must be defended against the charges that, first, one's own theory has been ascribed unjustifiable priority, and second, that if LEGAL reality is reducible to either an unending, purposeless power struggle or a stream of (equally purposeless) creative interpretation, then what is the point of it all? Attempts to provide adequate replies are far from conclusive.

Words of caution aside, recent LAW/law and literature scholarship has made the following contributions to the LAH and LCATH$_2$: (1) it has effected a measurable 'axial shift' in LEGAL theory away from a preoccupation with Ricoeur's 'scientific' discourse[36] to a perspective which reconnects LAW with ART; (2) in so doing, it has made the use of ART works, concepts and methods in LEGAL inquiry credible; (3) it has reinstated the acceptable use of metaphor and narrative in explaining LEGAL ideas; (4) it affirms that if the LAH is the best explanation for LAW, then one must first take ART seriously; (5) in flirting with politicization, it warns against subversion (instrumentalization); and finally, (6) it demonstrates that, as a LEGAL perspective, extreme scepticism/relativism destroys its targets at the expense of itself, since arguments for its own priority are impossible.

The movement has linked LAW/law with *one particular kind of ART* (literature) but its anti-aestheticism precludes any serious attempt to conceptualize LAW *as* ART. It more often reduces both LAW and literature to, not ART, but text. The LAH, rejecting anti-aestheticism, builds upon a reconstructed concept of ART and its value and thereby more radically connects LEGAL theory with the philosophy of ART. The LAH differs from the LAW/law and literature movement in taking *both* ART and LAW equally seriously.

Contemporary LEGAL inquiry is dominated by the challenge of scepticism, one response being an aspiration to recapture LEGAL expertise for the *Legal* insider. In *The Problems of Jurisprudence*, Posner describes an emerging movement which he calls 'neotraditionalism',[37] which insists on the self-sufficiency of LAW in correctly resolving internal disputes. A 'back to basics' approach which finds philosophy's trespass into inquiry about LAW unwarranted, unhelpful, if not positively distasteful.

Posner sees neotraditionalism's rise as a reaction to the decline in LAW as an autonomous discipline, which he believes has accelerated since the 1960s, and can be explained by reference to four factors, which collectively removed support for the orthodox autonomy thesis. First, 'the political consensus associated with the "end of ideology" has shattered';[38] second, the 'boom' in multidisciplinary interest in LAW;[39] third, the desire to be 'innovators rather than imitators';[40] and fourth, the 'rise in the prestige, authority and ... achievements of the natural sciences'.[41]

Posner identifies four principal facets of this neotraditionalism: (1) anti-reductionism; (2) LAW as a via media between unacceptable extremes; (3) LAW as practical reason; and (4) LAW as interpretive communities. The third has two distinct, but incongruous, threads: (a) prudentialism and (b) epistemological traditionalism.[42] A brief elaboration of each is useful.

'Anti-reductionism' is used

to denote the idea that law is its own kind of thing and cannot be reduced to something else - to philosophy, or economics, or politics ... Law is a collection of insights, procedures, and methods, of great antiquity and durability.[43]

This makes possible the claim that 'Law is art - the art of social governance by rules'. What does Posner have in mind in saying that neotraditionalism holds 'law as *via media* between unacceptable extremes'?

If law is an art, it is not a science; indeed it must stand in equal opposition to the two 'scientific' schools of thought (as neotraditionalists describe them) - critical legal studies, on the left, and law and economics, on the right. Because most lawyers are uncomfortable with extreme positions, the opportunity to reject Left and Right in favor of a position safely centrist, both politically and methodologically, has powerful appeal.[44]

Anti-scientism is implicit in the third facet, that LAW is a form of practical reason.

The neotraditionalists emphasize three closely related, orthodox Aristotelian faces of this variegated concept: first, the centrality of deliberation, conceived as a mode of enquiry and judgment requiring qualities of character as well as intellect; second, the cautious, prudential, incremental character of Aristotelian practical reason in contrast to Platonic radical speculation ... ; third, the importance of tradition as a corrective to theoretical speculation. Law as practical reason in this account celebrates adherence to the traditional values, methods, and vocabulary of legal reasoning and is suspicious of systematic approaches.[45]

The 'interpretive communities' facet builds on Fish's idea,[46] in that

the neotraditionalist seeks to reclaim legal interpretation from indeterminacy by arguing that even if not text possesses objective meaning, the community of lawyers to which constitutional and statutory texts are addressed can impose determinate meaning on these texts by virtue of the shared outlook of the community's members.[47]

Neotraditionalism's appeal is best explained by its pluralism, nostalgia, anti-interdisciplinary position, and restoration of status to *Legal* scholars,[48] yet ironically its theoretical grounds are derived from similar extra-LEGAL sources to those it seeks to escape from Posner's assessment of attempts to ground the four facets of neotraditionalism is as follows.

The first two facets are clearly related. It is easy to dismiss anti-reductionism by appealing to the old argument about 'gaps' in laws,[49] which undermines the claim that *no* other discipline can contribute to the understanding of *any* such problem. The second claim, regarding the accommodation between LAW and economics and Critical Legal Studies, is untenable because the polemical spectrum is untenable. Of more interest is the third facet: the idea of LAW as practical reason. In its prudentialist variant, (following Aristotle, Burke and Coke), it seeks to

> emphasize human fallibility, urge humility, counsel adherence to immemorial custom, deplores breaking with the past, recommend prudence as the central principle of politics and judgment as the central principle of law, elevate the particularism and (apparent) lack of system of the common law over the generalizing tendencies of statutes and codes, and stress the limitedness of intellect as a tool of social reform. Prudence, or judgment, is a mixture of intellectual and temperamental qualities rather then an intellectual quality alone, and the prudentialist attitudes sum to a posture of caution about embracing theoretical solutions to practical problems.[50]

The problem is that it is a 'mood rather than a method of analysis', although for Posner it is 'the right mood in which to do law'. The second variant (following Aristotle, Freid and Weinrib) makes the Aristotelian division of reason into, what in Freid's version[51] may be called deduction and 'trained, disciplined intuition', or 'practical LEGAL reasoning'. This is the *sole* domain of the lawyer, satisfying the neotraditionalist overarching desire for anti-reductionism. (Here, the practical reasoning thesis *leads to* the anti-reductionist thesis.) But, if LAW is *not* irreducible, then the anti-reductionist implication of both variations are undermined, and inevitably lead to 'imprudent activism' or 'false humility' on the part of those who seek to make judgments on laws. What room is left for judicial 'error'? How do we judge the judge?

The problem with the fourth facet, Fish's idea of LAW as an 'interpretive community', is

> that, when applied to law, the 'conversational' method and the limits of consistency and intelligible adjustment that constrain it leave a vast area in which opposite outcomes are equally rational.[52]

LAW, for Posner, requires maximum determinacy but the idea of LAW as interpretive community is indeterminate, and also incoherent with LAW's importance, trivializing it.

For Posner, neotraditionalism amounts to 'mostly aspiration' and is not 'an antidote to legal scepticism',[53] because 'the intellectual currents that feed the movement are themselves rooted in scepticism'. His pragmatism differs from neotraditionalism with respect to the prospective or retrospective *gestalt* of those who make judgments on laws. The Posnerian pragmatist is 'less the traditional legalist' because 'no more than the pragmatist will the neotraditionalist be able to rest securely on traditional certitudes. Today we are all sceptics'.[54]

In concluding this review, and by way of locating the LAH with respect to the key ideas outlined, I will summarize the principal points of convergence and divergence. Recent scholarship in LAW and literature has made six positive contributions to the LAH, yet it is the deep scepticism permeating the movement which is the marked point of divergence. Avoiding anti-aestheticism, the LAH takes ART much more seriously. The LAH shares the movement's claim that ART *does* bear upon LEGAL inquiry, as it shares the sense of the 'ordinariness of language', interpreting the latter within a new epistemology. It affirms the ordinariness of language, but avoids intellectualizing excess by emphasising, not the interpretive activity, but the experience of the *work*. The LAH stresses 'text' in understanding LAW, but holds that LAW is not reducible to text alone. Text is important to the extent that LAW *is* text, and the movement's insight into textual analysis is to this extent significant. The LAH also aspires to be 'user friendly' and to 'educate', but its ambition is tempered by its multidisciplinary implications, reflecting the inherent complexity of LAW. Against the movement, the LAH avoids extreme relativism, and *can* justify its concept of LAW as best explanation, thereby giving direction to LEGAL inquiry.

As for neotraditionalism, the LAH shares its general aim of justifying the importance of the practice, tradition and experience, but rejects its sceptical, anti-philosophical tendency. Where neotraditionalism seeks to restore to LEGAL inquiry the self-importance which the autonomy thesis brought, the LAH endeavours to further undermine the autonomy thesis but shares the desire to restore the prestige of LEGAL scholarship through providing new focus and methodologies: LEGAL inquiry as multidisciplinary inquiry into complex, compound LEGAL ART works.

The neotraditionalist belief that 'LAW is a *via media* between Economic Analysis of Law and Critical Legal Studies' is an oversimplified polemic which the LAH transcends through its new conceptual framework, offering new explanatory possibilities regarding 'efficiency' and 'power'. It follows Posner in rejecting the third facet of neotraditionalism: that there is a distinctive LEGAL form of reasoning. LEGAL reasoning is the application of logic to LEGAL problems which derive from experience of LEGAL works. LAW is *not* reducible to a type of reasoning ('practical' or otherwise) but is a distinctive kind of ART work, which we logically engage. Finally, while agreeing that LAW includes Fish's idea of 'interpretive community', there is no reduction of the work to the activity of interpretation, therefore it denies that LAW *is* a special interpretive community. Since it rejects Fish's scepticism, it avoids his indeterminacy by focusing upon real works.

Conclusion

Awaiting further argument, if the LCATH$_2$ is judged a *plausible* hypothesis for LAW, then this essay will have achieved its objective. Nonetheless, plausibility is an important and significant finding, since it reinforces the axial shift toward meshing LEGAL and ARTISTIC inquiry. Both 'plausible' and 'best explanation' are the end of the beginning, as the LAH and LCATH$_2$ offer a new framework for future inquiry into the morphology and development of the component elements of LEGAL ART: architecture; performance techniques, traditions and styles; modes of communication; boundary problems; and ethnic and cultural comparison of works. This is not to mention the possible resolution of classical jurisprudential problems, not least, bridging the natural/positive LAW distinction by explaining how moral judgment may be constitutive of ascribing ARTISTIC value, and thereby validity *as* ART, to the LEGAL work - an action type, possessed of structure and heuristic, and capable of multiple instantiation.

Notes

1. Bagnall (forthcoming).
2. Allot (1980), pp. 1-2.
3. Allot (1980), p. 4.
4. Allot (1980), p. 27.
5. Currie (1989), p. 67.
6. Bagnall (forthcoming).
7. Currie (1989).
8. Budd (1995).
9. Bagnall (forthcoming).

10. Currie (1989), p. 8.
11. Munro (1970) understood as conceptual criteria facilitating the description of structural differentiation in ART works.
12. Bagnall (forthcoming).
13. Posner (1990), p. 435.
14. Kelly (1992), p. xiv.
15. Hanfling (1992), p. 7.
16. Ward (1995), p. 3.
17. Smith (1979).
18. Boyd White (1973).
19. Ward (1995), p. 3.
20. Ward (1995), pp. 5-6.
21. Ricoeur (1978).
22. Posner (1988).
23. Posner (1990), p. 4.
24. Ricoeur (1978).
25. Rorty (1989).
26. Fish (1990).
27. Boyd White (1984).
28. Ward (1995), p. 15.
29. Ward (1995), pp. 15-16.
30. Fish (1980).
31. Posner (1988), (1990).
32. Ward (1995), pp. 21-2.
33. Posner (1988).
34. Ward (1995), pp. 22-4.
35. Ward (1995), pp. 22-3.
36. Ricoeur (1978).
37. Posner (1990), p. 424.
38. Posner (1990), p. 428.
39. Posner (1990), p. 429.
40. Posner (1990), pp. 431-2.
41. Posner (1990), pp. 432-4.
42. Posner (1990), p. 434.
43. Posner (1990), p. 434.
44. Posner (1990), pp. 434-5.
45. Posner (1990), pp. 435-6.
46. Fish (1980).

47.   Posner (1990), pp. 436-7.
48.   Posner (1990), p. 437.
49.   Posner (1990), p. 437.
50.   Posner (1990), p. 443.
51.   Fried (1981, 1988).
52.   Posner (1990), p. 451.
53.   Posner (1990), p. 452.
54.   Posner (1990), p. 452.

References

Allott, A. (1980), *The Limits of Law*, Butterworths, London.

Bagnall, G. (Forthcoming), *Law As Art*, Dartmouth, Aldershot.

Boyd White, J. (1973), *The Legal Imagination*, Little, Brown and Co., Boston.

Boyd White, J. (1984), *When Words Lose their Meaning: Constitutions and Reconstitutions of Language, Character and Community*, University of Chicago Press, Chicago.

Budd, M. (1995), *Values of Art: Pictures, Poetry and Music*, Allen Lane, The Penguin Press, London.

Currie, G. (1989), *An Ontology of Art*, Macmillan, London.

Fish, S. (1980), *Is There a Text in this Class: The Authority of Interpretive Communities*, Harvard University Press, Cambridge, Mass.

Fried, C. (1981), 'The Artifical Reason of the Law or: What Lawyers Know', *Texas Law Review*, Vol. 60, pp. 35-57.

Fried, C. (1988), 'Jurisprudential Responses to Realism', *Cornell Law Review*, Vol. 73, pp. 331-335.

Hanfling, O. (1992), 'The Problem of Definition', in Hanfling, O. (Ed.), *Philosophical Aesthetics: An Introduction*, Blackwell, Oxford.

Kelly, J.M. (1992), *A Short History of Western Legal Theory*, Clarendon, Oxford.

Munro, T. (1970), *Form and Style in the Arts; An Introduction to Artistic Morphology*, The Press of Cape Western Reserve University, Cleveland and London.

Posner, R.A. (1988), *Law and Literature: A Misunderstood Relation*, Harvard University Press, Cambridge, Mass.

Posner, R.A. (1990), *The Problems of Jurisprudence*, Harvard University Press, Cambridge, Mass.

Ricoeur, P. (1978), *The Rule of Metaphor*, Routledge and Kegan Paul, London.

Rorty, R. (1989), *Contingency, Irony, and Solidarity*, Cambridge University Press, Cambridge.

Ward, I. (1995), *Law and Literature: Possibilities and Perspectives*, Cambridge University Press, Cambridge.

Index